ZELDA POPKIN

ZELDA POPKIN

The Life and Times of an American Jewish Woman Writer

JEREMY D. POPKIN

ROWMAN & LITTLEFIELD
Lanham • Boulder • New York • London

Published by Rowman & Littlefield
An imprint of The Rowman & Littlefield Publishing Group, Inc.
4501 Forbes Boulevard, Suite 200, Lanham, Maryland 20706
www.rowman.com

86-90 Paul Street, London EC2A 4NE

Distributed by NATIONAL BOOK NETWORK

British Library Cataloguing in Publication Information Available

Library of Congress Cataloging-in-Publication Data

Names: Popkin, Jeremy D., 1948- author.
Title: Zelda Popkin : the life and times of an American Jewish woman writer / Jeremy D. Popkin.
Description: Lanham : Rowman & Littlefield Publishers, [2023] | Includes bibliographical
references and index.
Identifiers: LCCN 2022029244 (print) | LCCN 2022029245 (ebook) | ISBN 9781538168431
(cloth ; alk. paper) | ISBN 9781538168448 (ebook)
Subjects: LCSH: Popkin, Zelda, 1898-1983. | Jews--United States--Biography. | Authors,
American--20th century--History and criticism. | Women authors, American--20th century--
History and criticism. | LCGFT: Biographies.
Classification: LCC PS3531.O634 Z85 2023 (print) | LCC PS3531.O634 (ebook) | DDC
813/.52 [B]--dc23/eng/20220815
LC record available at https://lccn.loc.gov/2022029244
LC ebook record available at https://lccn.loc.gov/2022029245

Contents

LIST OF FIGURES

INTRODUCTION

Legends of Zelda

IN 1965, ZELDA POPKIN, MY GRANDMOTHER, UNPACKED HER TYPE-writer at the Yaddo Writers' Colony in upstate New York and began a new novel. Undeterred by the presence of two of the most celebrated male Jewish authors of the day—Philip Roth, who was working on what became *Portnoy's Complaint*, and Alfred Kazin, who had just published his memoir *Starting Out in the Thirties*—she set out to tell "the story of the American Jew from the ghetto to the country club," the epic tale of American Jewish life in the first half of the twentieth century. Her book, *Herman Had Two Daughters*, released in 1968, dramatized the conflict between East European Jewish immigrants and their parents, her gener-ation's ascent into the American middle class, their battle against the ris-ing antisemitism of the 1930s, the shock of the Holocaust, the challenge to American Jewish identity caused by the establishment of Israel, and the growth of a Jewish culture centered around organized fundraising.

Unlike Roth and Kazin, Zelda—the name she taught me to call her by even as a small child—told the American Jewish story mainly through the lives of women characters, particularly a spirited protagonist mod-eled after the author herself. She may have lacked the literary polish of Roth and Kazin, but, as she told an audience in 1975, at the end of her writing career, "This has been my century—this extraordinary century that some have called the cruelest century in the history of mankind. I've lived all of it. Not only as a spectator but as a participant."[1] Born to Yiddish-speaking immigrant parents in Brooklyn in 1898, Zelda Popkin started her public career during World War I, working to raise funds to aid beleaguered Jewish communities in Europe and Palestine and to provide support for Jews serving in the American military. She began to write just as American women gained the right to vote, and the articles she published in the early 1920s in the *American Hebrew*, the country's leading English-language Jewish magazine, highlighted the role of "Jewish Dolly Madisons" like Rebecca Gratz in American Jewish history and the contributions women had made to the Jewish community's wartime fundraising campaigns. At a time when most middle-class women did not work outside the home, Zelda was a full-time partner with her husband in one of the country's first public relations firms. The Popkins worked for Jewish causes, but also for commercial clients and political candidates, including both Franklin Roosevelt and Alf Landon.

As World War II began, Zelda Popkin was embarking on a new career as a novelist. Her Mary Carner detective novels, published between 1938 and 1942, featured an enterprising woman detective, making her a feminist pioneer in that literary genre. Once she realized the stakes in the war, for Americans, for women, and for Jews, Zelda left "escape" fiction behind to tackle larger themes. *The Journey Home*, a novel in which she dramatized the tensions between men who had seen combat and civilian women, sold a million copies in 1945 and 1946, making it the best-selling war novel by a female author. Zelda's next book, *Small Victory* (1947) is now recognized as one of the earliest American works of fiction with a Holocaust theme, and *Quiet Street* (1951), based on her visit to the country in 1948, was the first novel in any language about the creation of the state of Israel. At the same time, Popkin was confronting a personal drama: the unexpected death of her husband had left her alone, and her 1949 novel *Walk Through the Valley* foreshadowed the widowhood memoirs of late twentieth-century authors such as Joan Didion and Joyce Carol Oates.

The 1950s were a time of prosperity for most American Jews, but it was a discouraging decade for Jewish women authors. Even the topic of American Jewish women's lives was taken over by Herman Wouk, whose runaway best-seller *Marjorie Morningstar* delivered at best a mixed message about whether women could have both independence and happiness. By the time Zelda arrived at Yaddo in 1965, she was virtually forgotten; no publisher offered her an advance for *Herman Had Two Daughters*. But my grandmother was convinced that she still had something to say, and the commercial success of her book, which became a Book-of-the-Month Club selection and was recommended by some reviewers as an antidote to Roth's scandalous *Portnoy's Complaint*, gave her a sense of vindication. Younger Jewish women writers, such as Grace Paley and Cynthia Ozick, were coming on the scene, and the 1960s feminist movement, led by Jewish women such as Betty Friedan, was taking up themes about women's autonomy that my grandmother had explored years earlier. Zelda Popkin had been there first, however, and her story offers an extraordinary opportunity to explore Jewish life and the changing opportunities for American women in the first two-thirds of the twentieth century through the eyes of a woman who not only experienced these developments personally but who also took on the challenge of writing about them both as they were happening and then with the advantage of hindsight.

As a child, I was enthralled by my grandmother's tales about her exciting life. She had met Albert Einstein, Eleanor Roosevelt, and actual Communists. She had encountered Holocaust survivors soon after the war, and she made it sound as though she had single-handedly carved out the "Burma Road" to break the Arab siege of Jerusalem during Israel's war of independence in 1948. Later, after I became a history professor and my grandmother passed away, I started to ask myself how a Jewish woman author who had published one of the earliest American novels with a Holocaust theme and the first novel in any language about the birth of Israel could have been almost completely overlooked by my fellow scholars—even by a historian of American Jewish women who had unwittingly chosen the same title as my grandmother's million-selling novel for her well-documented monograph.[2] My experience in teaching courses on modern Jewish history, in which my "Zelda stories" make the material come alive for students, has shown me that her experiences are valuable in explaining broader issues. With the enforced time at home provided by the worldwide pandemic that began in 2020, I finally asked myself the same question my grandmother asked herself in 1953 when she decided to write her autobiography: "Why not . . . do, now, the book about Zelda Popkin that you've always been wanting to do?"[3]

Zelda Popkin's story brings to life larger stories about the remarkable rise of American Jews and the transformation of American women's lives in the twentieth century, with the vividness that comes from having a lively character at its center. At the same time, it is also a story about a woman whose powerful personality profoundly influenced several generations of my family. As I have sorted through Zelda's letters and papers, I have learned that not every story she told me about her life was entirely true. She was in Israel in 1948, for instance, but she did not get there until after the breaking of the siege of Jerusalem that she described in her novel. She and her husband, Louis Popkin, who died five years before I was born, made the publicity arrangements for one of Albert Einstein's lecture tours, but the photograph my grandmother loved to display, in which my grandfather is speaking to Einstein, shows the great physicist looking somewhat annoyed, as if putting up with a publicist was the price he had to pay to keep his promise to help raise funds for the newly founded Hebrew University.

Even if she sometimes burnished her stories to create what I have call "legends of Zelda," however, Zelda Popkin does have a story worth telling. She was one of the most articulate female members of the generation of Jews who fought their way into the American middle class during the decades of the 1920s and 1930s. She plunged into what a character in one of her novels called "the sordidness of money grubbing" as a professional in what was then the new field of public relations, and she was also an active journalist, contributing to the *New Yorker* and other leading magazines of the day. As she left the Jewish press behind, she illustrated the skill that ambitious Jews of the time developed at what we now call code-switching. She kept references to Jewish themes and to her own identity out of her articles, but she was nevertheless acutely aware of the danger of antisemitism at home and abroad in the 1920s and 1930s. Her husband helped draft Henry Ford's 1927 apology for spreading antisemitic propaganda and the Popkins were part of the campaign to force the antisemitic "radio priest" Father Coughlin off the airwaves in the 1930s. They confronted the American State Department's prejudices on a personal level when they tried to help relatives obtain visas to flee Hitler's Europe.

Zelda Popkin's detective stories and her million-selling novel, *The Journey Home*, made her an active participant in the process by which American Jews came to define much of American popular culture. Her books raised questions about women's careers and about what would happen as American women, and civilians in general, were reunited with a generation of men who had been transformed by the experience of war. Cautious about highlighting Jewish characters or themes in her earlier books, she returned from a 1945 trip to visit Europe's "displaced persons" camps determined to take on the issue of antisemitism, both in Europe and in American life. *Small Victory*, published in 1947, was one of the earliest American works of fiction in which Jews who had lived through the Holocaust appeared as characters. Four years later, *Quiet Street* took American readers into the struggle for the creation of the Jewish state, and, remarkably for its day, did so through the experiences of women. Discovering the book after it was reissued in 2002, an Israeli journalist was struck by "the lack of stereotyping so favored by [Leon] Uris or the bitter vitriol so often released by [Philip] Roth and Saul Bellow."[4] In her autobiography, *Open Every Door*, in *Herman Had Two Daughters*, and in her last published novel, *Dear Once*, my grandmother gave her own twist to the story of her generation, the Jewish children of the turn-of-the-century immigrants from eastern Europe who were now Americans, again focusing on women's thoughts and experiences, and thus bringing a very different perspective to the portrayal of the American Jewish experience from that of the male authors who dominated the literary scene in those years. Her final novel, *Dear Once*, published in 1975 when she was seventy-seven years old, featured a female protagonist whose life is shaped by a childhood experience of sexual molestation, an issue that a younger generation of feminists was just beginning to bring out of the shadows.

Zelda lived long enough for me to give her a copy of my first book. She died before I became not just a historian but also a scholar of life-writing and began analyzing her autobiography, *Open Every Door*, as a thought-provoking example of that genre. In writing my own book about Zelda, I have drawn on the version of her life story in her auto-biography, but also on many other sources. For nearly forty years, my grandmother wrote regularly to my parents. These letters and my parents' replies give me a sense of what was on her mind throughout the second half of her life. Zelda herself kept voluminous files about her book projects, including materials she gathered as she worked out her plots, correspondence with her literary agents and her editors, rough drafts, clippings of reviews, and letters from friends and readers, all of which are conserved in the Howard Gotlieb Twentieth-Century American Authors Collection in Boston University's Mugar Library. She also kept letters from her father, her sister Helen, who moved to Jerusalem in the 1930s, her son Roy, my uncle, and other friends, which add to the evidence about her life. Family photographs show her, usually with a cigarette at hand, as a "flapper" and a serious businesswoman, as a best-selling author, and as a spirited septuagenarian.

In writing about Zelda, I cannot pretend to complete scholarly detachment. I visited my grandmother regularly, first in the company of my parents and later, on many occasions, independently. My understanding of my grandmother has also been shaped over the years by conversations with other relatives. Everyone in our family had their own version of Zelda. My father, a professor of philosophy, never told me stories about his childhood, and he rarely talked about his mother; he did dutifully write to her at regular intervals, although not nearly as often as she wrote to him. Whereas my father shaped my view of my grandmother primarily through his silence, my mother loved to tell "Zelda stories," some of which she eventually wrote down, although she never published them. Her mother-in-law's behavior supplied her with amusing anecdotes that had the additional advantage of underlining the teller's patience and understanding.

The "legends of Zelda" that I heard from my relatives and my own memories of her demonstrate the effect that her powerful personality had on our whole family. This book is testimony to the hold she still has on my imagination, nearly four decades after her death in 1983; my sister calls it a "passion project," and I cannot deny that writing it has engaged me emotionally as well as intellectually. I am also a historian, however,

Figure 0.1. Zelda Popkin with her future biographer (1949): Zelda Popkin and her grandson Jeremy size each other up.

and I have done my best to use the tools of my profession in telling my grandmother's story. I have tried to evaluate my sources critically, bearing in mind, for example, that what Zelda says about her life in her autobiography does not always correspond to other evidence. I have also immersed myself in the burgeoning literature on twentieth-century American Jewish history, and especially the scholarship on American Jewish women, historical subjects very different from the history of the French and Haitian Revolutions that have been the main focus of my previous work.

One of the few silver linings of the pandemic months during which I did this reading was that there were suddenly numerous lectures and webinars about American Jewish history online, through which I "met" many of the leading scholars in the field, and I am grateful to those who took the time to mentor me, on Zoom or through email. I discovered a lively field that has transformed Jewish history itself as it has documented the remarkable growth of a community that went, in little over a century, from being marginal both in American life and within the wider Jewish world to being one of the two major centers of Jewish life and that developed a unique culture, at once embedded in the larger American society and yet in many ways distinctive. Few other subfields of history have been as open to gender studies as American Jewish history has become, and the literature on that subject enabled me to understand my grandmother's life in ways I had not imagined. I supplemented my reading in American Jewish history with an exploration of American Jewish novels and memoirs, which have added to my overall knowledge of the tradition from which I myself come and also given me perspective on the literary genres that my grandmother practiced.

My immersion in twentieth-century American Jewish history helped me see how many of Zelda's experiences illustrated larger processes in American Jewish and American women's lives. Zelda's interactions with her parents offer a window into the human reality of the immigration experience and the conflicts between European-born Jewish parents and their American-born children. Her and her husband's success in the public relations business provides a perfect example of how American Jews took advantage of the new opportunities they found here, and how they transformed American life in the process. Zelda Popkin's repeated retellings of her encounters with Holocaust survivors are a case study of the evolution of American attitudes toward that catastrophe, and her book on Israel raises issues about the Jewish state and its meaning for American Jews that are still relevant today.[5] Her life is a rich source of evidence about the experience of American Jewish women and offers perspectives that are frequently at odds with analyses based on men's lives. Men's memoirs, for example, give little hint of the revolution in parenting that made the 1920s "the age of the child" and presented my grandmother with many challenges; my uncle Roy's indignant response to her critique of progressive education, written when he was about eleven years old and preserved in her papers, is a vivid demonstration of the issues she faced. Zelda's struggles to make a living during the 1950s and 1960s, usually seen as a "golden age" for American Jews, are a reminder that older single women, even if they had achieved economic independence earlier in their lives, could find themselves left out of the period's prosperity.

This project is thus meant as a contribution to American Jewish historiography, but it is also a biography. Biography offers a chance to see how the large-scale events of an era played themselves out in an individual life, and how the actions of individuals contributed to what hindsight now tells us were the major developments of the time. It is a way to translate the currently fashionable concept of "intersectionality" into concrete terms: in my grandmother's case, we can see how she negotiated between the identities society gave her, as a woman, a Jew, and an American, and those she actively constructed for herself, as a professional with a career and a writer. In setting out to write a biography, I have drawn on another aspect of my professional career: my engagement with the field of life-writing studies. I originally became involved in this interdisciplinary field of study because of my interest in the autobiographical memoirs written by historians, a number of whom heeded the call of the French scholar Pierre Nora, one of the pioneers of the "history of memory," to explore their own memories as well as those of the society around them. Nora urged the historian to "acknowledge the close, intimate, personal liaison he maintains with his subject. Even more, to proclaim it, to meditate on it, to make it, not the obstacle, but the means of his understanding," a call he eventually responded to himself by publishing an intimate memoir.[6] From historians' autobiographies, I moved to the study of other forms of life-writing, including autobiography in general, diaries, personal correspondence, and the hybrid genre of family memoir. This background has helped me to interpret the motives behind my grandmother's various exercises in life-writing, including her autobiography, her heavily autobiographical fiction and her letters, and other sources I have used, such as my mother's diaries.

"Family memoir" is a form of life-writing that has become increasingly popular in the past few decades, but whether it constitutes scholarship is very much contested. Bliss Broyard's *One Drop*, about her father Anatole Broyard's effort to hide his partially African American ancestry and her own efforts to reconnect with other branches of his family, and Daniel Mendelsohn's *The Lost*, the account of his search for information about a branch of his family that perished in the Holocaust, were both popular and critical successes. Some academic historians, such as Mark Mazower and Modris Eksteins, have published family memoirs that have shown how insights derived from relatives' stories can illuminate larger historical questions.[7] After I gave my first conference paper on my grandmother's novels about the Holocaust and the creation of Israel at a meeting of the Association for Jewish Studies in 1999, however, I overheard a discussion among members of the organization's program committee about the danger of letting "grandmother studies" infiltrate a serious scholarly meeting. Having immersed myself in the lively stream of recent scholarship in the field of American Jewish history in order to write this book, I have learned that many of the best books on this topic have grown out of their authors' interest in aspects of their own families' histories, although their authors may not overtly acknowledge that fact.[8] Aside from the gender bias implied by the label "grandmother studies," there is no good reason to reject serious scholarship that draws on an author's family documents, as long as they are treated with the same critical rigor as other sources and are used to put the story of the author's family members in its historical context.

This book is in some respects a family memoir, but it is also meant as a biography, another genre much discussed by theorists of life-writing. One of the generally accepted conclusions from those discussions is that, as one critic has put it, "any biography uneasily shelters an autobiography within it."[9] This story of an American Jew who went back and forth throughout her life about what being an American and a Jew meant to her certainly reflects issues I have grappled with in my own life. There is also no doubt that Zelda's story speaks to me in particular ways because writing has been central to both of our lives, as well as that of my father, Richard Popkin, a much-published historian of philosophy.[10] I have also given much thought to the question of what it means for a male author to write the biography of a woman, even if—or perhaps especially if—that woman is a member of his own family.

Thirty years ago, the editors of a pathbreaking volume of essays on *The Challenge of Feminist Biography* endorsed pioneering women's historian Gerda Lerner's assertion that a feminist approach would allow women biographers to "address topics that most biographers seldom touch on, such as how women's private and public lives intersect," and the volume's editors acknowledged that, as they wrote, "we began almost inevitably to identify with and compare ourselves to our female subjects."[11] It is certainly no coincidence that all the biographies of American Jewish women I have read are by women authors.[12] Zelda sometimes called herself a feminist and the majority of her published writing, from her early articles on Jewish women in the *American Hebrew* to her late-life novels, was written from a woman's point of view. My grandmother, who marched for women's suffrage in her teenage years but who was often stridently critical of the new forms of feminism that surfaced in the last decades of her life, might not have appreciated the application of some of today's approaches to the interpretation of her life and writings. Nevertheless, it seems to me that if we now admit that women's lives and life-writing are as worthy of attention as the doings and publications of men, male scholars should not be afraid to take on the challenge of telling women's stories and drawing on the insights that a generation of feminist biographers have given us.

As a subject for biography, my grandmother presents both a challenge and an opportunity because she wrote so much about her own life, in so many different forms. She frequently created multiple versions of the same stories in her letters, in her nonfictional magazine articles, in her novels, and in her autobiography, each version intended for a different audience and meant to achieve a different effect. Over the decades, she often returned to the same themes—her childhood as the daughter of immigrants, the American encounter with Holocaust survivors, the impact of sudden widowhood—while presenting them in different ways.

At times, she sought to conceal important aspects of her history, particularly her Jewish origins; at other times, she stressed the same features. As I have tried to make sense of her life, I have come to see that, from an early point in her life, Zelda was always engaged in that most American of projects, the attempt to define her own identity. In that respect, the story of her life is not only a Jewish story and a woman's story: it is also a story about our country.

CHAPTER I

An American Jewish Childhood

WHEN ZELDA POPKIN APPLIED FOR A PASSPORT IN 1945, SHE DISCOV-
ered that she had an identity problem, one created for her by her Jewish
immigrant parents. The two official documents she needed to include
with her application—her birth certificate and her marriage license—
listed different first names. The birth certificate, issued in Brooklyn, New
York, in 1898, called her "Jennie Feinberg," whereas the marriage license,
from 1919, gave her maiden name as "Zelda Feinberg." To establish that
Jennie and Zelda were the same person, Popkin had to have her father,
Harry Feinberg, swear out a notarized affidavit in which he explained, in
his Yiddish-inflected English, that "A daughter, named Zelda was born
to us at Brooklyn N.Y. on July 5th, 1898. For purposes of Birth and
School registration this name was anglicized to Jennie. Since 1918, our
Daughter has continuously used and has been known under her given
name of Zelda."[1]

The discrepancy between my grandmother's two first names was
symbolic. Her parents, both of whom had come to the United States
from Russia as teenagers in the 1880s, gave their daughter an "American"
name that would fit with the culture of the society in which she would
grow up, a world very different from the one from which her parents
came. At the same time, however, they also gave her a name common
among Jews. A generation before F. Scott Fitzgerald's wife made the
name fashionable, "Zelda" was popular among East European Jewish
immigrants; it was probably an anglicized version of "Zlata," "golden," a
common girl's name in the Slavic-speaking world. The census-taker who

visited the Feinberg family at 142 5th Avenue in Brooklyn in 1900 wrote the two-year-old's name down as "Zelma," confirming that she was not called "Jennie" within the family, but in 1910, after she had been in school for some time, the census records listed her as "Jenny."

My grandmother's two names were tangible reminders of the fact that she grew up with two identities: one entirely American and one linked to her East European Jewish ancestry. By the time she was old enough to go to school, she must have absorbed the lesson that, in America, it was sometimes better to be "Jenny": the one scrap of elementary-school artwork she preserved, a small colored drawing, is signed with that name. In her late-life autobiographical novel *Herman Had Two Daughters*, the free-spirited woman protagonist who unmistakably represents the author is named "Jessie." But in real life, as Zelda's father's affidavit affirmed, at the age of twenty, she chose to leave "Jennie" behind and embark on adult life as "Zelda." She made that choice at a moment when she was deeply immersed in Jewish concerns and when she was committing herself to life in New York City, a Jewish community far different from the small towns in New Jersey and Pennsylvania where she had gone to school. Her choice would work out well for her, even though she made it in 1917, before she could have known that Zelda Fitzgerald was going to make her name a symbol of the Jazz Decade. By accident, my grandmother found herself with a name that would fit with the modernity of the 1920s and would make her stand out throughout her life.

When they gave their daughter her two names, my great-grandparents could hardly have imagined what kind of life she was going to lead as an American and a member of a new kind of Jewish community. Harry Feinberg and Annie Glass were typical members of the great wave of East European immigration that landed on American shores in the last decades of the nineteenth century. In my classes on modern Jewish history, I use them as examples of the Jewish immigrant experience. Pictures of my great-grandmother Annie's parents—her father with his bushy beard and her mother with her Orthodox Jewish woman's scarf on her head—and of Annie herself, in fashionable modern dress, with my four- or five-year-old grandmother make the story of Jewish acculturation visible for my students; excerpts from the autobiographical sketches my great-grandfather typed out in the English he never really mastered, even after sixty years in America, convey both the leap he had made from a world of the shtetl to the very different environment of the New World and also the difficulties he faced in making that transition.

Figure 1.1. Zelda Popkin's maternal grandparents, Israel and Sarah Glass (1910): Taken in Zelda Popkin's grandparents' apartment on Catherine Street in New York City's Lower East Side in 1910, this photograph shows that they had maintained the customs of East European Jewish life, even in America.

Figure 1.2. Zelda Popkin and her mother Annie Feinberg (1902–1903?): The clothes worn by Zelda and her mother dramatize the process of acculturation by which East European Jews became Americanized in the early twentieth century.

In the early 1950s, Zelda began writing her autobiography. "When I told my father I was writing the story of my life, he told me he was writing his—and showed it to me," she wrote to my parents. "Promptly, I snatched. Why the man was out peddling needles and pins in the blizzard of '88." Even though historian Hasia Diner's classic book showing how door-to-door peddling had been the gateway into American life for thousands of Jewish immigrants did not appear until decades after Popkin's death, she herself already knew the significance of that phenomenon: in 1927, she had published a magazine article, "The Jewish Covered Wagon," showing how, "at the roots of the proudest Jewish family trees of this land is the dim and shadowy figure of a peddler."[2]

Harry Feinberg's life story, which he wrote in several versions, is the story of thousands of other Jewish immigrants. He was born into a poor family in the small Lithuanian shtetl of Zizmor in 1871. His father, Isaac Feinberg, left the family behind to pursue his fortune in America when Harry was a small boy. In her own autobiography, Zelda Popkin devoted a few pages to the picaresque tale of her feckless grandparent, who careened from one disastrous business enterprise and one marriage to another, finally emigrating again, from America to Jerusalem, where he took his fifth wife and "died of gangrene of the big toe while the Palestinian riots of 1929 raged outside his door."[3] Left at home with his mother and his two sisters, Harry Feinberg was first sent to a cheder or religious school, and then to a more modern teacher from whom he learned to read and write in Yiddish, Russian, and German. In 1885, when Harry Feinberg was fourteen, his mother died, and relatives shipped him and his two sisters to their father, who was then running a kosher butchery in Elmira, New York. A few days after Harry arrived in Elmira, his father "bought for me several packs of matches and sent me out on Water Street to begin my business career." Quickly realizing that he could not depend on Isaac for support, Harry went out on the road as a peddler in upstate New York for several years. Like many of the peddlers described in Diner's book, he had fond memories of some of his adventures, particularly the night he spent sheltering from the "worst blizzard in the history" with a farmer who stayed up late talking to him and told his family "that last night was the first night in his life that he had the best enjoyable evening and that was with a Jewish boy."[4] Tramping from door to door was a hard life for a teenage boy, however, and Feinberg eventually moved to New York City.

In New York, Harry Feinberg found various jobs in which he "learned business." "In 1890 I met my Wife Annie Glass . . . and we kept Company until this day," he wrote fondly in his "History of Harry

Feinberg and Annie S. [sic] Feinberg," another of his short autobiographical sketches. Like her husband, Annie Glass was a typical East European Jewish immigrant. She and her brother Bernard left their native Kovno in 1887 or 1888 and landed in New York, where she found work, like so many other female Jews, in a shirtwaist factory. Whereas Harry Feinberg seems to have stayed away from politics, Annie Glass's "heroes were Johann Most and Emma Goldman," leaders of the "Anarchist crowd" to which her brother was attracted, and she took part in demonstrations for the ten-hour working day.[5] The young couple married in 1894, two years after Harry acquired American citizenship. His Americanization was furthered in 1894 when he joined the Knights of Pythias, a fraternal organization that welcomed Jews; he remained a member for over sixty years. Zelda's older sister, Pauline, was born in 1895; she herself came along three years later.

Harry and Annie Feinberg's experience deviated from the dominant pattern among East European Jewish immigrants because they did not remain in New York City. After unsuccessful ventures as an insurance agent, an ice-cream parlor owner, a wholesale stationery dealer, and the operator of a "library of popular and classical music," Harry Feinberg decided to try his luck in smaller communities, "on account of my health," as he later wrote. Zelda remembered a brief interlude on a farm in New Jersey, where her father tried raising chickens, but he soon moved the family to the town of Plainfield, where he "opened a general man's store and struggled hard with two nice loving little girls to bring up rightly." Plainfield in the first decade of the twentieth century was what Lee Shai Weissbach, author of *Jewish Life in Small-Town America*, called a "three-digit community": the 500 Jews living there were enough to sustain a synagogue, and Harry Feinberg took the initiative in organizing a school for the Jewish children. In her autobiography, Zelda remembered a childhood of Friday afternoons when "the house was redolent of baking bread and fragrant chicken soup" and Sabbath dinners with gleaming brass candlesticks and a freshly ironed white tablecloth. "So six million Jewish homes looked and smelled on Sabbath Eves in those pastoral years between the Russian pogroms and the rise of Hitler."[6]

Had she stayed in the Brooklyn neighborhood where she had been born, my grandmother would have been immersed in Jewish life. In a small town where a few Jewish families formed "a Jewish island in a Protestant sea," however, interaction with non-Jews was unavoidable. The teacher at Stillman Grammar School in Plainfield was clearly impressed with my grandmother's intelligence, since she was allowed to skip several grades, an indication that she must have been fluent in English from childhood on; as an adult, she could speak Yiddish, but not particularly well. Her teacher told Zelda's parents that she was "do[ing] all in my power for the adoucement of your little people," a polite way of saying that the rough edges of their Jewish immigrant background needed to be sanded off. In her autobiography, Zelda wrote that "being an orthodox Jewish child in an American little town was not without some complications." To avoid admitting to other children that she hadn't received any presents for Christmas, "whatever books and games I was given in the fall I hid and brought forth on Christmas Day," she recalled, and she and her sister Pauline took advantage of the generosity of the ladies at the Women's Christian Temperance Union, who gave them candy and toys in exchange for taking "the pledge" never to touch alcohol, a promise my grandmother flagrantly violated throughout her adult life.[7] Even though she did not become a teetotaler, the WCTU taught her from an early age that women in America could play a role in public affairs.

Zelda remembered her father as a store-owner "without aptitude" for his trade, who could be harsh and impatient with his children, behavior she had trouble reconciling with his "liberality to every charitable enterprise." His indifference to success and willingness to give to charities often left the family "short of cash for food, money and rent." It also infuriated Zelda's mother, "short, plump and vocal about what she wanted to get out of life, which was financial security and which she never achieved." Annie Feinberg worked in the family store, leaving Zelda and her older sister to do most of the housework. According to my own mother, who developed a wealth of midrashim about her mother-in-law, Zelda found both her parents impossible and insisted that her mother was "a stupid woman." My mother, who knew Annie Feinberg in her later years, remembered her as being "famous for her inability to say anything that constituted a decent compliment." Zelda's younger sister, Helen, however, thought that "if my mother would have had the education that we three had, she would have done a hell of a lot more than any of us did."[8]

Zelda was sure that her birth disappointed her father, who "being an only son, had demanded a boy to perpetuate his name." Like most Jewish immigrant parents, however, the Feinbergs made sure their daughters were educated. Although his own schooling had come to an end when he left Lithuania for America, Harry Feinberg was an enthusiastic autodidact who filled the family house with multivolume reference works; when my parents died, I discovered that the set of the 1906 *Jewish Encyclopedia* on their shelves had originally been one of his acquisitions. In her autobiography, Zelda remembered paging through the "twenty salmon pink portfolios of Famous Paintings of the World" and illustrated histories of the Civil War and the San Francisco earthquake. From the public library, she got children's books, "Elsie Dinsmore, The Little Colonel series, and even that new adult author, Conan Doyle," whose Sherlock Holmes mysteries gave her nightmares. Her father also followed current events avidly, and Zelda claimed that her earliest memory, dating from when she was three, was of her older sister explaining to her a newspaper photograph of the assassination of President McKinley in 1901.[9]

In 1912, when Zelda was fourteen, her parents moved from Plainfield to the coal-mining town of Wilkes-Barre, Pennsylvania, where her father managed a department store owned by two of his cousins who had established themselves in the neighboring community of Scranton. Even after this arrangement fell apart in the mid-1920s, Zelda's parents stayed in the Wilkes-Barre area, where her father was employed as a social worker by the local Jewish community, and she continued to visit there until they died in the 1950s. Instead of Plainfield, a "little and green and snug" rural community, the teenaged Zelda had to adjust to an environment where airborne coaldust "filtered into the house, filled the pores of one's skin, grayed the wash on the line."[10] Wilkes-Barre's Jewish population was several times larger than that of Plainfield—2,000 in 1907, rising to 3,000 in 1920, according to figures in the *American Jewish Year Book*—and the town had several long-established synagogues, as well as a Hebrew Ladies' Society and a Zionist group.

Other Jews who grew up in Wilkes-Barre often had bleak memories, both of the philistine atmosphere of the Jewish community there and of their treatment by the other ethnic groups in the population. One, a future physicist, rebelled against his father, a pious used-goods dealer whose ambition was that his "sons should own the largest furniture store in Wilkes-Barre." Another told the local paper that he was regularly beaten up by "the sons of immigrant coal miners who got their antisemitism from their mothers' milk."[11] Even though the Feinberg family's home was in the city's small "red-light district," Zelda and her sister integrated themselves easily into their new environment. "We joined the Y.W.C.A, the Y.W.H.A., the Sororis Literary Society. We gave parties and went to parties, made friends at school and, because the music teacher was Welsh, learned to sing 'Men of Harlech' lustily," she recalled. Social notes in the local newspaper recorded her presence at numerous events for high school girls and her service on the arrangements committee for the YMHA's "Halloween Hop."[12] One wonders whether her parents thought of her status as the manager of the YWCA's girls' basketball team as evidence of her successful integration into American culture or as a sign that she was abandoning the values of the Jewish culture in which they had attempted to raise her.

Whereas Zelda's recollections of Plainfield mentioned only Jews and Protestants, Wilkes-Barre introduced her to the social and ethnic mosaic of industrial America. Long after she had left for New York City, she would write magazine articles and works of fiction set in the city on the Susquehanna River, drawing on her recollections of its clannish Jews, its snooty Protestant elite, its Italian gangsters, the hard-scrabble farmers in the surrounding countryside, and, above all, its Irish and Slavic coalmin-ers.[13] She never forgot her first sight of the miners marching in a Labor Day parade, singing a militant union song. "The men who mine coal have since that day been my family," she wrote in her autobiography. In 1943, a fellow Wilkes-Barrean, folklorist George Korson, sent her a copy of his classic book, *Coal Dust on the Fiddle*, inscribing it "To Zelda, a great lady, a grand friend and kindred spirit who shares my enthusiasm for the coal diggers." When she became a novelist, Zelda would devote years to a book about the Molly Maguires, the Irish militants whose movement was bloodily repressed in the 1880s, a project that never saw publication. The coalminers offered her a chance to identify with a downtrodden group different from her own Jewish milieu. She remembered how easily girls from the mining "patches" were tempted into prostitution, because "the gilt and plush elegance of a whorehouse looked like heaven" to them. Perhaps the muscular men of the mines, with their "healthy bodies, their songs, their dialects," offered the adolescent girl a more impressive vision of masculinity than her father and other Jewish men she knew.[14]

Zelda spent only four years, from 1912 to 1916, in Wilkes-Barre, but those years were crucial ones in her life. She graduated from high school there in 1914, at the age of sixteen, and it was in Wilkes-Barre that she was hired as the first woman reporter on the local newspaper, the *Times Leader*, and began her writing career. Landing a job with a local paper was not uncommon for young American Jews at the time; more likely to have completed high school than many of their non-Jewish peers whose families put less value on formal education, especially for girls, they constituted a useful pool of talent. Edna Ferber, thirteen years older than Popkin, began the writing career that led her to a Pulitzer Prize as the first woman writer for the newspaper in Appleton, Wisconsin, and Ben Hecht started acquiring the experiences that helped him write *The Front Page* when he was hired at age seventeen by the *Chicago Daily Journal*. Even the modest success of the store Harry Feinberg ran in Wilkes-Barre made him sufficiently important as an advertiser to persuade the publisher of the *Times Leader* to employ his daughter, particularly since she was willing to work for three dollars a week, "the all-time low in beginners' salaries in journalism," as she wrote in her autobiography.[15]

"I was sixteen, fresh out of Wilkes-Barre High. My skirts were down to my ankles, my hair pinned in a bun, with a hair-combings rat to fill it out, and cast-iron corset to give me shape. I was far from grown up," Zelda recalled forty years later. Women's rights were a lively topic at the time—male Pennsylvania voters rejected women's suffrage in a 1915 referendum—but newsrooms were traditionally a male preserve. "In 1914, there were no females on general assignments in our part of the state. The few who got into the newspaper plants did social notes and advice to the lovelorn," Zelda wrote. "Mac," the formidable city editor of the paper, was not happy at having to employ a woman and did what he could to scare her off by sending her on the most unpleasant assignments available. "I covered a dozen homicides before I was 18," Zelda told an interviewer toward the end of her life, and her sister Helen remembered watching one of the paper's editors "wav[ing] a tearsheet containing one of her stories practically in her face, then he gave her one of the worst bawling outs I have ever heard and when she was almost in tears he came over, put his arm around her shoulder, and said, 'Don't let it happen again, little lady.'"[16] Zelda was determined not to fail, however, and eventually she won over her gruff boss "because I was willing to run around," unlike her male colleagues, who "took it easy, as much as they could."[17] The lesson of her experience at the *Times Leader* was that a woman could succeed in a man's world if she was willing to work hard and ignore casual harassment; it was a formula she would carry over into her adult life.

Even though the *Times Leader* was a small-town paper, it had already launched the careers of several successful writers; in her autobiography, Zelda named two local Jews, Sam Hoffenstein and Louis Weitzenkorn, who had made the leap from Wilkes-Barre to New York. After two years in the *Times Leader*'s city room, Zelda was ready to make the same move. The Wilkes-Barre paper said goodbye to her with an article headlined "Bright Girl Reporter Going Higher," but her interview with the dean of Columbia's Pulitzer School of Journalism was a rude awakening. Forty years later, the memory of being told to "Go back home and get married," preferably to "a man whose people are as much like your people as you can find," still rankled as a reminder of how both her sex and her ethnic background closed doors to her. She failed the entrance exam for Barnard College, and had to fall back on "Columbia's cellar door," the school's extension division. Despite their own difficult circumstances, her parents scraped up a few dollars to subsidize her, and she was able to board with her mother's sister. No New York paper would hire her, but Louis Weitzenkorn, whose example had inspired her, took pity on her and published a few pieces of her writing in a Socialist publication where he had found work.[18]

Even though she had to live on candy bars at the end of each month when her money ran out, what mattered to Zelda was that she was in

New York, "Main Street of the world of ideas, offering sustenance and sanctuary for the man who is willing to think." A city emblematic of modernity was taking shape around her: "The Woolworth skyscraper was being built, the Flatiron was up." At first, she lived on the fringes of the city's life, attending classes and supplementing her parents' stipend by working in the basement of Gimbel's department store, "tying sales tags on shoes." Then one of her fellow students at Columbia invited her to her parents' home for dinner, and a new world opened up for her. Her friend's father was Morris Hillquit, a leading figure in the Socialist Party and the pacifist movement that opposed American entry into World War I. Zelda would never become a committed radical, but the lessons about politics that she absorbed listening to Hillquit would stay with her. When he ran for mayor of New York in 1917, she threw herself into his campaign. "At last I was having fun in New York, an insider, caught up in the stirring and doing."[19]

Still determined to become a writer, Zelda jumped at the chance to be introduced to a young man who "worked on a weekly magazine and had all sorts of literary contacts in town." Louis Popkin "was stocky and brisk with bright hazel eyes, full of laughter, dark curly hair, a Latin face with mobility and warmth, but no conventional handsomeness." Like Zelda, he was the child of East European Jewish immigrants. If Zelda's parents struggled to make a living in their new country, Louis Popkin's seem to have made no effort at all. In Russia, his father had been "a *felsher*, which is a combination leech doctor and practical nurse." His specialty was temporarily dislocating young Jewish men's arms so that they would not be drafted into the army. In America, there was no demand for this talent, and Charlie Popkin left it to his children to find ways to support the family. Louis, the first of the Popkin family's five children to be born in America, started earning money by making deliveries for a neighborhood butcher at age five; by the time he was seven, he was a newsboy. "He almost became an outcast and a thief," Zelda claimed, but instead he managed to put himself through high school and then through night school at City College, whose 1913 yearbook lists him as a member of the student council.[20] By the time Zelda began dating him, Louis Popkin had already transcended his poverty-stricken background and propelled himself into a position that gave him contacts with the most distinguished members of New York City's Jewish "establishment." He was on the editorial staff of the *American Hebrew*, a magazine that represented the outlook of the "uptown" German-Jewish elite, and he was doing publicity work for the Joint Distribution Committee, the organization established in 1914 to provide aid to the Jews of Europe and Palestine who found themselves caught up in the maelstrom of the First World War.

How had a poor boy from an East European immigrant family penetrated into this milieu? A newspaper clipping from 1937 that Zelda preserved in her files—she may well have written it herself—gives a clue:

> *Twenty-five years ago the Philip Cowens were observing the silver anniversary of their marriage. . . . A young lad named Louis Popkin was hired by the happy couple to check the guests' hats. . . . And there were some famous hats to be checked. . . . One belonged to Jacob Schiff, another to Dr. Cyrus Adler, a third to Felix M. Warburg, a fourth to Solomon Schechter, still another to Cyrus Sulzberger. . . . The lad Popkin was overwhelmed at the honor. . . . But in the excitement of the moment, he was overlooked when the time came to don the feedbags.*

According to the story, the Cowens apologized for forgetting to feed him and promised to invite him to their golden wedding anniversary. "When the aged couple sent out invitations to their golden anniversary, there was one for Louis. . . . And when the appointed hour came, he was at the festive board (with his wife) . . . thankful that he no longer had to check hats and that, after having waited a quarter of a century, he didn't come down with a bellyache or something else to keep him from partaking of that long-deferred repast."[21] Philip Cowen was the founder of the *American Hebrew*, and the guests enumerated in the article were leading lights of the American Jewish community; perhaps the talents that would let Louis Popkin carve out a successful career in public relations allowed him to leverage the contacts he made at the Cowens' dinner into a chance to join the *American Hebrew* staff.

Aside from whatever opportunities the dinner at the Cowens' may have given him, Louis Popkin was not lacking in ambition. In 1915, he and some friends wrote to Israel Zangwill, then one of the most famous Jewish writers, seeking his support for a plan to create a Jewish magazine of their own.[22] Within a few months, he had become the first publicist hired by the Joint Distribution Committee, the organization created to unify American Jews' efforts on behalf of their coreligionists in the war-torn Old World. It was the beginning of a relationship with the "Joint" that would last down to the tragic years of the Holocaust. The position brought him into regular contact with many of the leaders of the Jewish community whose hats he had checked at the Cowens' anniversary dinner. By 1918, after America entered the war, he was doing publicity for a second organization, the Jewish Welfare Board, which provided support for Jewish soldiers serving in the army.[23] As he courted my grandmother, Louis Popkin was thus engaged directly with major issues affecting the Jewish world.

Zelda was lucky to have met a young man whose intentions were honorable, unlike Pearl "Polly" Adler, a Russian Jewish immigrant exactly her age who was determined, like Zelda, not to stay in an underpaid dead-end job and whose life course was determined by an encounter with a smooth-talking gentleman who steered her into the life of prostitution that eventually made her America's most celebrated brothel-keeper.[24] Nevertheless, it took over a year before Zelda was ready to accept Louis Popkin's proposal. Her family in Wilkes-Barre was not pleased at the prospect of her marrying a man from such a poor family, and she wasn't sure she was ready to give up the independence she had just begun to enjoy. "At nineteen, with all of the world before you, it is not easy to narrow your orbit to the walled city of matrimony," she wrote in her autobiography. Not yet permanently settled in New York, she was still spending a good deal of time in Wilkes-Barre, where the *Times Leader* noted her comings and goings and reported an occasion when she "pleasantly entertained a few friends at her home," serving them a "dainty lunch."[25]

New York fueled her literary ambitions, although Wilkes-Barre still provided her with her best opportunities of appearing in print. In May 1917, she showed that she had mastered the journalistic skill of manufacturing a story out of the story of how she had missed the story when the *Times Leader* published her entertaining account of her unsuccessful attempt to witness French war hero General Joffre's appearance on the Columbia campus. Later that year, she found a way to contribute to the war effort by writing the script for a "patriotic pantomime play" put on in Wilkes-Barre by girls from the local YWHA and directed by her sister Pauline; the fact that, just a month earlier, she had been supporting Morris Hillquit's anti-war campaign in New York City apparently did not faze her. The diary of her future brother-in-law, William Pinsker, who was courting her older sister, Pauline, gives a glimpse of the young woman's outspokenness. When he spent an evening at the Feinbergs,' "Jennie—or Zelda, as she now calls herself," told him that "my talking too much is a vice," Pinsker recorded. "She is a perfectly frank girl and a very nice one; still, I do not think most people who know her like her. All will say that she is clever, she as well as the rest of the world." (The *Times Leader*, which had always referred to her as "Jennie Feinberg," gave her name as "Zelda" for the first time in an article in September 1917.)[26]

Zelda may have put him off at first, but Louis Popkin was persistent. When Zelda's parents said they would not approve the marriage if she did not have a job that would give her some financial security, he got her hired as his assistant at the Jewish Welfare Board, where, by the end of 1918, he had risen to head of the publicity department. "There are those who say he married me because it was cheaper than hiring me, which may be the case," Zelda remarked in her autobiography. A personnel roster for the organization noted that she "Writes copy. Serves as reporter," and listed her salary as $125 a month.[27] In her autobiography, Zelda wrote, "Our marriage began early in 1918. Our wedding took place in the fall of 1919," indicating that the couple lived together for over a year before any official ceremony, hardly a common situation in that day and age. This was probably another reason why, as William Pinsker recorded in his diary when his engagement to Zelda's sister was made official, that Annie Feinberg "has not yet forgiven Zelda for marrying Lou Popkin."[28] Marry they did, however, on 19 October 1919, at the Broadway Central Hotel in New York City. Despite her mother's earlier reservations, Zelda's parents paid for a proper ceremony, and her mother had her own wedding band split to make a ring for her daughter. One of New York's most prominent rabbis, Joseph Silverman from the fashionable Reform

Temple Emanu-El, described in the wedding announcement as "an intimate friend of the groom," officiated, further evidence of how successful Louis Popkin had been in making connections with the New York Jewish elite. "The bride wore a travelling suit, a black satin picture hat and a corsage bouquet of orchids and lilies-of-the-valley. The young couple are enjoying a southern trip," the Wilkes-Barre paper reported. Perhaps in return for her parents' toleration of the somewhat belated celebration of her union with a man of whom they had initially disapproved, Zelda agreed to serve as the secretary for a "family association or league," a pet project of her father's, who saw it as a way of strengthening ties with his relatives through "mutual helpfulness."[29]

Whatever her parents thought, Zelda had every reason to be pleased with the direction her life had taken. She had escaped from the confines of her immigrant family and from Wilkes-Barre and found both love and a career in New York City. Although her work for the Jewish Welfare Board did not make her a recognized author, it gave her a chance to exercise her writing skills, and her husband's connection with the *American Hebrew* promised her opportunities that she would soon begin to exploit. By moving in with Louis before they were officially married, she had obviously flouted the religious precepts of her parents, but they may have been somewhat mollified by the fact that her liaison with him had anchored her to the world of Jewish concerns; in raising money for the Joint Distribution Committee, the young couple were helping to sustain the East European Jewish communities from which the elder Feinbergs had come. Perhaps they were also pleased that she had chosen to be married under the Jewish name of "Zelda" they had given her, rather than embracing the more American-sounding name of "Jennie" they had felt obliged to put on her birth certificate.

CHAPTER 2

Zelda Popkin

Modern American Woman

ON 11 NOVEMBER 1918, ZELDA WAS AT LUNCH WITH THE MAN SHE already regarded as her husband, even though it would be almost another year before the young couple would marry legally. "A newsboy came running in with extras," she recalled in her autobiography. "We went out into the delirious streets. We danced and shouted and sang with the crowds because the war was over." She would always remember the date of the Armistice that ended the First World War as one "which belongs to me . . . for on it I saw, not aware that I saw, what my future would be."[1] For the rest of her life, she treasured a small etching of the crowds in the New York streets on Armistice Day, done by the American Jewish artist William Meyerowitz, a friend of hers, which now hangs on my wall. Zelda knew that the life opening up for her would be a spent with the man she loved: they were living together and had already decided to pool the skills they had developed working for the Jewish Welfare Board to open a public relations firm.

The Armistice Day celebration also gave Zelda a chance to launch her career as a freelance magazine journalist. A week earlier, she had had her first signed article in the *American Hebrew*, the country's leading English-language Jewish periodical, a promotional piece for the Jewish Welfare Board. Now the magazine gave the Wilkes-Barre *Times Leader*'s one-time crime reporter the opportunity to show that she could capture a great moment in history, and she rose to the challenge. "Waving in one hand the Stars and Stripes and in the other the blue and white flag of Zion—shouting, singing, dancing and sobbing—the East Side welcomed the dawn of peace," she told the magazine's readers. "The East Side, that had given its sons to the great conflict; the East Side, that had given its small earnings for Liberty Bonds, War Savings Stamps and War Relief Drives—the East Side that had repudiated time and again the stigma of disloyalty, rejoiced with the nation when peace came—peace with victory. And the East Side celebrated as only the East Side can—with tears and laughter." Tears from "a grey-haired, red-eyed woman" who had just learned "her Yossel is killed"; joy "in the cafés—the Cosmopolitan, Levitt's and Strunsky's—where . . . there was singing and shouting until nearly dawn. Poet and playwright, ghetto diplomat and actor, with hands on one another's shoulder, drank (wine and tea flowed lavishly) to the future of democracy."[2]

With a man by her side, a career plan mapped out, and a foot in the door of the literary world, Zelda was confident that the future would offer women like her possibilities her mother's generation had never dreamed of. "I was emancipated," she wrote in her autobiography. "I had bobbed my hair . . . when Henri of Hotel Brevoort in Greenwich Village was the only barber in town who would cut women's hair and even he asked whether you had your mother's consent. I smoked Fatimas . . . though headwaiters in some restaurants scowled. . . . I had marched in the suffrage parades. I was, I told myself, modern and uninhibited." Henri, "pioneer bobber and aristocrat of hairdressers" according to the *New Yorker*, practiced his trade in the center of the neighborhood where members of the avant-garde women's movement known as "Heterodoxy" regularly encountered each other. Whether Zelda knew of the group or not, she certainly adopted many of its attitudes.[3] The fact that she and Louis were Jewish did not seem like a handicap. She and her husband had grown up in America and attended public schools designed to turn them into fully acculturated citizens. Both of them had given up the religious practices that might have hindered their integration into the mainstream of American life. During the war, they had worked for the Jewish Welfare Board, providing for the Jewish soldiers whose service in the military justified expectations for greater acceptance of Jews as full members of American society. The contacts they made during the war with influential members of the German Jewish elite, such as Jacob Schiff and Louis Marshall, promised to open doors for them that might otherwise have been closed to two young East European Jews from poor families.

History would prove more complicated than Zelda could have imagined on Armistice Day in 1918. The "war to end all wars" created new conflicts that would affect her life. The achievement of suffrage was a victory for women, but even the most self-confident and emancipated of them still found themselves facing obstacles that did not lend themselves to attack through marches and ballot initiatives. There were new opportunities for American Jews, but also new threats of prejudice. In 1926, a Jewish woman author a few years older than she published an autobiographical novel, *I Am a Woman—and a Jew,* that wrestled with the questions that Zelda faced in her own life. The novel's main character, like Zelda, had grown up with Orthodox immigrant parents. She had broken away from her family's religious orthodoxy and married a man they did not approve of—a Gentile, in her case. She had ambitions to be a writer but wound up pursuing a career in social work, one of the new professions that was developing in the early twentieth century, before belatedly establishing herself as a journalist in New York City. Her loving husband encouraged her ambitions but also wanted to remain the "head . . . of our life and of our home." Other women challenged the novel's heroine to explain "how a woman could be a mother and a wife and at the same time work side by side with her husband in his profession." She had to cope with the conflict between having a demanding job and raising her children. She encountered antisemitic prejudice, and eventually she recognized the impossibility of abandoning her connection with Jewishness, even though she could not find meaning in Jewish religious beliefs. Whether or not Zelda read Leah Morton's novel, it shows that the challenges my grandmother faced in the interwar period were those faced by an entire generation of bright, ambitious American Jewish women.[4]

Like the heroine of *I Am a Woman,* Zelda entered into marriage partly as a way to make a career. The end of the war meant the winding down of the Jewish Welfare Board's activities, but she and Louis were ready to venture out on their own. They were confident that the lessons they had learned about organizing publicity could be applied more widely. Aside from a few well-known names, like Ivy Lee and Sigmund Freud's nephew Edward Bernays, the public relations field in 1918 "had few full-time practitioners. . . . We were all pioneers. . . . What techniques were best were still to be learned," Zelda wrote in her autobiography.[5] As they anticipated the opportunities they could find in the new profession of molding public opinion, the Popkins were also anticipating the growth of a new world, one that would be radically different from the one in which they had grown up. They would make their lives in New York City, the capital of modernity, with its skyscrapers, its subways, and its busy streets. They would be part of the largest Jewish community in the world, where the immigrant culture of their parents was rapidly being replaced by new ways of being Jewish. As a woman, Zelda would enter the postwar decades as part of the first generation to possess the right to vote: after the victory in New York in 1917, the Nineteenth Amendment, passed in 1920, would allow her and all other women to participate in the first postwar presidential election.

By the time she wrote her autobiography in the 1950s, Zelda could look back ironically on "the halcyon years when we listened to the Happiness Boys on the radio, when the neighborhood barber was considered a reliable source for a stock-market tip." She knew that the 1920s had given way to the Great Depression, to the rise of fascism abroad and an increasingly strident antisemitism at home, and to a second world war even more destructive than the first, especially for Europe's Jews. Women had gained new opportunities, but questions about their place in society remained. For her and Louis, however, the first years after the Armistice were a time of excitement and promise. In 1912, Louis had been overlooked when dinner was served at the Cowens' anniversary party; at the end of 1918, Jacob Schiff, the head of the American Jewish Committee and one of the distinguished guests whose hat he had checked on that occasion, entrusted the young couple with the task of drafting a plea to President Woodrow Wilson, in the name of the American Jewish community, for protection for the rights of minorities in the new countries being called into life by the peacemakers at Versailles.[6] Whatever shape the new postwar world would take, the Popkins were confident that they would be in the middle of things.

On the strength of Schiff's commission, which was their first paid assignment, Zelda and Louis rented a one-room office at 42–44 West 39th Street for their Planned Publicity Service and hired a secretary who turned out to know stenography but very little English. Louis took charge of "hunting business or conferring with what business we had" while Zelda "sat at the desk, writing news stories." Within a few years, they had relocated to 103 Park Avenue, at the corner of 41st Street. It was a strategic location, a block away from the offices of the Joint Distribution Committee and the Jewish Agency, two major organizations that frequently sought publicity, as well as the Jewish Telegraphic Agency, the news service for Jewish publications. The location also put the Popkins close to Times Square, to the office of the *New Yorker*, to which Zelda would soon become a contributor, and to the theater district. A photograph from the period shows Zelda working her telephone, with a pile of the day's newspapers and a pack of the cigarettes that her fellow public relations maven Edward Bernays was hawking to young women in front of her.

Years later, my uncle Roy told me how his easygoing, good-humored father, assisted by an older partner, Abraham Fromenson, charmed the clients, while Zelda wrote copy and nagged customers to pay their bills. In her own memoir, published around the same time as Zelda's, Doris Fleischman, Bernays's wife and business partner, remembered the difficulties of "being an exception in a masculine world" and how she "learned to withdraw from situations where the gender of the public relations counsel was a factor."[7] My grandmother probably had to accept the same constraints: Louis appeared in published photographs with Albert Einstein, Rabbi Stephen Wise, and president Herbert Hoover, but Zelda did not.

Although the celebrated Edward Bernays was Jewish, advertising was not a profession that particularly welcomed Jews. A survey of employment discrimination published in 1931 quoted the president of the Association of National Advertisers, a Jew himself, as saying that he could think of only six or seven coreligionists who held important positions in

Figure 2.1. Zelda Popkin at work (c. 1925): The professional woman of the 1920s used modern technology—the telephone—to do her work. The pack of cigarettes on her desk symbolized her emancipation from earlier norms of women's behavior.

the field, and an article in a leading Jewish magazine explained that "All good agencies bar Jews. Ask them why and they say their clients won't stand for it."[8] Throughout the next two decades, the Popkins continued to work for "establishment" Jewish causes, which probably provided most of their income. To the end of her life, Zelda remained nostalgic about the "giants of American Jewish life" she met through their publicity work. Louis Popkin regularly attended board meetings of the Joint Distribution Committee, where he had begun his career; a treasured family photograph shows him standing behind Albert Einstein and Stephen Wise at a fundraising event where the famous scientist encouraged donations to the new Hebrew University in Jerusalem.

The two Popkins wrote articles publicizing Hebrew Union College, the center of the Reform movement, and prepared press releases for programs sponsored by New York City's Temple Emanu-El and for Beth Israel hospital. Louis Popkin regularly interviewed prominent Jewish figures for the *American Hebrew* and the Reform movement's *American Israelite*. Although they depended heavily on Jewish clients, the Popkins also sought out other business. Over the years, they did publicity work for a number of non-Jewish causes, including Anne Lindbergh's China Famine and Flood Relief campaign and the Spanish Republicans during that country's civil war, and for an American archeologist who had found

Figure 2.2. Louis Popkin with a famous client (1925?): The Popkins arranged publicity for Albert Einstein's fundraising talks on behalf of the newly founded Hebrew University in the 1920s. Einstein is seated with Rabbi Stephen Wise, a leader of the American Zionist movement.

the Biblical city of Lachish. A press release announcing a course on public relations that Louis Popkin taught at the City College of New York
in 1929 listed a number of their commercial clients: the American Master Hairdressers' Association, the National Association of Men's Straw
Hat Manufacturers, the Association of Leather Goods Manufacturers
of America, the Arnold Constable department store, and the Broadway
National Bank and Trust Company.[9]

The Popkins also worked for a number of state and local political
candidates in the New York area. In 1924, they organized the New
York "speakers' bureau" of the Progressive Party's Robert La Follette,
whose third-party campaign won over 16 percent of the national vote.
The Progressive Party's program, which included public regulation of
utilities, higher taxes on the wealthy, and "equality for women and men,"
anticipated the activist liberalism of the New Deal to which Zelda would
remain loyal to the end of her life, but by 1940, "we'd urged election of
Democratic, Republican, Independent, Liberal candidates, public relations being another trade in which your bedfellows are whoever picks up
the tab," she wrote in her autobiography.[10] In 1932, she scored a coup for
Arnold Constable, one of their most loyal clients, by persuading Eleanor
Roosevelt to buy her inauguration gown there. As a result, the "small,
middle-income Fifth Avenue department store" edged out fancier establishments to become the First Lady's regular supplier. This connection
did not prevent the Popkins from doing work for Alf Landon when he
ran against Franklin Roosevelt in 1936: the Republican campaign con-
tracted with them to keep out the "peculiar vermin whose attitudes came
from Mein Kampf [who] kept crawling from the woodwork into the
campaign offices." A year before going to work for Landon, Louis Popkin had politely declined a request from the opposite end of the political
spectrum, telling Earl Browder, head of the American Communist Party,
that "I do not think it is practical at this moment to talk about what a
Communist President would do."[11]

"I went to the office every day and my name was on the letterhead,"
Zelda wrote in her autobiography. At the time, she was one of the
minority of American women with a professional career. A 1925 article
that claimed that "a Jewish girl who has to go to work after her wedding

looks upon herself as the unhappiest creature on earth" exaggerated the situation, but in 1920, only 9 percent of married women in America earned wages, and the 781-page 1928 edition of *Who's Who in American Jewry* listed a mere handful of women working in professions other than social work and community organizations, including only one "publicist." Although Zelda clearly rejected the idea that women should not do paid work, she was not entirely comfortable with the occupation she found herself pursuing. Unlike the many middle-class American Jewish women who found roles beyond their homes in these years by serving as unpaid volunteers on behalf of causes such as birth control and pacifism or in Jewish women's organizations such as synagogue and temple sisterhoods and Hadassah, activities that expressed their personal values, my grandmother had to learn to make the compromises that success in the business world required.[12]

In a 1928 advice manual for women choosing a vocation, her fellow professional Doris Fleischman called public relations "an enthralling occupation for the woman who has constructive ideas and the desire and force to make them result in concrete activities, facts, laws, and products."[13] Zelda did not always find it that way. As a former journalist, badgering reporters to get coverage for clients and being under pressure to "make small men big and black resemble white" bothered Zelda. When she wrote that line in 1956, she might have been remembering her article on "The Jew and Aviation," published in 1927, shortly after Charles Lindbergh's historic flight. Zelda's assignment was to celebrate "the first trans-Atlantic air passenger," a controversial businessman named Charles A. Levine, who financed the second trans-Atlantic flight and then insisted on replacing the plane's navigator "by stepping into the plane attired in his business suit just before the takeoff. This spectacular feat," Zelda wrote, "if it served no other purpose, helped to focus attention on the Jew's contribution to aviation," although it also resulted in the plane landing many miles from its intended destination.[14]

Over the years, Zelda put her name on a number of magazine articles that were clearly puff pieces, such as a piece lauding New York department stores for making themselves into community cultural centers that sponsored free lectures and offered cheap art prints to upgrade customers'

Figure 2.3. "The Jew and Aviation" (1927?): Associating herself with airplanes was one way for Zelda to show that, as a Jew and a woman, she was part of the modern world of the 1920s.

aesthetic tastes. It was not only capitalists who benefited from Zelda's publicity talents: a pair of articles about Soviet cinema that she signed in 1930 and 1931, at a time when the Communist regime was working strenuously to improve its image abroad, hyped the achievements of Russian filmmakers and their contributions to the making of a new society whose audiences want to see "the driving force of history rather than the pomp, and above all . . . [the audience member] craves facts; facts that will help him to improve the conditions of his life, facts that will set him before a wide window through which he may watch the reconstruction of his country."[15]

Louis Popkin, according to Zelda, had no scruples about their occupation. When her husband argued that "We're professionals, doing a job. A doctor doesn't think well of V.D. Yet he treats it. A lawyer disapproves of murder. Yet he defends murderers," Zelda countered that doctors and lawyers were serving a higher cause, whereas "the public relations man has no excuse for much he does except that he's been paid. Anyone with cash in hand or credit at the bank can hire him to exalt the shoddy, to promote a dangerous set of ideas, even work up a war." Louis, like the characters in *For Immediate Release*, a 1937 novel that described their profession as "lying and parasitic and acting . . . phoning people. Annoying people. Pushing," had fewer reservations. "He stirred a pot with gusto and the headier, the more incredible, the brew which came from it, the greater his enjoyment," Zelda recalled. "Most of the time he believed sincerely that his work was public service. He could sell anything to anyone, including himself." His 1930 article, "Henry J. Gaisman, The Edison of the Safety Razor Field," which put its subject on the level of Albert Einstein, was a demonstration of the lengths to which he was willing to go.[16]

Despite her qualms, Zelda clearly enjoyed some of the ventures into ballyhoo in which she collaborated, particularly the story of the "Shifters," a wholly imaginary conspiracy supposedly dedicated to undermining the morals of young women. She and Louis, according to her account, concocted this "Flapper Ku Klux Klan" to attract attention to the efforts of one of their clients, the Working Girls' Vacation Society. The young publicists and their friends had a fine time making up a whole lexicon of phrases—"wurp," "sock-dragger," "cake-eater," "the slat slimped on me"—and a secret badge—a paperclip worn on the lapel—that supposedly identified Shifters who seduced women into frittering away the money that would have allowed them to spend the summers in healthy surroundings. Helpful reporters filed stories about the Shifter menace that ran in papers all over the country; even the august *New York Times* took the bait. "Since nothing is more tempting to the publicity hungry than inquiry into the morals of youth," Zelda wrote, the Shifters were denounced by the president of the Board of Education of the City of New York, the World Sunday School Association, and the Reverend Robert McCaul of Brooklyn. "Then the slat slimped," she concluded: the story died when the Popkins ran out of ideas to keep it going. Nine decades later, however, the Shifters resurfaced in the *New York Times*: in 2012, an unwary columnist republished the story, and, when confronted with the relevant pages from Zelda's autobiography, refused to concede that he might have been taken in.[17]

Even as she worked as a full partner in the public relations business, however, Zelda also developed an individual career as a freelance journalist. Louis Popkin may have started out as a journalist—it was the occupation he listed on his draft registration card in 1916—but he did not have the same passion for writing as the woman he married. His articles in the *American Hebrew* show that he also did not have the same talent for it. Zelda's first articles appeared in that magazine, and, for the most part, they concerned Jewish women. An article on women who had served in France during the war observed "that whenever a Jewish girl entered any field of service she speedily made her mark and in practically every case was assigned to work of still greater importance and responsibility." A piece on women's involvement in Jewish fundraising hailed "the most ambitious task ever undertaken by the Jewish women of New York," an article entitled "Mother Love in Mean Streets" used data gathered by the city's health commissioner to show that "the typical Jewish mother is a real and wonderful mother," and a book review critiqued the latest novel by the Jewish writer Fannie Hurst, "this gifted young demigoddess." In 1921, Zelda was the only woman contributor to the *American Hebrew*'s special issue on American Jewish history. Her survey of "Jewish Dolly Madisons" anticipated the conclusions of subsequent women's historians, showing that "women wore lovely gowns and costly jewels, gossiped, coquetted, kept house, raised families, sewed, read, went to college, raised money for the synagogue, helped the poor, envied and tried to enter the sphere of masculine activities."[18]

Zelda made no mention of her extensive contributions to Jewish publications during the 1920s in her autobiography. It is clear, however, that the *American Hebrew* in particular played a crucial role in the development of her writing career. That a young woman who, only a few years earlier, had campaigned enthusiastically for the Socialist Morris Hillquit would find a supportive environment at that magazine in the early 1920s was surprising. Founded in 1873, the *American Hebrew* had long been regarded as the mouthpiece of the country's wealthy and acculturated Jewish elite. The advertisements for luxury automobiles, gold jewelry, and exclusive country clubs that filled its pages portrayed a world of wealth and privilege to which Zelda and Louis did not have access. Under the editorship of Rabbi Isaac Landman, who took the position in 1918, the *American Hebrew* was outspokenly anti-Zionist and opposed to socialism and communism.[19] While Zelda and Louis were working for Robert La Follette's Progressive campaign in 1924, the magazine reflected the Jewish elite's traditional sympathy for the Republican Party. It identified with the Reform and Conservative movements, which promoted forms of Judaism adapted to American conditions, whereas Zelda and Louis had no personal interest in religion at all.

Although there was much in the *American Hebrew*'s content with which Zelda probably disagreed, there were several features of the magazine with which she could identify. Whereas many of the leaders of the establishment Jewish community thought the best response to the hate campaigns of Henry Ford and the Ku Klux Klan was a dignified silence, the *American Hebrew* never hesitated to speak out against antisemitism. When Zelda and Louis became active in combatting Jew-hatred in the 1930s, they undoubtedly drew on lessons they had learned from Isaac Landman. Most importantly for Zelda, however, the magazine took a progressive position on women's rights. An unsigned editorial in 1925 announced that "It is nothing short of an inspiration to see how women are taking hold of the world's work with an alacrity paralleling the zeal with which they have always participated in the domestic problems and pleasures of life. . . . They are both active and prominent in every sphere of the complexities that total our modern, western civilization. The war tested their powers and abilities in occupations and interests other than the home; the postwar period, short as it has been, has proved them capable enough to hold their own with the men along the line of the world's endeavors. Argue as you will with the proposition of homemaking versus a career—the facts, as opposed to the theories, indicate that women today are no whit behind the men in the field of commerce, in the professions and industries, even in politics." In 1922, a Reform rabbi used the magazine's pages to argue that women should have the right to be ordained.[20]

The *American Hebrew* put its feminist principles into practice by giving several women opportunities to become regular contributors and to write extensively about women's achievements. Zelda probably published more pieces in the magazine during the years from 1918 to 1926 than any other woman writer, however. Unlike Myra May, who churned out a series of articles about successful professional women, Zelda's contributions were varied. She did news articles, she reviewed books for the magazine's literary chronicle, and she joined better-known authors such as Fannie Hurst and Ben Hecht in entertaining readers with short stories. She and Louis even had the chutzpah to insert themselves into the magazine's society pages, normally reserved for the doings of the great and the good in the Jewish community. A short item in 1921 announced that "Mr. and Mrs. Louis Popkin, of New York City, are spending the summer at Suffern, N.Y.," and a paragraph in 1924 informed the world that "A second son was born to Mr. and Mrs. Louis Popkin, of 1145 Vyse avenue, at the Nursery and Child's Hospital, Thursday, December 27," adding that "Mrs. Popkin is a well-known writer of fiction and book reviews, and her many articles signed 'Zelda F. Popkin' had won her distinction in the literary world."[21]

The news of my father's birth elicited a letter from Stephen S. Wise, the most prominent American rabbi of the day, which reflected the way in which the Popkins' publicity work had put them in touch with leading figures in American Jewish life:

Free Synagogue, West 69th Street, New York, December 31, 1923

My Dear Young Friend:

Even though I can't typewrite as well as your big brother, I may yet give myself the pleasure of congratulating you upon your arrival. If in the course of what I trust may be a very long and altogether blessed journey through life, you require that help which lies in having your virtues heralded, do not fail to call upon the Planned Publicity Service, and such influence which I may have with its perpetrators will be at your command. If its managers continue to overcharge during the next few years with the same zest and ruthlessness with which they do now, it will have been possible for them to discontinue the service long before you require any heralding or trumpeting.

In the meantime, I am, with most hearty greetings to you and to your parents,

Faithfully yours, Stephen S. Wise[22]

Zelda's feature articles on Jewish figures and institutions usually had a positive tone, and some of them, particularly those she contributed to the *American Israelite*, were probably part of the Popkins' public relations work.[23] The short stories she published in the *American Hebrew*, heavily influenced by O. Henry and Fannie Hurst, were undistinguished and hardly hinted at a promising career as a fiction writer.[24] Her numerous book reviews in the *American Hebrew* and the articles about theater and movies she did for the *B'nai B'rith Magazine* gave her more scope to express herself effectively. She applauded the Italian modernist playwright Luigi Pirandello's works and praised the French novelist Romain Rolland for his recognition of the vitality that Jews brought to European culture. The American naturalist author Theodore Dreiser earned her approval because he "works like a surgeon, dissecting life minutely, exposing its festering sores with an unshrinking scalpel," but the prominent orchestra conductor Walter Damrosch's memoir proved, she said, that his field "is music, rather than literature." Her fellow Jewish woman author Fannie Hurst's second novel, *Lummox*, won high marks, but Zelda could not help remarking that Hurst's earlier work had been "submerged for many years in a morass of highly paid slushy sentiment."[25]

Not surprisingly, in view of the magazines where she published, many of Zelda's reviews dealt with works on Jewish themes. In an article about the nineteenth-century French actress Rachel, she expressed her frustration with the fact that "as quickly as a Jew becomes great or successful in any sphere, he ceases, in all but the *Dearborn Independent*, to be heralded as a Jew. He is a great Russian, Frenchman, Pole—but never a Jew." A review of Ada Sterling's *The Jew and Civilization* praised the author for putting the emphasis "not so much on what modern Jews have achieved for civilization, but on the important thoughts, systems, plans and movements which have been originated by Jews." The future author of the first American novel about the 1948 Israeli war of independence dismissed an overwrought thriller set in 1920s Palestine: "An attempt to erect a modern melodramatic novel on the ruins of the ancient Temple of Jerusalem has resulted in a decidedly tedious and unconvincing work." But she recognized the significance of the immigrant novelist Anzia Yezierska's story collection, *Hungry Hearts*, which "takes its place beside Mary Antin's *The Promised Land* and Abraham Cahan's *The Rise of David Levinsky* as a descriptive narrative of the spiritual hunger of the immigrant Jew. And yet it does more than either of these books, for it stimulates the hope that at least a great writer has risen out of Israel to right the wrongs that lesser scribblers have done," she told the *American Hebrew*'s readers.[26]

What she meant by "wrongs" was made clear in her discussion of the smash Broadway hit *Abie's Irish Rose*, which succeeded, she complained, because "the world likes to laugh at the Jew and in the mispronunciations, the mannerisms and mental processes of his adaptation to his American environment it has found cause for abundant mirth." Al Jolson's blackface performance in the first sound movie, *The Jazz Singer*, emphasized by a photograph accompanying her article, didn't bother her: she saw it as evidence for the proposition that there was "an intimate relationship between the wailing ecstasy of jazz and the song that comes from the heart of the Jewish people." She was more critical of the film's unrealistic depiction of "the alacrity with which an Orthodox congregation welcomes a beardless cantor."[27]

An extended review of *The Coming of the Lord*, a now-forgotten novel by a South African Jewish woman author, Sarah Gertrude Millin, offered Zelda an occasion to make some of her most outspoken statements about the Jewish condition. Explicitly acknowledging the parallels between the racial situation in South Africa and America, Zelda noted that, according to Millin, Jews were welcomed by the whites in South Africa for their "organizing talents and indomitable energy," but their attitudes changed when Jews achieved real economic and professional success. She quoted Millin's conclusion: "'And it is this which makes the position of the Jew so difficult. He does not stay down. The will to succeed, the capacity for growth are in his blood. Yet, if he achieves either, he also achieves suffering. There comes a point in his enlargement where his presence begins to irritate his host.' Thus simply, does Mrs. Millin state her conception of the Jewish problem, which to her is the problem of an unwanted race," Zelda concluded, adding that the book, "written with profound compassion, but without sentimentality, with complete and mature judgment, but without smugness or smartness, with richness of language and of dramatic narration," was "one for which salutations are to be offered to the brilliant Jewess who is its author."[28]

By the time Zelda published her summary of Sarah Millin's pessimistic conclusions about the prospects for Jews in Gentile societies in 1928, she was shedding the constraints of the identification with the Jewish community that her publicity work and her contributions to the Jewish press had created. She had begun moving beyond her original identification with Jewish subjects and with women by placing articles in a wider range of periodicals early in the 1920s. In her autobiography, in which she never mentioned the *American Hebrew* or other Jewish magazines, she recalled her own excitement when she sold her first article to the *Nation* in 1922, a story about a miners' strike in eastern Pennsylvania. She also remembered Louis's alarmed reaction when he realized that she was finding a way to earn money and build a reputation based on her own work: "'You're independent,' he growled. 'I suppose next you'll want your own apartment.'" Zelda realized that "whatever might take me from him, even a little . . . was something of which he was afraid," and vowed to limit her writing to the spare time left over from work and family obligations.[29] Nevertheless, she pursued her writing career with determination. On the 1920 census form, both she and Louis had given their occupation as "publicity office," but in 1930, when Louis listed himself as a "publicity director," she put down "journalist." Before the end of the 1920s, she had published articles in *Survey*, the well-respected periodical of progressive social reform, in the *New York Times*, in H. L. Mencken's *American Mercury*, and in the *New Yorker*. During the 1930s, her byline also appeared in *Theatre Guild*, *Harper's*, the *Outlook and Independent*, *Travel*, and *Independent Woman*.

The earliest of the dozen or so articles that Zelda published in the *New Yorker* were a revelation to me when I discovered them, and I can see why my grandfather might have feared that they would have set his wife on a course that would take her away from the public relations business. Her very first *New Yorker* contribution was one of the magazine's earliest articles on a Jewish theme: it described the fashionable nightclubs that were replacing the Yiddish tearooms on the Lower East Side. In 1926 and 1927, the magazine that had quickly made itself the epitome of the city's sophisticated spirit featured a series of sketches Zelda called "Reflections of Silent Citizens," in which she employed the modernist literary technique of stream-of-consciousness interior monologue to imagine the thoughts of a department store floorwalker, a bus driver, and an apartment-building "super." In these pieces, she captured the frustrations of individuals caught in dead-end jobs, like the floorwalker who had to "walk around all day smiling like a sap" when "I oughta be on Wall Street. Making real money," or the "super" worrying that his boss, after supplying him with coal "full of clinkers" that would barely burn, would "raise the devil on account of me using so much coal." These sketches also caught the spirit of the city through the complaints of a taxi-driver reluctant to take a fare to the Bronx, where they "cut a new street there every half an hour expect you to know about it" and a bus conductor lamenting that "they're tearing everything down. Pretty soon there won't be only apartment houses. . . . Museum one side, apartment houses other side." Ben Yagoda, author of the most comprehensive history of the magazine, singled her out as one of the first contributors to perfect the art of capturing "the sound of speech" on paper that became one of the distinguishing characteristics of the *New Yorker* style.[30]

Slight as they are, the "Silent Citizen" sketches have a freshness and imagination that Zelda's short stories in the *American Hebrew* and much of her later work often lack, and when I read them, I wondered whether my grandmother could have grown into an avant-garde modernist writer if she had stuck to this vein. Instead, the first book she would complete, published in 1928, less than two years after her last "Silent Citizen" piece, was pure hackwork: a volume entitled *The Story of Hair: Its Purpose and Its Preservation*, which she ghost-wrote for one of the advertising agency's clients, a hairdresser named Charles Nessler who claimed to have invented the permanent wave. In her best advertising style, my grandmother plugged Nessler's invention as "a great advantage to the busy woman who ordinarily would be compelled to curl her hair every day or even to sleep with hair curlers in order to be what she considers well-groomed for the coming day."[31]

Zelda continued to publish occasional pieces in the *New Yorker* during the 1930s, but they were less adventurous than her "Silent Citizen" sketches. Like many other *New Yorker* contributors, she found it difficult to anticipate what the magazine's editors wanted. "For some reason, my contributions of recent years haven't clicked with your editorial staff," she told Katherine White in 1936. White accepted her next submission, but cut out a reference to toilet paper because "we always try to avoid functional mention of this sort." "I am sorry you don't believe in letting your readers know the facts of life," Zelda replied. Thirty years later, near the end of her career, she warned would-be writers against the magazine's "mood" stories, of which many of her contributions had been classic examples. "The 'mood' story is as fragile as a butterfly's wing, demanding a delicate hand as well as a touch of genius. Also, in a way, it's lazy fiction, growing of contemplation of one's navel, rather than the exercise of moving out to where the action is."[32]

A modern woman by virtue of her professional career, Zelda was also determined that her marriage would correspond to the new ideals of equality and companionship. "We had signed for partnership," she wrote in her autobiography, which, to be sure, gives only one partner's story about the marriage that ended, as a result of Louis Popkin's early death, long before she described it. In her own telling, at least, there was no remnant of Victorian inhibition in the couple's sex life; some reviewers in the 1950s were put off by her evocation of the "love play, exploration . . . the drowsy after-closeness which is the best of it." In the kitchen, the two "cooked together and washed up," a sharing of responsibilities that was certainly not emulated in my own parents' lives a generation later. The Popkins moved into a flat on the top floor of the building on 1145 Vyse Avenue in the Bronx where Popkin had earlier lived with her Aunt Ida, part of a "row of brown brick three-story houses between tenement canyons." In a 1922 short story about a "curb lizard," a poor Jewish mother trying to find some fresh air for her baby, Zelda gave a disabused description of her Bronx environment: "when, a scant twenty years ago, the northward extension of subway lines brought in its trail apartment houses, shops, motion picture theatres and young homemakers, progress neglected to supply parks, lawns and backyards for a great army of new perambulators. Hence, by the grace of janitors and the providence of chair manufacturers, the sidewalks became the airing place of the subjuvenile Bronx." Despite its lack of amenities, the Bronx attracted Jewish families eager to leave the overcrowded Lower East Side of Manhattan. When my father found himself in private school with "upper middle class Jews" from Manhattan, he realized that "our nice middle class life in the west Bronx was slum dwelling compared to the large elegant Central Park West apartments and upper East Side town houses of my classmates."[33] Nevertheless, the Popkins and the other middle-class Jews who populated the west Bronx were considerably better off economically than those who had to settle for apartments in the eastern parts of the borough. The 1930 census listed a young German domestic servant living with them, probably to care for the children; she was later replaced by an African American cook whose cupcakes my mother remembered as one of the benefits of her acquaintance with my father.[34]

In 1924, shortly after the birth of their second child, the Popkins bought a house of their own on a block of Sedgwick Avenue in the Bronx, across the Harlem River from the northern tip of Manhattan, where they would live until Louis's death in 1943. In keeping with the easy-money ethos of the 1920s, they seem to have borrowed the entire purchase price of $20,500. Unlike the apartment on Vyse Avenue, the Sedgwick Avenue house was in a residential neighborhood without much street life, Jewish or otherwise. It was "huge, oblong, of brick, stark and ugly as a barracks," buffeted by cold winds in the winter, located across the street from a psychiatric hospital for war veterans. "We live conveniently, we jested, between the river and the madhouse," Zelda wrote in her autobiography. But the "prodigious view" from the house's windows inspired a painting, "Spuyten Duyvil," by her friend Theresa Bernstein and also the only poem I have found in my grandmother's files, an apparently unpublished piece of free verse that, like her early articles in the *New Yorker*, reflects her awareness of the period's literary trends and the pleasure she took in the changing panorama she enjoyed every day. In the poem, "Manhattan Vista," she evoked both the "green hill upon a city street" on which her house stood and the "distant rumble" of the subway "down below where rich Manhattan / Lavish, spreads her man-made treasures." During the day, she could see "the Palisade cliffs crowned with trees" across the Hudson; at night, she could look downhill and see the lit-up Velodrome, home to the marathon races that were one of the fads of the 1920s, "a bowl where pennants fly / Saluting man-size boys who whirl around on bicycles." Bernstein's striking painting of the scene depicts all the details mentioned in Zelda's poem, including the Velodrome.[35]

"Manhattan Vista"

I have a green hill upon a city street
Where maple branches tap my study window
And crickets whirr the summer night through
And the subway is a distant rumble,
Down below where rich Manhattan
Lavish, spreads her man-made treasures.
Three waters sprawl beneath my windows—
The turgid Harlem, joined to Hudson
By the circlet of Spuyten Duyvil
And a bridge of shadows like a Whistler painting.
Dawn, dimming the jewels of city night
Flings a slender church spire up against the sky
Beyond the drab stone canyons where New Yorkers dwell.
A factory whistle hoots. Chicago flyers,
Their Pullman beds unmade, flash by
With sleepy travelers blinking at the muddy river.
A lazy tug crawls toward the Hudson,
Towing a raft of rosy building bricks.
The subway serpent halts beside the bridge;
Impatient autos pause. The draw swings,
Full of majesty, leaving a city's traffic parted

For a tiny boat with tall and graceful masts.

Noon and the full sun now reveals
The Palisade cliffs crowned with trees
A sooty power house, coal piers, galvanized garages
Drenched all in a flood of gold.
An excursion boat darts round the Island
Fluttering white handkerchiefs,
Sounding a huntsman's horn.

Evening pours purple and scarlet
On the crazy house across the street—
A benediction for distracted victims of democracy.
A broad white band of light appears
Advertising motor oil; in the windows of a tire factory
A blue glare seethes like flames atop a witches' cauldron.
Out of the dark, a phosphorescent circle
Glows, filled with stamping shouting men
Jammed into a bowl where pennants fly
Saluting man-size boys who whirl around on bicycles.
Twinkling night . . . images quivering in the water.
Silence . . . a cat in travail in a neighbor's yard
Three o'clock freight that rips the veil of sleep.

I have a green hill top on a city street
Where round the corner frowsy women loll
And air their babes on sunlit rubbish heaps.

Zelda's venture into verse expressed her love for the city she had made her own, but in her autobiography, she emphatically declared that she and Louis had never been part of "the gaudy, exhibitionist fringe" of its Jazz Age culture; although she and Zelda Fitzgerald had shared a first name, they had lived in different worlds. In her 1968 novel *Herman Had Two Daughters*, my grandmother allowed herself to imagine what her life might have been like if she had been able to join the expatriate writers' milieu in Paris. But New York had its own allure. New subway lines opened in 1917 made it easy for the young couple to reach Manhattan. They had a favorite speakeasy, Attilio's on Sixth Avenue in Greenwich Village. "Because there was Prohibition and what is forbidden is fun, we chose to drink," she wrote. They socialized with other newlyweds like the artists William Meyerowitz and his wife Theresa Bernstein, who both made portraits of Louis; in return, Zelda published a laudatory article about Bernstein in the *American Hebrew*.

"The men discussed whether to buy a radio set, what kind, for how much," Zelda recalled. "The women discussed sex, which, being safely married, they had permission to be curious about. Marie Stopes, Westermarck, Vandervelde had written books, scientific and dull, but with directions and details. . . . We haunted the theater . . . we subscribed to opera, went dancing, the one-step and the fox trot and the waltz." Like other young women, Zelda sported "knee-length, flat-chested dresses and divers' helmets over Irene Castle bobs."[36]

Although she wanted to be an emancipated woman, my grandmother also wanted children. Like a proper modern woman, she gave birth in a hospital, not at home as her mother's generation had. More than thirty years later, she was still eager to share with readers the details of her labor pains, "a wrenching torment, an ebb, a lull, before it came again, stronger and more violent." When she first nursed the new baby, "the primeval forces stirred," but Zelda did not claim that nature taught her everything she needed to know. "Love is not sufficient. You need techniques," she wrote. "Pop learned, as well, because we shared everything." At first, the couple alternated days in the office; later, they hired a regular babysitter and "went to the office together and came home together to enjoy our child," an arrangement that sounds routine in today's world but one that was unusual in the early 1920s. The search for child care may have inspired her 1925 article about the challenge of finding household help, in which she commented that "the household where there are small children will invariably pay well."[37] Jewish women were pioneers in adopting birth control methods, and the fact that the couple never had another child after the birth of their second son, when Zelda was just twenty-five, strongly suggests that my grandmother was one of them.

Figure 2.4. Louis Popkin (1920s): The artist William Meyerowitz and his wife, Theresa Bernstein, were friends of Zelda and Louis in the 1920s. Both artists made drawings of Zelda's husband. In 1925, Bernstein did a painting of the view from the Popkins' house overlooking Spuyten Duyvil in the Bronx.

Being modern parents in what was dubbed at the time "The Age of the Child," a catchphrase Popkin would later skewer mercilessly in numerous magazine articles, meant following the prescriptions of the behaviorist psychologist John Broadus Watson, who dictated that children be bottle-fed at strictly regulated intervals and left to cry in between. "No cuddling or pampering. . . . Thumb-sucking was high crime, ranking with theft and murder." By the time the Popkins' second child was born, however, the permissive theories of John Dewey had begun to replace Watson. "Panicky parents, deprived of sense and judgment by bullying psychologists, set out to 'free' the child. Let him be uninhibited." Like many other American Jews of her generation, Zelda also absorbed the new psychological ideas of Sigmund Freud and his renegade disciple Alfred Adler, whose success demonstrated the influence Jews were coming to have in American culture in general. "A smattering of watered-down Freud" made parents fearful that saying "no" to their children "was the straight, sure path to complexes." The result, in her memory, was that "our little boys were hellions, destructive, rude, untidy, hard to live with."[38]

The issue of education became a test of Zelda's commitment to modernity, and an opportunity for her to write about a subject on which her status as a mother gave her special authority. The topic was also one that allowed her to escape the confines of the Jewish identity she had constructed for herself in her contributions to the *American Hebrew*: childrearing was a universal concern. Even before her children were old enough to be enrolled in school, Zelda published several articles about her fellow Wilkes-Barrean and high school friend Lillian Rifkin's Montessori-inspired "barn school" in her home town, where "children are learning through their own creative impulses to develop naturally into self-reliant, thinking, cooperative men and women, prepared in the broadest sense to understand and cope with life."[39] One of her funniest *New Yorker* pieces dramatized the search for the perfect preschool for her two boys, "a modern school to develop their individualities, stimulate their creative instincts, fit them to live harmoniously in the modern world" that would also "save our furniture from total destruction." Present-day New York parents could still relate, no doubt, to her parodic account of her visits to the Pastoral Playground, the Misses Spoonfeeders' school, the Rousseau Institute, and the School for Celebrated Children, where "all our teachers have been psychoanalyzed" and "all our children are problem children." In retrospect, she regretted the school she chose

Figure 2.5. Zelda Popkin and her sons, Roy (foreground) and Richard (c. 1930): The perplexities of parenthood were one of the themes Zelda wrote about during the 1920s and 1930s. She embraced and then rejected several different philosophies of childrearing.

because its woman director struck her as so sympathetic. "What our children learned at her school or whether they learned at all we were never sure," she recalled.[40]

The onset of the Depression led the Popkins to cut back on expenses and transfer their boys to the local public school. The results provided Zelda with material for several more magazine articles, including a humorous piece in the *New Yorker* titled "Wonderful Institution, Our Public Schools," in which she announced jubilantly that "Dewey and Watson simply don't mean a thing around our house any more. Alfred Adler and Sigmund Freud are just ghosts out of a troubled past. . . . No more of this hazardous business of treating your children as equals for us. . . . Just let them get familiar! The principal's office, Superintendent O'Shea, Mayor Walker, the Board of Aldermen, and the government of the United States stand solidly behind us, to a man, when we tell the offspring it's time to go to bed." In a more serious vein, her article on the "Panic of the Parents" lamented that "we got ourselves all mixed up on matters of discipline, sex and religion, and not knowing exactly what to teach, we begged the question altogether. We lost even the privilege of loving our children." She now criticized parenting "experts," disparaged the pacifist campaign against letting children play with toy soldiers and the fad for "child study groups for parents," and concluded that "the old relationship of parent and child, with sentimentality and spankings, all wrong in theory, was more satisfactory all around than the modern relationship of parent and problem."[41]

Before long, however, Zelda became disenchanted with the public schools as well. When students in one of her sons' classes set off stink bombs and "an entire school was sickened," she concluded that the principal was more concerned with protecting his teachers' pension rights than with whether they could control their classrooms and transferred her children again, this time to the famous Walden School, "the *avant garde* of experimental education, the *most* progressive school." Zelda was evidently not entirely satisfied with this solution, either, but by now, her sons had begun to stand up for their own views. In a short essay on "Respect for Teachers: A Contrast," her older son explained that, even though Walden School students addressed their teachers by their first names, "in Walden, despite the nicknames, breaking of rules, and a sometimes noisy classroom, there is far more respect given the teachers" than in PS 86. Roy Popkin eventually graduated from Walden; my father, more academically inclined, remembered the school's curriculum as an effort "to slow down my intellectual development" by forcing him to spend time knitting, weaving, and making ashtrays. He was happier when he was able to enter the honors program at the public DeWitt Clinton High School in the Bronx.[42]

As her children grew, Zelda became increasingly conscious of the impossibility of dictating their interests. A 1932 article in *Harper's* acknowledged the revolt "of this particular generation of boys and girls which, like no other that ever lived, has been rocked in the cradle of culture" by parents determined to expose their children to classical music, art museums, and theater. Instead, her sons were interested in sports, toy trains and trucks, comic books, and humorous radio programs like *Amos 'n' Andy* and *The Rise of the Goldbergs*. Despite her best efforts, her sons accumulated a library of books "which have never appeared on any recommended list," such as the Tom Swift science fiction novels. A growing boy, she had learned, wants "that thing which culture-bound adults too lightly dismiss—a feeling of participation in the swiftly moving world in which he lives. . . . Our children," she concluded, "born with all the honest vulgarities of the human race, and with an instinctive resistance against being made into snobs and prigs, identify themselves readily with these mob interests," and she quoted her ten-year-old son Roy's observation that "all people are a little bit vulgar" to clinch her argument. A year later, however, she sounded the alarm about "children of the racketeer age" for whom "playing at crime is . . . the favorite pastime" and who were "growing up with admiration and amusement toward lawlessness." This article ended with a lament about "the diminution of religious training" and a plug for social worker Henrietta Additon's Crime Prevention Bureau, which was sending speakers into the schools to "strip the gangster of his halo."[43]

Despite her salute to the value of religious education in her article on "the racketeer age," Zelda had made sure that her own children did not learn the rules and traditions of Judaism with which she had grown up. The progressive education movement "tossed out folklore, myth, religion even, since these, it felt, prolonged the superstitious yesterdays. . . . Having set no standards, taught no Ten Commandments, we pushed our luck," she wrote in her autobiography.[44] The 1920s were the years of a synagogue-building boom in New York, but there is no indication that the Popkins ever belonged to a congregation, and their sons never had Bar Mitzvah ceremonies. Once she had begun to publish regularly in the mainstream press, Zelda seems to have stopped writing for magazines like the *American Hebrew* and the *B'nai B'rith Magazine*. "My parents were emancipated from Jewish orthodoxy, and pretty hostile to it," my father wrote in his own brief memoir. Nevertheless, he recalled, "We lived . . . in an almost totally Jewish world, consisting mainly of similarly emancipated Jews. My parents were actively involved in the Yiddish culture in New York, knew the writers, the playwrights, the actors. Unfortunately, they failed to share this part of Jewishness with their children."[45] The period's pervasive antisemitism was the one aspect of being Jewish from which my grandmother could not shield her children. She was adamant that "in our own daily lives, we had never been personally touched by the shriveling blight of domestic anti-Semitism," but she heard her older son wisecracking that "You can't tell your Jew without a pogrom," and had to react when her younger boy "read the dispatches from Germany" after 1933 and asked "'Why are they doing this to Jews?' . . . Possibly we should have taught him the history, imparted the age-old fears, but in the milieu in which our children lived that seemed irrelevant," she wrote.[46]

Even if they shunned religious practices and insulated their children from New York's lively secular Jewish culture, however, the Popkins always had multiple connections to the Jewish world. More than Zelda, Louis Popkin's work regularly involved him with Jewish organizations. He was one the volunteers who served occasionally as arbiters on the Jewish Conciliation Board, an institution to which New York Jews could appeal to settle disputes among themselves that they did not want to take to civil courts. The minutes of the Joint Distribution Committee's board of directors show that he regularly attended meetings for many years, although he was not an official member of the board. In November 1931, JDC officials asked to him to arrange a "frank talk" with editors of the

Yiddish papers in New York about "the European and Russian Jewish situations." For unknown reasons, he was unceremoniously dismissed from the "Joint" in 1935, however, despite his protest at "the absurdity of engaging a new and totally inexperienced staff for the most difficult campaign in the twenty years of this organization's existence." In that same year, he won praise from James McDonald, the League of Nations' High Commissioner for Refugees Coming from Germany, for publicizing McDonald's protest against the world's indifference to Nazi Germany's persecution of its Jews.[47]

There are fewer traces of Zelda's engagements with Jewish organizations, although one of her *New Yorker* articles dealt with the Jewish Conciliation Board on which her husband had served.[48] That article, which appeared in 1932, was, as far as I know, the last piece dealing with Jewish concerns that she would publish until after her encounter with Holocaust survivors in Europe in 1945, although in 1937 she offered that magazine a humorous depiction of a lavish New York Jewish wedding that apparently never ran. Family connections kept her involved with Jewish life, however. Popkin's father was among the founders of the Conservative synagogue in Wilkes-Barre in the early 1920s. After his partnership with his cousins ended and he failed for one last time at running his own store, he was hired as a community social worker for the Wilkes-Barre Jewish community. The letters he regularly sent her came on stationery with the letterheads of the Wyoming Valley Jewish Committee, the Hebrew Loan Society of Wyoming Valley, and the United Jewish Social Service Agency for Luzerne County, all of which shared the same address. When Zelda went home on visits, she generated conflicts with her parents because of her disregard for the kosher laws. "I pleaded with you not to use all of [the pans in her parents' kitchen]," her father wrote in one letter, "because I wished to keep especially the large one for Pesach."[49]

Zelda's sisters were both, in different ways, more overtly engaged in Jewish life than she was. Her older sister Pauline's husband, William Pinsker, who had been intimidated by Zelda's sharp tongue when he first met her, became a significant figure in the world of Jewish community organizations. In the 1920s, he was the director of the Jewish community center in Savannah, Georgia, and in 1931 he became head of the YMHA in Paterson, New Jersey, where he spent the rest of his career. In 1935, he served as president of the National Association of Jewish Center Executives, stressing in his annual report that "the Jewish Center has worked mightily as an instrument for the preservation of Jewish life, rather than as an agency of assimilation." After an initial visit to Palestine in 1929, Zelda's younger sister, Helen, expressed her Jewish identity in a different way: in 1934, she made *aliyah*. At the time, Zelda was not sympathetic. "We were not Zionists," she wrote in her autobiography. "'The whole world should be made safe for all people,' was what we said. 'Jews don't need a separate homeland, a place of refuge. Their home is wherever they live.'"[50] Nevertheless, the fact that she had a sister living in Jerusalem meant that she could not entirely ignore the Zionist project of creating a Jewish homeland, and in 1948, it would give her the opportunity to witness the first months of Israel's history.

Behind the scenes, however, Zelda remained concerned about issues that affected American Jews. One suggestive item is an anonymous newspaper clipping from 1932 headlined "The American Jewish Tragedy," found in one of her files of articles by and about her. This long article, published in the *Jewish Criterion*, the newspaper of the Pittsburgh Jewish community, is attributed to "Two Professional Jews," and a handwritten note on it reads "Please return to Louis Popkin." I cannot prove definitively that the article was written by my grandparents, but it was certainly penned by an author with an intimate knowledge of the world of Jewish fundraising and some of its wording strongly resembles a speech about the problems of American Jewish life that Zelda gave in 1966. The article dissects the impact of the Great Depression on American Jewish institutions. "The millions that were poured out in the last two generations are no longer forthcoming. . . . Swept by a panic born of fear, or actual deprivation of income, the Jews of America are abandoning their community obligations and destroying their reputation for largesse." The root of the problem, according to the article, was not lack of money. "American Jewry is truly singing its swan song today because it is leaderless, and because its youth has no connection with or interest in the vital spiritual essence of Judaism."[51]

Anticipating a critique of American Jewish fundraising campaigns that Zelda would incorporate into her late-life novel *Herman Had Two Daughters*, the article complained that Jewish donors were motivated solely by the recognition they received: "Giving helps the giver to feel strong and powerful." Regretting the absence of successors to Jacob Schiff, Nathan Straus, and Louis Marshall, leaders with whom the Popkins had worked at the start of their careers, the authors lamented that "the giants of Israel had vanished." Perhaps unwittingly pointing a finger at themselves, they ended their jeremiad by acknowledging that the many fundraising campaigns conducted since the World War "did not stimulate one iota the creative spirit which is the very essence of Jewish survival."[52] The article's diagnosis of the situation facing the American Jewish community in the early years of the Depression was hardly original, but it corresponds to what subsequent historical scholarship has shown about the era. The Popkins would have been as well situated as anyone at the time to understand the issues the article described, and a good part of their income depended on the continuing vitality of Jewish institutions.

My grandmother's autobiography does not mention the kinds of issues raised in the 1932 *Jewish Criterion* article, but she does claim that she and her husband were active in combatting the rising tide of antisemitism that pervaded American life in the decades after World War I. The most threatening manifestation of anti-Jewish hatred in the 1920s was the industrialist Henry Ford's propagation of the conspiracy theory embedded in the forged *Protocols of the Elders of Zion*, which Ford's nationally distributed newspaper, the *Dearborn Independent*, translated into English and published in installments starting in 1921. American Jewish leaders wrung their hands about Ford's campaign but were unable to find an effective way to counter it until Ford himself, for reasons that remain disputed, approached Louis Marshall, the head of the American Jewish Committee, and offered to disavow his attacks. Zelda asserted that it was her husband and his partner Abraham Fromenson who composed the text of the apology that Ford signed in 1927, although Marshall presented it to Ford as his own work.[53] When the William Morrow company hired the Popkins to obtain blurbs for a book denouncing the danger of the rising Nazi movement in Germany in 1932, they were shocked to receive a letter from the famous American novelist Theodore Dreiser insisting that the Jews ought to be expelled from the United States, a proposal Dreiser claimed to think "should not, I hope, involve bloodshed or enormous cruelty." Zelda kept this damning piece of evidence in her files and eventually donated it to the library of the Hebrew University in Jerusalem.[54]

Nothing shows the somewhat contradictory feelings that the nature of American Jewish life and the threat of Hitler aroused in Zelda Popkin's mind better than an apparently unpublished article she composed about the mass rally organized in Madison Square Garden by the American Jewish Congress on 27 March 1933 to protest Nazi treatment of the German Jews. The Popkins had written a press release publicizing the meeting, but Zelda had doubts about its impact. In a tone that varied from cynicism about the organizers, "a little vague themselves about the purpose it would serve," to furious indignation at the treatment being inflicted on Jews during the first months of Hitler's regime, she described how the event had brought together "Russian, Polish, Roumanian, Galician Jews, remembering what once had been done to them in their own lands . . . on behalf of these co-religionists of theirs who would not admit them to membership in their best clubs." While she approved of the protest's goals, she compared it to "a snowball on its way downhill," growing "tremendous in size, somewhat lopsided and quite cold." It was, in her view, "the tamest protest meeting ever held . . . dignified to the point of meekness." She attributed this in part to the fact that the size of the Garden meant that the crowd was too far from the speakers to be easily stirred by them, but the real reason, she concluded, was that American Jews had changed. American Jewry had outgrown "its love for dramatic expressions of its feelings" and had "learned to leave shouting and horse-kicking to the Communists." But the participants also knew that even this largest protest meeting in American Jewish history "was a gesture, nothing more, a way of getting their case stated in the newspapers."[55]

With the leaders of the American Jewish community uncertain about how to oppose Nazi antisemitism without risking a nativist backlash in the United States, the Popkins had no opportunity to publicize the cause;

only at the end of the 1930s would they find an anti-fascist movement they could wholeheartedly support. During the mid-1930s, Popkin, who wrote later that "by nature I am not a reformer," enrolled in a different campaign: she joined a prominent New York woman magistrate, Anna Kross, in an effort to reform the treatment of women arrested on charges of prostitution. This was the one "women's issue" with which Popkin was publicly involved during the interwar years. She devoted more space to it in her autobiography than to any of her other activities during this period, and, in addition to working with Kross to prepare a lengthy report that was eventually submitted to New York mayor Fiorello La Guardia, she published a number of articles on the cause in the *New York Times* and other periodicals.[56]

Speaking for herself and Kross, Zelda condemned policies "directed against the woman, the individual prostitute, rather than against the evil she represents." While her articles were unsparing in their denunciation of the futility of repressive measures and the corruption of a system that left streetworkers at the mercy of the police, they were not particularly sympathetic toward the women themselves. "A score of black girls and white girls straggle in and fill two rows of benches in front of the rail," she wrote in "Vignettes from a Woman's Court," an article that appeared in one of the era's leading women's magazines. "Their clothes are poor, ill fitting. They wear no more makeup than any other females of their economic and social strata. . . . Few of them are even remotely pretty." Kross's goal was to replace the traditional women's court with an "informal tribunal, consisting of a physician, a psychiatrist, and a lawyer, staffed by trained medical social workers . . . to prescribe proper and adequate treatment for the cure, protection, and rehabilitation of each individual." Having researched the treatment of prostitution in other countries, Zelda ended this article by praising the policies adopted in the Soviet Union, where "woman . . . is no longer an inferior, no longer a chattel, no longer a dependent, but man's equal in opportunity, work and wages, and before the law." In her autobiography, she admitted that she and Kross soon learned that even in the Soviet Union, "when hundreds of men without wives gathered in a single place for long periods, prostitutes appeared." La Guardia ignored the Kross report's recommendations, and Kross was still struggling to bring about reforms two decades later, when my grand-mother wrote her autobiography.[57]

Cautious by now about identifying herself publicly as a Jew, and usually reticent about tying herself to women's causes, Zelda had no hesitation about writing articles that positioned her as a commentator on American life. At a time when Edna Ferber, a dozen years older than Zelda, was making a fortune from novels set in different parts of the country that added up to a portrait of America's regional and eth-nic diversity, my grandmother did something similar on a smaller scale. Coal-mining towns in Pennsylvania; fishermen in Gloucester, Massa-chusetts, where the Popkins spent their summer vacations; fiddlers in the Appalachian mountains—all became grist for her mill. An article with the clickbait title "Tent Show Turns to Sex," published in 1930, made the argument that the melodramas performed by touring companies throughout rural America were "our own folk drama—the full length portrait of the American soul." From the vantage point of the urban sophisticate she had become, she imagined actors performing for "lean farmers, unshaven, often unwashed, who come clad in working overalls, collarless, who slump in their seats, worn out by all day's haying in the hot sun, who are childishly eager to be amused . . . plump farmers' wives in housedresses and aprons . . . young couples who have come twenty miles in the Ford over rough roads . . . the village undertaker, and the choir singers . . . the garage mechanic and his son and daughter. Their audience is talkative, lively, and it has the wistfulness of people who work hard and have little recreation."[58] Herbert Hoover was still president when this article was published in September 1930, but it already breathed the spirit of the populist murals that artists hired under Franklin Roosevelt's WPA program would paint on post office walls throughout America.

Among the groups to which Zelda turned her attention in the early 1930s were African Americans. Far from ignoring African American culture, American Jews in this period displayed what now seems like a disturbing enthusiasm for appropriating it as their own. Evenings at Harlem nightclubs, most of them owned by Jews, were one form of this; the ubiquitous blackface performances by Jewish singers and actors, most notoriously Al Jolson in *The Jazz Singer*, the first talking picture, were another. Popkin never wrote about Jewish blackface spectacles, but, on a 1931 visit to her sister Pauline in Savannah, Georgia, she took in a performance of *Heaven Bound*, a pageant based on African American spirituals, and her article about it in *Theatre Guild* magazine is often cited in histories of the period's African American culture. Her description of Blacks as a people "which still is held by distorted jungle superstitions . . . child-like, easy going, unstable," showed that she, like most American Jews of the time, had absorbed prevailing racial prejudices, but she was clearly moved by what she witnessed on the stage. "It is a religious drama, sincere, fervent, eloquent, conceived in simple faith, presented with simplicity and with affection. It is concerned with the only thing the whites have given the Negro freely to live with and adore—his religion. . . . Beyond a doubt, 'Heaven Bound' is the first great American folk drama. . . . It is done by the colored people for colored people and without regard for white approval."[59]

The magazine articles Zelda wrote about Jews after she stopped contributing regularly to Jewish magazines in 1928 can be seen as an extension to her own ethnic group of her interest in the diversity of American life. In 1927, she expanded her earliest contribution to the *New Yorker*, a description of "East Side Night Life," into a much longer piece on the "Changing East Side" for the *American Mercury*. In this article, she depicted the transformation of the quintessential East European Jewish immigrant neighborhood into a middle-class, commercially oriented district. "The settlement-houses in which an earlier generation flapped its wings are now teaching the art of serving salmon salad and applying cosmetics to a youth that yearns only to look and eat and amuse itself like its uptown neighbors," she told readers of H. L. Mencken's magazine. "Americanization has come at last to New York's East Side." Night clubs and cabarets had replaced the cafés where penniless radicals had argued about politics, and young Jewish women no longer wanted to marry intellectuals. "The girls want furs and diamonds and servants. They don't want to work or sacrifice as their mothers did." For the sake of local color, she mentioned the survival of Jewish Orthodoxy among some of the East Side's population, but for her, the typical Hasidic *zadik* was "a shrewd showman" who "plays the stock market and uses his holy wisdom to guide his speculations in real estate."[60]

Zelda's 1932 *New Yorker* article on the Jewish Conciliation Court was her last publication on an overtly Jewish theme until after World War II. In one sense, it was another exercise in translating the life of a segment of the American poor for the benefit of more sophisticated readers; in another way, it was her most explicit commentary on the distance she had traveled from her own origins. "Old men with long white beards and haunted eyes; old women wrapped in shabby plush coats and kerchiefs; portly, squat, unshaven middle-aged men; and wives, portly too, middle-aged, and equally scornful of grooming": these were people she had grown up with, but not those with whom she wanted to be identified. They had come to the Court, on which her own husband at one time served as a mediator, because it was a place where they hoped to find understanding of "the woes of a race which makes up a quarter of New York's population, and carries on in a modern city racial traditions and religious customs that are thousands of years old. In the shadow of steel skyscrapers, the mystic rites of the Chasidic sect are practiced; under the roaring elevated trains, in bare hovels that are called stubels, rabbis preach and pray . . . who never looked on the face of a woman," she wrote, emphasizing the gulf between Jewish tradition and the conditions of modern life.

The final case Zelda described for the benefit of the *New Yorker*'s cosmopolitan readership was that of "a tailor in Avenue C, a small, heavy-set man with a scraggly beard," whose daughter was bent on marrying an Italian boy. "Love? Who talks of love? What is love beside obedience to parents, beside the sin of marrying a Gentile?" When the young man showed the Court judges the document attesting to the couple's civil marriage and the court ruled that "the case has settled itself," all the distraught father could do was announce, "My daughter is dead. . . . I go home to cover the mirrors and light the candles." Having dramatized for her readers the inevitable outcome of this collision between Old World Jewish customs and the realities of modern American life, Zelda concluded, "There was human interest for you!"[61]

The insider knowledge Zelda displayed in her articles about the Lower East Side and the Jewish Conciliation Court would have allowed readers to identify their author as Jewish. When she reappeared in the *New Yorker* in 1936 and 1937 with a series of articles drawn from her personal experiences in Wilkes-Barre, however, she managed the remarkable feat of erasing all clues to her ethnic origin even as she made her own life the subject of her writing. A story about her father's habit of hoarding historically significant newspapers for his "collection" not only avoided any reference to her family's religion but dropped hints that might have made readers conclude that they were Christians. The hook for the article was the fate of her father's archive, washed away by a flood in 1936 except for "a Christmas calendar, produced in kindergarten—green leaves, red holly berries, and a brown 'Merry Christmas' punched into cardboard with a thick needle." An article about one of the newspaper stories she had covered for the Wilkes-Barre *Times Leader* mentioned that she was unfamiliar with the poorer parts of town because "I had been playing around with a Y.W.C.A. and pretty refined high-school crowd." These *New Yorker* articles, examples of the "personal history" genre that is still a regular feature in the magazine, were an important extension of Zelda's writing talents: she was learning to turn episodes from her own life into stories and to limn characters, like the poetry-writing murderer who called himself "Poor But Honest John," who would hold readers' attention.[62] But they were also demonstrations of how skillful she had become at "passing," at concealing truths about herself that didn't fit the image she wanted to project.

By the late 1930s, as she neared her fortieth birthday, Zelda Popkin had come a long way from her own origins as the precocious daughter of Jewish immigrants who might well have sat *shiva* for her if she had married out of the faith. She had avoided a rupture with her family, but other than that, she had traced her own path, as a modern woman liberated from the religious bonds that defined her parents' lives. She had found a mate willing to embrace the ideal of egalitarian marriage, she had raised her children according to the latest scientific prescriptions and then helped denounce those prescriptions' inadequacy, and she had carved out two professional careers for herself, as a partner in a public relations firm and as a journalist. She had used her Jewish connections to launch both careers, but then she had successfully made the transition from being a "Jewish" journalist to being an "American" writer, capable of commenting on her own group from the same cosmopolitan stance that she took when writing about white countryfolk or black spiritual singers and of writing about her own life as if she had been born into the country's majority culture.

Both Zelda's personal achievements and her ambivalence about her Jewish identity reflected the ambiguous position of Jews in American life during the interwar years. Acutely aware of the opportunities their country offered them, especially in contrast to the dire situation of Jews in Europe, American Jews remained uneasy about asserting their particularity.[63] At almost the same time as Zelda was writing her autobiographical articles for the *New Yorker*, the better-known novelist Edna Ferber, whose small-town childhood in Appleton, Wisconsin, had many resemblances to Zelda's, was publishing her autobiography, *A Peculiar Treasure*, in which she openly acknowledged her Jewish origins and denounced antisemitism, "a thing to fill one with a profound sadness and pity for the whole struggling human race."[64] Compared to Zelda, Ferber had had very little personal engagement with Jewish life during the interwar years, but the rising dangers she sensed in the world of the late 1930s drove her to make a kind of public statement that her younger and less celebrated contemporary decided to avoid.

CHAPTER 3

Politics, Murder, and War

A Career in Popular Culture

LIKE EDNA FERBER, ZELDA POPKIN WAS ACUTELY AWARE OF THE DAN-
gers facing the world as the 1930s neared their end. For her, as for American society in general, the last days of peace and the years of the Second
World War were a time of extremes. Breaking out of the confines of her
role in the Popkin publicity firm, she established herself as a successful
popular author. Between 1938 and 1942, she published a half-dozen
mystery novels, making herself a recognized contributor to a genre that
was rapidly becoming a mainstay of American popular culture and a pioneer whose woman detective, Mary Carner, like her creator, functioned
successfully in a man's world. Even as the fictional Mary Carner was
reassuring readers that evil deeds would be punished, however, Zelda saw
her country thrust into a new global war, one even more menacing for
Jews than the one during which she had begun her career, and her family
broke up, as her husband Louis died and her sons left home to start the
independent lives for which their progressive schooling had prepared
them. In her mid-forties, my grandmother unexpectedly found herself
living the life of a single woman that she had told her future brother-in-
law Bill Pinsker she would have a quarter-century earlier. In a country
mobilized for all-out war, she had to grapple with the question of how
women could contribute in a crisis where supposedly masculine virtues
like courage and selflessness were at a premium, a question she would
answer, for herself and for thousands of readers, in a best-selling novel

that established her as a writer of "serious" fiction. At the same time, pulled back into the world of Jewish organizations she knew so well, she also found herself forced to confront the antisemitism that flourished in wartime America and news of the catastrophe overwhelming the Jews of Europe.

As she recounted in her own autobiography twenty years later, in 1937, political disasters broke her spirit and left her in a personal crisis. "When Madrid fell, the road lay open for catastrophe. For those of us who were Jews, the despair was greater than for those who were not, since Spain was no separate defeat. It was linked to the tragedy in Germany." Her chronology was a little off—Madrid did not surrender until 1939—but General Franco's forces held the city under siege from November 1936 onward and the Spanish Republican cause was clearly on the defensive. Zelda was not a political militant, but she and Louis had become heavily invested in the struggle there. "We had been tapped to create a favorable climate of public opinion in the United States toward lifting the arms embargo against Loyalist Spain," she explained in her autobiography, published during the McCarthy years of the 1950s when it took a certain amount of courage to admit to having backed a "red" cause. "We were selected because we were competent professionals without party tags." The Popkins' publicity firm badly needed the work at the time, since the Depression had dried up the demand for their services, but they were also eager to take on the assignment because, as Louis Popkin said, "It gives us a chance to work on something we care about." In the early months of 1937, the Popkins churned out numerous press releases for the American Friends of the Spanish Republic, denouncing the neutrality policy that kept the Spanish government from purchasing arms in the United States and countering the claims of Franco's supporters.[1] Zelda carefully preserved a set of large-format propaganda posters from Spain and eventually passed them on to other family members, hardly imagining that the crudely racist depiction of a Moroccan soldier from Franco's army in the one she gave me would someday make it unsuitable for public display.

The failure of their efforts on behalf of Spain was especially bitter for Zelda because she and Louis had come to realize that the "red-headed

Comintern man" who had taken charge of the campaign was more concerned about "making certain that his boys handled all the cash and shaped all policy" than with getting the Roosevelt administration's arms embargo lifted. "That was a pity," she wrote, "because we cared very much and he ate our hearts out. Being human," she continued, "I took sick, out of weariness as much as anything." Louis Popkin's business partner Abraham Fromenson had died in 1935, and Louis himself was suffering from health problems that affected his hearing, leaving Zelda as the only person her husband could call on to "grind out endless copy and serve as his ears and quick nudge." Although she did not mention it in her autobiography, her teenaged sons were probably also causing her anxiety. At a moment when she was heartbroken about the Communist takeover of the pro-Spanish movement, both of them were applying the lessons about thinking for themselves they had learned from the Walden School by having youthful flings with the Party. Her rambunctious older son, my uncle, imitated his parents by starting a precocious journalistic career: he got himself hired as a sportswriter for the *Daily Worker*, publishing under the name of "Roy Parker." Roy took pride in the fact that the Communist paper had gotten his account of "Joe [Louis]'s smashing one-round victory over the Nazi boxer" Max Schmeling onto the streets ahead of any other New York paper. My father, two years younger, hosted meetings of a high-school cell of the Communist-dominated American Student Union in Zelda's living room, and both boys tried to convert the family's African American maid to the cause.[2]

Whatever the reasons for the collapse she recalled in her autobiography, Zelda found herself confined to bed for three months. On her doctor's recommendation, she took up reading detective stories. Soon, she "decided it would be fun to see whether I could write one. By the time I was well, I had entered a part-time life of crime."[3] Over the next six years, she published six mystery novels with appropriately lurid covers and titles: *Death Wears a White Gardenia, Murder in the Mist, So Much Blood*. Popkin's engagement with crime fiction coincided with the first golden age of the genre in America. Dashiell Hammett, Raymond Chandler, Erle Stanley Gardner, and others were giving detective novels a new status; they were no longer simply "pulp fiction" for semiliterate readers.

The invention of the inexpensive paperback book in 1942 would bring mystery writers, including Zelda, a greatly enlarged audience. Her success as a detective-novel writer established her as a recognized author and gave her a long-lasting relationship with J. B. Lippincott, a respected firm that would publish all but one of her fourteen books. Her mystery novels provided a welcome supplement to the family income at a moment when the looming war was curtailing demand for commercial public relations work and driving her husband Louis to apply unsuccessfully for jobs at various Jewish and government agencies.[4]

Zelda's budding career as a mystery novelist did not end her involvement in public relations and, in fact, once she recovered her health and packed her son Roy off for an unhappy freshman year at the University of North Carolina in the fall of 1938, thereby getting him away from the *Daily Worker*, she and Louis found new ways to support the campaign against fascism. The boxing match between Joe Louis and Max Schmeling on which Roy had reported had put the Popkins in touch with a young activist named Morty Zerwick, the press agent for the Anti-Nazi League, a group which staged protests against the rallies regularly organized by "America First" and pro-Hitler movements in New York. Zerwick's group had threatened to picket the Louis-Schmeling fight, and the match's promoters wanted to avoid the bad publicity. Louis Popkin persuaded Zerwick to agree to let the match go ahead, provided that 10 percent of the proceeds were donated to refugees from Nazi Germany. "Joe Louis grinned. Schmeling squealed, but he needed the cash," Zelda wrote. Zerwick, whom Zelda remembered fondly as "Embee," from his initials, joined their firm. "It was a marriage made in heaven, a merry, agile-witted young man and a merry, agile-witted older one," she recalled.[5]

With Zerwick to help them, the Popkins threw themselves into promoting the activities of the Friends of Democracy, an anti-fascist organization created by a Unitarian minister named Leon Birkhead. From his home in Kansas City, Birkhead had battled the Ku Klux Klan in the Midwest and, in 1937, he moved to New York City to expand his efforts, which prefigured those of present-day organizations such as the Southern Poverty Law Center. The Popkins "helped to bring Birkhead and Friends of Democracy east, set it up, keep it going. We fine-combed the country to raise funds for it," Zelda recalled in her autobiography. They wrote press releases circulating the organization's "Democracy Pledge," warning that "in nation after nation, human decency and dignity have been sacrificed to totalitarian rule," and that "forces from within and from without are at work in America organized to accomplish this same end." The pledge concluded with a call to "set forth our faith in Democracy, commend it to all as the course for internal stability and rely upon it always as the chief bulwark of liberty, justice and peace."[6]

One of the main targets of the Friends of Democracy was Father Coughlin, the "radio priest" whose antisemitic broadcasts had made him a national figure. "Patiently, Birkhead assembled the facts, put them together, published them, to prove beyond doubt that the priest of Royal Oak was a transmission belt for Nazism," Zelda wrote. The Popkins drafted press releases addressed to the Catholic hierarchy and the Federal Communications Commission, which finally ordered Coughlin off the air. Together with Birkhead and one of his "undercover men," Art Derounian, whose specialty was infiltrating far-right groups in order to gather information about them and who worked out of an office in the same Park Avenue building as theirs, they gathered information about "candidates running on what might be generally described as a Fifth Column platform" in the 1940 elections, such as Joseph McWilliams, an avowed Nazi sympathizer and one-time ally of Coughlin.[7]

As the Popkins tried to combat Nazi sympathizers at home, they were also involved, like many American Jews, in a personal effort to save relatives trapped in an increasingly dangerous Europe. When she came to write her panoramic novel about American Jewish life, *Herman Had Two Daughters*, in the 1960s, Zelda incorporated into her text a letter from the American consul in Berlin in the late 1930s, Raymond H. Geist, not only denying the request for a visa for one of Louis Popkin's cousins but insinuating that my grandfather must have been lying about the relationship, since he had spelled the cousin's family name differently from the way it was listed in official documents (he had substituted a final "y" for an "i").[8] In the end, these cousins were able to reach the United States, and any time Zelda found herself close to the docks in New York City, she would tell a story about how their young children, as they debarked to start their new lives in America, caught sight of a German ocean liner flying the Nazi flag and waved excitedly, happy to see something familiar and unaware of the danger from which they had just escaped. Zelda and the adults in the family, of course, understood that danger only too well, and that understanding energized her commitment to combatting American fascists and supporting American democracy.

Because it illustrated that commitment to American democracy, Zelda devoted more attention in her autobiography to a political campaign that she, Louis, and "Embee" Zerwick ran in 1940 than to any other episode in their career as publicists. As she told the story, the fall of France in the spring of that year had brought home to them the danger that democracy "might vanish overnight" if their country did not prepare to enter the fight. "American politics, in 1940, on even the lowest local level, was tied to preparations for the war." The Popkins and Zerwick were asked to galvanize the campaign of the underdog Democratic candidate for governor of Connecticut, Robert A. Hurley. Starting with a contact obtained thanks to a distant relative of Zelda's family—the network her father had dreamed of holding together through the "family association" he had had Zelda try to create twenty years earlier proved its value—they quickly took over Hurley's campaign operation. The media have changed in the decades since, but the tactics Zelda recounted—photographs of the candidate, "posed solo, given flattering lighting to bring out character," "research . . . to ferret out the silly and shameful spots on the opponent's escutcheon," and the drafting of "vigorous speeches, one issue per speech, with homely anecdotes, employing short, familiar words, so that the candidate may not mispronounce"—have remained much the same.[9]

Zelda spent much of the fall of 1940 in New York City, keeping the office going, while Louis and "Embee" based themselves in Connecticut. This explains why the only personal letter between my grandparents I have found comes from the campaign, when Louis realized that they would not be together for their anniversary. "Darling, I love you just as dearly—and more dearly—as on the day we were married—Do come out—if you can," he wrote, before launching into details about his efforts. At the climax of the campaign, FDR himself made an appearance, giving

Zelda an opportunity to witness how, "using his massive shoulders, his strong arms for locomotion," the president, a survivor of polio, pulled himself to the podium. Hurley won, and Zelda was proud that her and Louis's efforts had put into office a man who spoke "on behalf of the common man and for the ideals of democracy." A week after Pearl Harbor, Hurley brought employers and Connecticut labor unions together to sign the "Connecticut Compact for Victory," "the first voluntary no-strike-for-the-duration agreement in the United States." According to Zelda, Louis came up with the idea and "Embee put it into strong, simple words." She was proud that they had contributed to this "footnote written into the history books," but it was not enough to carry Hurley to victory in his 1942 reelection campaign. She remembered the governor, on his way to make his concession statement, telling her disabusedly, "We put our trust in the little people. Now we know they're damned small." As the letters she received from "Embee" a few years later reveal, she was also deeply disillusioned by Hurley himself: his campaign never paid their firm for the work they performed in 1942.[10]

As she struggled to help defend democracy, however, Zelda was also pouring her energy into writing detective stories to provide readers with harmless distraction. In addition to giving her a new identity and a new source of income, her detective stories gave her a new way of writing about aspects of American society she had covered in her journalistic articles and, above all, a new opportunity to depict women's lives. The first five of her mystery stories, written as Americans still enjoyed an uneasy peace in a world at war, featured an enterprising female protagonist, Mary Carner. In the earliest of Zelda's books, *Death Wears a White Gardenia*, Carner was introduced to readers as a department-story detective, charged with keeping an eye on light-fingered women customers. This gender-appropriate role made her involvement in finding the killer who left a body in the store's shipping room seem natural. In the four subsequent novels, however, Carner found herself embroiled in murder cases outside the confines of the Blankfort store's massive building on Fifth Avenue between 46th and 47th Streets, leading feminist detective-novel scholar Kathleen Gregory Klein to sniff that Zelda treated her heroine's crime-busting career as no more than a "hobby."[11] In the stories, male policemen and district attorneys often initially dismiss Carner as an intruding busybody, but New York City cops and officials, impressed by her contribution to solving the department-store murder, vouch for her in her other cases. Carner's male boss in the store's security department, whose "saturnine" appearance matches that of Zelda's husband, Louis, grouches about her absences from her job, but not too loudly: by novel three, he has married her and become her loyal supporter, even keeping an eye on the daughter they have adopted while Carner chases clues.

By the time she began writing her detective stories, Zelda had been publishing magazine articles for nearly twenty years. Writing book-length fiction was a new venture for her, however, and in her autobiography, she described the detective novels as an "apprenticeship" that helped prepare her for more serious fiction projects. "From writing mysteries I learned plotting and pace, the art of storytelling, and in gathering materials I entered worlds I might otherwise never have explored," she wrote. To lend her stories verisimilitude, she purchased a copy of *Legal Medicine and Toxicology*, "the medical examiner's encyclopedia of the effects of poisons, blunt instruments and artillery," consulted a toolsmith to decide which sculptor's implement would make the best murder weapon, and listened carefully as a friend with expertise explained what would happen to a corpse left in an abandoned furnace for six months. She also "began to haunt the courts, to learn the processes of investigation and trial, to see the faces, hear the voices of men and women who killed."[12]

Composing her detective stories gave Zelda free rein to ponder the darker side of human nature, what she called "the unknowableness of the heart of man."[13] The acquaintance with the ideas of Sigmund Freud demonstrated in many of her magazine articles in the 1920s and 1930s helped her imagine husbands and wives eager to dispose of inconvenient spouses, parents bent on dominating their children's lives, crooked businessmen and politicians, and suspected Nazi sympathizers. The most diabolical of her murderers devises a scheme to trick innocent people lured by the bait of a promised inheritance into publicly admitting sins they had not committed. Zelda's policemen, if they were not simply hopeless bumblers, were often in cahoots with criminals, and her district attorneys often let their political ambitions dictate their actions.

Zelda's detective novels were essentially locked-room dramas featuring a circle of suspects, each of whom was close to the scene and had a plausible motive for committing the crime. There was nothing subtle about her characterizations of the people her heroine encountered. Many were described in animalistic terms: both men and women were "horse-faced," men were "ape-like" or "squirrel-faced," women were "mice," "frogs," or "wrens." Accused suspects' eyes invariably blazed with anger and their voices rose to shouts. Three stories were set in the New York City she had come to know so well; indeed, in *No Crime for a Lady*, the last of the Mary Carner books, she lodged Carner and her family on the street "between the river and the madhouse" in the Bronx where she and her own family lived, and wove a plot involving political clubhouse intrigue that reflected her knowledge of the underside of New York public life. The other three books took her and her characters to out-of-town locations familiar to her: a flood-prone Pennsylvania town on the Susquehanna River, like Wilkes-Barre; a beachfront resort on Massachusetts' North Shore modeled after Gloucester, where she and her family took their summer vacations; and a wealthy Long Island suburb.

As she peopled her stories, Zelda created a mosaic of East Coast American society circa 1940. The three stories set in New York City featured Irish cops, Italian restaurant owners and mobsters, Jewish store clerks, Slavic cleaning ladies, and African American janitors, their speech often rendered in caricatural accents. For all the ethnic diversity of her characters, readers were well advised to keep their eyes on the wealthy WASPs in the stories: the philandering department-store owner Jonathan Blankford, the flamboyant playboy Saxon Rorke, the jovial family lawyer Eli Yarrow, and the beachfront-community *grande dame* Esther Lyndall all turned out to have been up to no good.

The most original aspect of Zelda's detective novels was her treatment of her women characters. She was not the first woman detective-novel writer, and Mary Carner was not the first woman detective, but Carner goes about her business in a matter-of-fact manner that made a statement about women's abilities to function in a traditional male role. At a time when few women were real-life detectives, Zelda's decision to write about a department-store crime-stopper provided a plausible explanation for Carner's career: to deter shoplifters, New York department stores employed women who could unobtrusively patrol parts of their establishments where men would have drawn too much attention. Women's intuition plays little role in Carner's solving of her cases. In the Mary Carner novels, male policemen and prosecutors are the ones who jump to conclusions based on intuitive assumptions, whereas Carner withholds judgment until real evidence emerges. Zelda depicted her detective as a careful listener, alert for details that the men overlook—why, in *No Crime for a Lady*, does one neighbor say that the murder victim's garage was kept locked, when every other witness asserts that it was always open and accessible?—and a skillful questioner, able to spot the inconsistencies in suspects' responses.

Aside from insisting on Carner's intelligence and independence, however, Zelda did little to flesh out her "young sleuthess," as one reviewer called her. "A pretty girl, trim, slender, poised and well mannered. . . . A bright, sophisticated looking person, she dressed impeccably . . . a bland, attractive young woman": Mary Carner was hardly a match for Sara Paretsky's V. I. Warshawski or many other women detectives who would succeed her. In a letter to her publishers in 1944, when she had decided not to continue the series, Zelda admitted that she had "got rather tired of Mary Carner. She was getting too much like one of the Rover Boys." Carner came with no back story: she had no discernable ethnic identity, no family, no close friends or lovers, no quirks or special interests. Perhaps the greatest mystery in the Mary Carner novels is the question of how Carner manages to maintain her poise and her "secure knowledge that the world was—despite its gangsters and its Hitlers—a good and friendly place," even as she resigns herself to the fact that no one she encounters, other than her boss and eventual husband Chris Whitaker and her admirer among the ranks of New York's finest, Patrolman Reese, can be entirely trusted. Carner accepts the reality of a system in which men hold most of the power, and she allows herself to be married to her boss by the start of the third novel, *Murder in the Mist*, by which time she has also acquired a five-year-old adopted daughter, implausibly named Baby Doll, without the inconveniences of pregnancy and diaper-changing. (Only readers with instincts as keen as Carner's would have noticed that the child's father, killed fighting for the Spanish Loyalists, was named Martin Pincus, making Carner's adopted child, in all probability, half Jewish.)[14] Despite marriage, motherhood, and the move to a comfortable middle-class house outside of Manhattan, however, Carner keeps her department-store job.

Even if Mary Carner was not a vivid character, having her at the center of the stories allowed Zelda to depict the lives of many other women in America besides her heroine. Her female suspects and victims were often more interesting than her ostensible heroine. The opening scene of *Time Off for Murder*, the second of the novels, finds Carner at a luncheon meeting of the Contempora Club, a networking organization for professional women. Her colleagues include the owner of a beauty salon, a playbroker, a newspaper columnist, a "stylist for the country's leading silk manufacturers," a "chief of social service at a large public hospital," a magazine editor, and a prison psychologist, all of them uneasy about the absence of their president, an attorney who is missing, as readers soon learned, because she has just been murdered. Zelda's aim was not simply to celebrate these women's successes. She used her novel to make a powerful statement about the price they paid for their careers:

> *When one looked closely, fatigue was plain in their eyes, in the hard line, circling the rouged lips that moved glibly in bright patter, that drooped in tired parentheses when they believed themselves unnoticed; in the parchment lifelessness of the skin under their makeup. Tired women, driving themselves too hard toward fame and fortune. All of them smoked at least a pack a day. They lived—omitting the few who resided under a parental roof with an aging mother or father—in modern, two and a half room housekeeping apartments and spoke with wistful pride of their domesticity. They entertained at intimate little dinners and Sunday night suppers. The food was sent up from the restaurant on the street floor of the apartment house. They had well-stocked liquor closets, mixed drinks with a bartender's expert hand, but rarely took more than two in an evening themselves. . . . Few of them wore wedding rings, not even those who had had a husband or two. Simply that it was bad business to flaunt the marital*

state. Nor had those who still wrote themselves down as "spinster" taken vows of celibacy. Men were amusing. One dined, danced, went to theatre, sat at bars, golfed, motored with them, all with a brittle gayety that had its overtones of hopefulness that this male would turn out to be the someone special. The man who was big enough to share a household with a wife who had a career, or make her forget she had ever wanted one.[15]

Zelda knew that many working women were even worse off than the successful professionals she portrayed in this passage. In a 1940 article in *Independent Woman* magazine, the publication of the National Federation of Business and Professional Women's Clubs, she provided facts and figures to show that "a woman's wage is often too low for even her own support, and often doubly and trebly inadequate when she has dependents" and concluded that "there is still room for improvement before the 'American standard of living' can have a meaning for many millions of women who work in this, the richest country in the world." Honest as Zelda was about the price that even better-paid women might have to pay for professional success, her intention was not to warn them against seeking it. When the Contempora Club's invited male speaker tells the members that they should have stuck to "the agreeable pursuits of domesticity which nature has ordained for you," explaining that "As females, you would have, save for your wretched contrariness, been relieved by nature and custom from the cruel necessity of contending in the marts of commerce. You would have been spared the sordidness of money grubbing. You would have been sheltered from life's ugliness. You would need to know nothing of man's inhumanity to man. Yet, deliberately, you have tossed away your natural good fortune," the women's eyebrows shoot up in "interrogatory arcs" as they reject this classic exposition of male obtuseness.[16] Even if one were to interpret as a cautionary tale the sad fate of the attorney Phyllis Knight, whose desiccated body would be found six months later in the furnace of an abandoned apartment building, readers would have recognized that she was avenged by the determined professional Mary Carner, in a book written by another determined woman, Zelda herself.

In 1940, when she wrote these lines, Zelda could count herself as one of those women married to a man "big enough to share a household with a wife who had a career." She had herself listed in the 1940 census as "writer, fiction," and on the dust jackets of her mystery novels and in interviews to promote them, she put her public relations skills to work to create the image of herself as a woman who had it all: a good marriage, a happy family, a fulfilling career, and a promising future as a writer. Readers of *Time Off for Murder* were told that the author "left Wilkes-Barre to attend Columbia University in New York. She gave up college to engage in war-work publicity, married her boss, started a publicity bureau with him, and raised two sons. Through more than twenty years, she has worked with her husband, Louis Popkin, on a wide variety of publicity accounts, among which were leading department stores in the metropolitan area. Mrs. Popkin has done a great deal of free-lance writing for magazines and periodicals and is a frequent contributor to the *New Yorker*. . . . Her knowledge of police procedure was augmented by close contact with New York City's police department and courts, through her collaboration with a New York City Magistrate on a sociological survey of vice and crime."

Perhaps to help readers identify more easily with her, in the blurb for *Dead Man's Gift*, published a year later, Zelda reassured them that "I practice the housewifely arts, even to the occasional darning of socks, in a small house on a rural street in New York," and added, "I am passionately interested in politics, a passion exceeded only by my devotion to the fortunes of the Brooklyn Dodgers." Interviews in the newspapers in Wilkes-Barre, where her family was known, provided the only references to her Jewish origins: the *Times Leader* referred to her work with the Jewish Welfare Board and its rival, the *Record*, said that she had been "a frequent contributor to the *American Hebrew*, the *Jewish Tribune*, and *B'nai B'rith Magazine* . . . and was for a considerable period stage and motion picture reviewer for the Anti-Defamation League of the B'nai B'rith." She certainly dazzled my mother, who began to frequent the Popkin home at this time. Zelda "exuded personal warmth, and absolute certitude. She was the first woman I knew who could entertain a roomful of people with her conversational wit. She could also tell excellent dirty jokes, often with a Yiddish flavor. She was earthy, warm and, especially in the early days, when I was young and shy, I enjoyed being in her orbit," my mother wrote after Zelda's death.[17]

Within a few years, after Louis Popkin's death and her sons' departures to start their own lives, Zelda would find herself living precisely the existence of the ambitious single women she described in *Time Off for Murder*. In several widely read magazine articles and in her 1949 novel *Walk Through the Valley*, she would revisit the question of the costs and benefits of a professional woman's life. In her detective stories, however, the career women were just one part of a broader panorama of female experiences. The department-store setting of her first Mary Carner novel offered Zelda the opportunity to portray a wide variety of female characters besides her heroine. She was aware that women could be as tempted by crime as men: in the how-to manual of shoplifting techniques that she provided her readers, light-fingered females figure prominently. The aggrieved wife of the murder victim and the murderer's spoiled mistress both come under suspicion as Carner unravels the case. Those characters were essentially caricatures, but Zelda's depiction of the store's female employees had greater realism. "Feminine executives departed with the salesgirls and packers each night at a few minutes after five," she observed. "As they hurried toward the subway, these working women invariably encountered another stream of women, plodding from the Second and Third Avenue 'Els' and buses, over to the great office buildings and glittering shops along the Avenue. These new arrivals were peasant women, with broad cheekbones and soap scrubbed faces, heavy and shapeless of body, or thin, worn-to-the-bone, parchment gray old drudges, dressed in ancient garments—a purifying army, which took over the stores and offices of the city after the fashionable shoppers and smartly clad stenographers had all gone on home."[18]

In *Time Off for Murder*, the second Mary Carner mystery, which had, as one reviewer noted, an "all feminine cast," the victim is one of those unmarried professional women from the Contempora Club whose longing for love leads her to fall for a wealthy playboy with criminal connections. Zelda used the opportunity, as we have seen, to sketch the situation of professional women in general. The novel's plot also allowed her, however, to confront readers with the reality of the lives of the women hauled into the city's Women's Court, where a female magistrate, modeled after Popkin's friend Anna Kross, uses words familiar to readers from Zelda's magazine articles about the court a few years earlier. "We go through the motions of giving them a trial, sending them to prison, and in a few months they're back again," the judge in the book remarks. "Reform? How can we expect them to—as long as low wages and drudgery are the only alternatives we offer them? And the poorest and stupidest are the ones we see here."[19] *Murder in the Mist*, the only one of Zelda's crime novels with a female perpetrator, also offered readers a red herring in the form of a grotesquely obese female recluse who, we learn, had actually committed a murder in the past in reaction to the bullying inflicted on her. Zelda brought some of the same psychological insight that allowed her to turn this woman into a relatively sympathetic character to her portrayal of the memorably named Xenia Tibor in her final mystery, *So Much Blood*. Physically unattractive and highly suspect in the death of her unfaithful husband, who is found clutching her broken eyeglasses in his hand, Tibor impresses the narrator with her intelligence and her ability to explain why her situation, as a (presumably Jewish, although this is not spelled out) war refugee, has forced her to associate with dubious characters.

Despite their highlighting of female characters, however, Zelda's mystery novels were not feminist tracts. In the passage in which the male speaker tells the highly accomplished women of Mary Carner's Contempora Club that they should have stayed in their homes, the women arch their eyebrows but say nothing. Occasionally, however, Zelda allowed one of her characters to make a statement on behalf of women's right to lead their own lives. In the first of the Carner stories, the detective and the police are questioning the roommate of the murdered credit manager's mistress, who has admitted that she spent the night with one of the male suspects in the case. "The Inspector shook his head: 'You're a pretty unmoral person, aren't you?' 'Call it that if you wish. I think I'm just being honest with myself and the rest of the world. A woman capable of supporting herself can do as she pleases about friendships with men,'" the young woman replies.[20] A few years later, after Louis Popkin's death,

Zelda would use almost the same words in discussing the right of widowed women like herself to sexual freedom.

Although the issues that she and other women of the period confronted in their lives figured importantly in Zelda's detective novels, the Mary Carner books were essentially meant as entertainment for their readers. History hovers at the edge of the stories: a mention of department store workers' anxiety about losing their jobs as the Great Depression lingers on in *Death Wears a White Gardenia*, published in 1938; a reference to a newsreel of German soldiers goose-stepping through Prague in *Time Off for Murder*, which appeared in early 1940. America was already at war when the last Carner mystery, *No Crime for a Lady*, came out in early 1942, but the manuscript had been completed before Pearl Harbor. Comfortably settled on the street in the Bronx where Zelda and her family lived in real life, Mary Carner is jolted by an explosion, but it is the result of a neighbor's plot to rid himself of his wife, not a foreign enemy's bomb.

Zelda's Mary Carner novels sold well and established her credentials as a contributor to American popular culture. Her first mystery, *Death Wears a White Gardenia*, got nationwide distribution when it was packaged as a Sunday supplement for newspapers in several major cities. Her books were among the first titles included in the Dell Publishing Company's "map-back" paperback series, started in 1942 and distinguished by maps of the crime scene on their back covers. Inclusion in that series put Zelda in the company of leading practitioners of the genre; other authors in the Dell series included Agatha Christie, John Dickson Carr, Dashiell Hammett, and Erle Stanley Gardner. Zelda became sufficiently prominent to be one of only three women authors included in a how-to guide, *Writing Detective and Mystery Fiction*, published in 1945.[21] Two of her Mary Carner novels were translated into French as parts of a short-lived Belgian series in 1946, and one of them appeared in Italian translation in 1952. Although the books have never been republished in English, they enjoyed a posthumous success abroad in the 1990s when all six were put out in translations by a well-known German firm and three came out in French.[22]

By the time Zelda published her final murder mystery, *So Much Blood*, in 1944, both the world and her personal life had been turned upside down. The United States was now at war, and she was now a widow: Louis Popkin had died of a sudden heart attack in January 1943. "I really don't know how we're going to swing it without him. For more than half my life, I hadn't a thought or emotion Louis didn't share," she wrote to a friend.[23] Leon Birkhead and an unnamed rabbi conducted his memorial service. Over the years, Zelda would write so much about her experience of widowhood that she would come to refer to herself as a "professional widow." By the time she wrote about Louis's death in her autobiography, thirteen years after the event, she had published a number of magazine articles and a novel directly drawn from her memories, and she would revisit the topic in her late-life fiction in the 1960s and 1970s. In exploring the subject so extensively, she was a pioneer: the "widowhood memoir" would only become a recognized genre decades later, after feminism had validated the public discussion of women's emotional experiences.[24]

Apart from the letter just cited, however, I have found no other documents about Zelda's emotional reaction to my grandfather's death prior to a determinedly upbeat article published in October 1945, when she had decided to mine her experiences for writing purposes. In the account in *Open Every Door*, her autobiography, she depicted herself as a psychological wreck, plunged into "a time of starkness, of despair," seized by fits of anger as she asked "how had this dared to happen to us?" She became dependent on "the yellow pills, the blue and red" to help her sleep. She missed "the satin softness of the flesh on flesh" in bed at night, and she sometimes contemplated suicide.[25] In later life, in a letter to my father, she vented her anger at her older son, Roy, who "married before Louis' body was cold. He knew you'd have to go into the army but he never gave a second thought to what would happen to me." My father, for his part, harbored the conviction that Zelda herself was to blame for Louis's heart attack. "He holds Z's bad temper responsible for his father's death. She nagged and pushed and always wanted more money, he says. No doubt some truth, some exaggeration in these memories," my mother noted in her diary in 1976.[26]

The wartime atmosphere proved to be conducive to Zelda's recovery. In between grousing about basic training, Louis's young partner "Embee" Zerwick reminded her that others also "miss[ed] with a terrific longing such a warm, friendly understanding guy like he was." Along with Embee's letters, reading the news made her aware that her experience was not unique. "Why, this has happened to women everywhere. We're in a war. In every country, there are women who mourn the men they loved." Two months after Louis's death, Zelda was offered a position with the Joint Distribution Committee, for which she and Louis had worked during the First World War. "It gave me reason for getting out of bed each morning, donning girdle, stockings, shoes, a dress or suit, hair neatly combed, enough makeup to hide the sleeplessness and the tears," she wrote.[27]

With her older son, Roy, supporting himself and preparing to marry and her younger son, Richard (my father), about to graduate from Columbia and go into the army, Zelda did not need the large house overlooking the East River where she had set the action of her 1942 detective novel *No Crime for a Lady*. According to my uncle, she simply took the house keys to the bank, told them she was abandoning the property, and found herself a room in a residential hotel in Manhattan. "When it came to preparing for the moving, I was in a vandal's mood," she later wrote. "Get rid of everything. . . . I don't need anything. I've lost what I valued most." Frustratingly for her future biographer, she seems to have jettisoned most of her personal papers from the years prior to the publication of her first book in 1938. Working for the "Joint" filled up her days, even if the issues she dealt with could hardly have done much to lift her mood. No one in America was better informed than the Joint staff about the Jewish catastrophe unfolding in Hitler's Europe. A memorandum that Zelda wrote in September 1943, proposing a radio broadcast that would go beyond lamenting the massacre of Jews in Europe and "focus attention on those who have survived, who will be the nucleus of the European Jewry which we must help to build," showed that she was fully aware of what was happening overseas.[28]

The war weighed on Zelda in other ways as well. Her older son, Roy, had been found unfit for military service, but by the summer of 1943, my father was in basic training camp in Virginia, and my grandmother was writing the first of the letters to him that I have found. It is partly jocular and, for a letter from a mother to a teenaged son, surprisingly frank: "I am very pleased that you have so quickly and satisfactorily begun your education in gold-bricking, which I understand is the first thing any man in his right mind learns in this army. Also that you passed short-arm inspection. I was worried about that, wondering if we'd forgotten to equip you with any of the vital necessities." But Zelda knew that my nineteen-year-old father had been badly shaken by his own father's death a few months earlier and that, as his letters to my mother show, he was nervous about the prospect of being sent overseas. My grandmother tried to give him strength, telling him, "it is one of the inevitables in your life, my darling, and we Popkins take inevitables in our strides, making every experience, even the heartbreaking ones, a source of ennoblement and enrichment."[29] No doubt she was addressing that encouragement to herself as well as to her son.

By the end of the summer of 1943, Zelda was receiving alarming news from the military base in Virginia where my father had been sent for basic training and had fallen seriously ill. "This is the very bottom," she remembered telling one of her officemates. A week after writing her grim memo about the European Jews, Zelda and my father's eighteen-year-old fiancée, Julie, traveled to Virginia for a brief visit with him. The visit was not reassuring: they found him in the hospital, so sick that he would soon be given a medical discharge from the army.[30] On the way back, the two women had tickets on the "Congressional Limited," the Pennsylvania Railroad's crack express train. The train was crowded with servicemen on leave and civilians of all sorts. Zelda and her future daughter-in-law sat with a famous acquaintance, the Chinese philosopher Lin Yutang, whose children had attended the progressive Walden School along with my father and his brother. Just north of Philadelphia, a journal box on one of the speeding train's axles overheated, causing a derailment. My mother and grandmother were handing their order to a waiter in the dining car when "there was a tremendous jolt," as my mother recalled more than forty years later. "I still have a perfectly clear vision of seeing his eyes widen in shock as he seemed to fly toward the front of the car."

The wreck, the worst rail disaster in the United States in decades, cost the lives of seventy-nine passengers and crew. "From her writer's viewpoint," Zelda told a radio interviewer, "the most vivid impression she got was that, contrary to Hollywood and popular opinion, no one screamed. Terror . . . froze everyone into absolute silence": she was clearly already thinking about the day when she would put the experience into a novel.[31] When she returned to the Joint office, the coworker to whom she had said that the news about her son's illness was "the very bottom" remarked that her experience showed that things could always become even worse.

As the fate of the Jews in Europe and of her son in his army base weighed on her, and as her own close call in the train wreck added to her sense of the uncertainty of life, Zelda returned to her typewriter and to the activity that had become central to her. *So Much Blood*, the first book she wrote after Louis's death, proved to be a transition in her career: its plot still adhered to the conventions of the detective genre, but she was clearly straining to move beyond them. As she was working on the book, she gave a talk in which she "denounced the whole notion of wanting to escape or trying to escape at the time when Nazi barbarism was rising and spreading and we were faced with the choice of being engulfed by the wave of the future or fighting for our lives." The central figure of her new novel, she told her editor, "hates Fascists and doesn't care who knows it."[32] In order to move toward wartime themes, Zelda abandoned Mary Carner and the issues about women that the Carner novels had raised. The narrator and central figure in *So Much Blood* is an American army medical lieutenant wearing a leg brace as a result of a wound sustained in the landings of November 1942 in French North Africa.

Zelda's son Roy, with whom she shared the manuscript, was glad she had dropped "bright-eyes Carner" in order to produce "a psycho-thriller" like those of the classic suspense novelist Eric Ambler, "the first with a war-time background and American locale."[33] Zelda experimented, not very successfully, with first-person narration, although the wounded veteran sounds more like the third-person narrator of her earlier mystery novels than like a real person. The plot revolves around the attempted murder of John Alling Pride, an industrialist who is making crucial contributions to the war effort. His activities so strongly paralleled the well-publicized achievements of Henry J. Kaiser, the builder of the mass-produced "Liberty ships" that carried wartime supplies to Europe, that Zelda's author's note explicitly disavowed any resemblance to him. The guests assembled for a weekend at Pride's Long Island estate include an unsavory war profiteer and a trio of suspicious foreigners, as well as several other individuals with potential reasons for doing away with their host. The narrator describes the exotic Xenia Tibor's philandering husband, Lorenz, as "an import, Hungarian, I believe, who didn't wait for Hitler to tell him that New York was a healthier place than Budapest to practice psychoanalysis," thus tagging him as Jewish without explicitly saying so; Zelda still assumed that reaching a broad public required downplaying the Jewishness of her characters and remaining silent about her own ethnic origins. In the sinister atmosphere that pervades the Pride estate after Lorenz Tibor is found lying in a pool of blood, even the narrator finds himself a plausible suspect, a twist unimaginable in the Mary Carner novels. The murderer turns out to be a Nazi sympathizer straight out of the pages of Art Derounian's 1943 exposé *Under Cover*, "a goddam idiot" who "thinks we're all wrong. A hater. Hates this country, the government." (Derounian's book was published under the pen name John Roy Carlson.)[34]

The murder in *So Much Blood* thus involved stakes much higher than those in the Mary Carner stories. If the nefarious Scott Neissen had managed to ply the patriotic industrialist Pride with as much of the blood-thinning medicine dicoumarin as the unfortunate Lorenz Tibor ingested, the American war effort would have been seriously imperiled. Lippincott saw the promotional possibilities of a thriller so closely linked to the war and made *So Much Blood* one of the first titles in a new collection of "Main Line Mysteries," promoting it as "a mystery for the connoisseur." The choice of a wounded warrior as the narrator and the hero whose last-minute intervention saves John Alling Pride was calculated to tug at the heartstrings of patriotic readers and to appeal to men in the military, who were by 1944 an important part of the audience for popular fiction. Despite his leg brace, Lieutenant Sam Tate gets the girl—Pride's sexy red-headed daughter—at the story's end, foreshadowing the uniformed-boy-meets-girl plot that would make Zelda's first "straight" novel, *The Journey Home*, a million-seller a year later.

By the time *So Much Blood* appeared in the spring of 1944, Zelda was beginning to adjust to her new life as a single woman. When her younger son was discharged from the army after his illness, she decided she needed to move out of the hotel rooms she had been occupying since moving to Manhattan. To those familiar with the present-day New York housing market, her account of how a sidewalk "for rent" sign led her to a spacious apartment on fashionable Gramercy Park for a hundred dollars a month is harder to believe than any of her fiction writing; it would be the first of her homes that I would visit.[35] My father did not stay with her long: he married my mother, a Jewish girl from the Bronx, in June 1944. (When Zelda's formidable mother Annie Feinberg met my mother, her response was "Who would have thought Dickie would get such a healthy girl?") Zelda's older son, Roy, had married a Gentile woman a year earlier, and they now presented her with a granddaughter. Zelda was not entirely pleased. "Grandmother means mothballs, shawls and on the shelf," she wrote in her autobiography.[36] She would teach all her grandchildren to call her Zelda, rather than "Grandma."

In her autobiography, Zelda claimed that the second year of her single life was worse than the first. With both of her sons now permanently out of the house, her loneliness became more acute. "What would I like to be?" she wrote. "Less lonely, for sure. The need for men, enjoying them, is a part of me." By the time she wrote these lines, ten years later, she must have realized that she was never likely to find another partner, but in 1945, at least according to her, there were possibilities. "Men phoned, old acquaintances and new. Widows are fair game for the hunter. The assumption is they need to be consoled. They do," she wrote. There was a serious love affair with a married man whom she called "Paul" in her autobiography, the husband of one of her friends. Plot lines derived from this experience were woven into two of her subsequent novels before she described the affair in her autobiography. My mother claimed to know that none of Zelda's retellings of the affair corresponded to the facts; the only thing I can say for sure is that she never remarried.[37] But her unhappy experience certainly gave her new ideas for writing about women's lives.

It was not a frustrated love affair but an ultimately consummated one that took center stage in *The Journey Home*, Zelda Popkin's most successful novel, which she worked on in the second half of 1944 and the early months of 1945. Like *So Much Blood*, *The Journey Home* had a wartime setting, but Zelda meant it to be a true novel, "not the slick puzzle, out of the fingertips and top of head, but from the gut, the beginning of the deeper searching, what am I, what do I think and feel?"[38] The press coverage of the train wreck she had survived gave her not only a dramatic climax of her story but an idea for a plot that would highlight the question of how men who had faced combat overseas would be able to form relationships with civilians who had not known the horror of war, and especially with women who had remained on the home front.

A *New York Times* story, "Survivors of Wreck Tell How Servicemen Helped," must have helped Zelda imagine a novel built around that event. The *Times* emphasized the efforts of the military personnel on the train, who were quickly recruited to help rescue trapped victims, although two of the servicemen interviewed confessed, as corporal Otis Tellis put it, "I could not stand the sight of the blood all about, and I had to leave." The only woman interviewed, Carolyn Brown, raised the issue of how women had reacted to the crash: she said that most of them "became hysterical." Zelda and my mother had not personally participated in caring for the injured. My mother, when she wrote her own account of the crash in 1987, recalled that she and Zelda "saw nothing of the carnage," since the dining car in which they found themselves was not badly damaged. "In those days, although we were both able-bodied women, we were not asked to come out to help." For the inventor of Mary Carner, however, it was not difficult to imagine how such a crisis might allow a woman to demonstrate her mettle. The train setting also gave her an opportunity to write about the experience of military men. An incident on another rail trip that Zelda took in the spring of 1944 helped crystallize a second major plot thread in her mind. During her trip, "a Marine and a naval officer . . . both on the make," invited themselves into her roomette, an experience the middle-aged widow found "flattering" and which gave her the idea of making the encounter of a serviceman and a woman on a train the heart of her story.[39]

As she worked on her book, a generation of young servicemen, many of them Jewish, such as Irwin Shaw, Herman Wouk, and Norman Mailer, were preparing to transmute their experiences into classics such as *The Young Lions, The Caine Mutiny,* and *The Naked and the Dead.*[40] It took a generous helping of chutzpah for Zelda to imagine that a woman who had never seen a battlefield could channel the thoughts of a male character who had flown through the murderous flak over the Ploesti oil fields. Her former business partner "Embee" Zerwick had written to her from Germany, "I hope you haven't written about the war without having seen something of it actually. Nobody can ever write anything of the war that will be believed by anyone who's ever been in it. . . . For instance try writing what it feels like to have stumps instead of hands." It was her experience of the "Congressional Limited" disaster that convinced her she could meet this challenge. "I gave my people the civilian substitute for a bombing—a train wreck, and those who grew up under the ordeal of terror and personal danger were only those who had in themselves living materials of growth," she wrote.[41]

To prepare herself for writing, Zelda began clipping magazine and newspaper articles about military men's reactions to the stresses of war and about the experiences of soldiers' wives and war widows. A *New Yorker* article, "No Place Like Home," filled her in on the arrangements for military men granted home leave and informed her that their first question was invariably "where they can buy a bottle." An unsuccessful request to a private foundation for a copy of its report on "war neuroses in North Africa" indicates that she wanted the latest data about the impact of the war on soldiers' psyches, a subject she knew something about from having lived for many years across the street from a psychiatric hospital where veterans from the First World War were treated.[42] She planned from the start to have a train wreck provide her story's climax, but at first, her detective-story experience led her to consider making it a "spy-sabotage story," even though suspicions that the Congressional Limited crash had been deliberately caused were quickly dismissed. Then Zelda took another long trip, from New York to Miami, Florida, to visit a center for returning servicemen. As she later told her publisher's publicity person, "I prowled the Miami train, day and night. I walked and I talked, with men in uniform and women in mink. In Miami, I spent my time in the Air Force Redistribution Area, hung about the little bars and drug stores and restaurants where the returned airmen congregated, talked at length with local people who were concerned with the servicemen and their families and problems. I came back by coach and sat up all night in the ladies room with a group of service wives who were talking straight off the chest." By the time she got home, she had the material for a book whose "broad pattern will be 'Grand Hotel'—a variety of lives and human problems brought together under one temporary roof, enduring a devastating common experience which violently affects all of them and resolves some of their problems."[43]

As she pitched her project to her publisher, Zelda explained that she wanted to use her book to draw a damning portrayal of "an America which has eaten well and slept soundly in a world of hunger and horror . . . it will tell about those Americans to whom the war has been one long money-making and spending binge, who have cloaked their meretricious escapism in palaver about 'upholding civilian morale.'" But she knew that "the joy-riders aren't all of war-time America. . . . Wives and children of men in the armed forces have endured hardship and loneliness and dread. Refugees have been among us, like ghosts at the banquet table. In the factories, on the railroads, workers have pushed their strength to superhuman levels to meet the demands of total war." Her central character would be "a bombardier, returning from Europe, full up with horror . . . a young man of cultured background, intelligence and sensitivity, who has destroyed the enemy's cities and killed its women and children."[44]

Zelda's story would bring this tortured soul together with "a sleek and smart young woman, an advertising writer, veneered with patriotic clichés, who has, like so many of us, skimmed glibly over the surfaces of the war." In another pitch for the book, Zelda wrote that her female protagonist would be a woman who has been "writing those ads about Flexees and Parfum Delice to glamorize your grueling work at the A.W.V.S. or the Boeing plant. She rings clever little changes on the 'don't-you-know-there's-a-war-on?' gag, and pulls the charming little suggestion that 'What we need is a little bombing to wake us up,'" Zelda wrote in an early sketch for the book. Through the romance-novel-worthy encounter between these two figures, Zelda hoped to dramatize "the enormous gulf between the ten million men who have endured war and the one hundred million men and women who have known only the petty irritations of a safe country in wartime." Although Zelda's ambitions to portray a cross-section of American society at war and to highlight the divide between male warriors and female civilians portended a sufficiently complex story, she added that "it has become impossible for me to write a book without a homicide" and made up a subplot involving "the most sordid of all murders—a murder for robbery."[45]

Once installed in her new apartment, Zelda set to work furiously: "Six months of seven days a week writing and re-writing and nights of insomnia." By the time Germany surrendered, in May 1945, *The Journey Home* was in production; it reached bookstores just as the war in the Pacific was nearing its end. The timing could not have been better: a novel featuring a romance between a soldier and a young woman was the perfect counterpart to the famous *Life* magazine photograph of a sailor kissing a young woman in Times Square to celebrate V-J Day. Zelda had assured her publisher that "the pace of the book will be swift—as swift as a train ride," and she delivered: in just 224 pages, she introduced readers to dozens of characters, let them hear a variety of opinions about the war and its impact, drew them into the conflicted relationship between her bombardier, Don Corbett, and the attractive fashion stylist Nina Gilmore, and then brought matters to a climax with her re-creation of the "Congressional Limited" train wreck.[46]

Into the crowded coach where Don Corbett's black-market train ticket placed him she crammed a young serviceman's wife with two small children, a young war widow and her older mother-in-law, a greasy-haired gambler, and a motley collection of sailors, Marines, and army men. As the restless Corbett roams the train, he encounters women of all kinds, a German refugee determined to warn Americans against any compromise with fascism, an elderly doctor who tries to establish a bond with Corbett by mentioning that he served in World War I, and a number of privileged passengers enjoying the luxury of private Pullman sleeping compartments. He meets a bloviating senator and his wife and daughter, an Englishwoman desperate to avoid returning to her endangered country, a wealthy industrialist, and a newspaper publisher, a stand-in for Roy Howard of the Scripps-Howard press chain whom my mother remembered seeing on the "Congressional Limited." Because her characters start their journey in the South and travel on a train with African American porters and waiters, Zelda found herself dealing for the first time in her novels with aspects of race relations that were less obtrusive in the North, the setting of her previous books.

There was no doubt in Zelda's mind about what a man who had spent two years at war would be looking for on his first day of liberty in the United States. Her novel's first line was "Don Corbett went straight to the bar." As he downs his rotgut whisky, his thoughts turn to "girls . . . *American Girls.*" He manages to convince himself that the women winking at him in the railroad station bar are not what he wants, but as soon as he boards his train, he begins assessing the prospects. Decent enough to leave women he recognizes as servicemen's wives alone, he is nevertheless determined to find himself a real "dish," and finally, on page 36, "an X marked the spot. The X was a pair of superlative legs." A strained conversation ensues, as Corbett fails to conceal his contempt for sheltered civilians and pretty Nina Gilmore puts him on the spot by asking how he earned the service ribbons on his uniform. Nevertheless, Corbett is reluctant to give up his pursuit and he finally screws up his courage to ask, "May I touch your legs?" With "something like pity" in her expression, Gilmore grants him his wish, joking awkwardly that "the best isn't any too good for our boys."[47]

Just as the train wreck gave my grandmother the idea for her novel, this passage gave an American women's historian, Melissa McEuen, the idea for her monograph, *Making War, Making Women: Femininity and Duty on the American Home Front, 1941–1945*: in her introduction, McEuen says that *The Journey Home* "became the frame for my argument" about the way images in wartime advertising and propaganda manipulated both women and men. Not only does Nina Gilmore correspond to the wartime stereotype of the idealized American woman—heart-shaped face, matching lipstick and fingernails, tasteful clothing and jewelry—but her profession of "stylist" means that she was responsible for persuading other women to put their money and energy into making themselves desirable for the men away at war. "It's no less than our duty, our patriotic duty, to keep things going the way they were before, the way you expect them to be," Gilmore tells Corbett, in words that echo the arguments that cosmetics manufacturers made in their bids to be classified as essential to the war effort.[48]

Corbett, on the other hand, bears "the scars of war on his face: the network of lines, the grooves in his cheeks, the wry twist of his mouth." The soldier in Zelda's previous novel, *So Much Blood*, had been physically wounded and wore a leg brace, but the damage Corbett has sustained is psychological, made visible through his compulsive habit of rubbing his thumbs together. He has been traumatized by the horrors he has witnessed during his combat missions—"flak so thick you could walk on it," a fellow crewman whose head was blown "clean off his neck" by a 20 mm shell—and by questions he can't answer about the justification for the war. As a schoolboy in Brooklyn, he tells Gilmore, his best friend was "a Japanese kid"; even though the news of Pearl Harbor made him enlist, he cannot make sense of the fact that "I'll have to go out and kill Sandi." At best, he considers himself "a guy who's doing a dirty job for his country."[49] He knows his bombs have fallen on women and children as well as military targets.

Corbett's encounters with civilians on the train do nothing to improve his mood. He overhears complaints about shortages of gasoline and consumer goods, schemes to profit from the war—at one point, Nina Gilmore herself gazes at the "fruit salad" of service ribbons on Corbett's shirt and talks about designing "a line of War Hero Prints" for women's clothes—and expressions of racial prejudice. By the end, as Corbett tries to figure out what he could say to the widow of a soldier he has encountered that would justify her husband's sacrifice, he wonders why anyone should die to protect the rights of such people. Zelda's editors worried that "Corbett appears as too harsh a character. In spite of the fact that he is war worn, he might have more sympathy for his fellow travelers. It would strengthen his case," one of them wrote to her, anxious that her book not offend potential readers.[50]

As Zelda intended, everything about her two principal characters emphasizes the seemingly unbridgeable chasm between civilian women and military men. Readers could sense, of course, that the couple were destined to fall in love, but Zelda knew better than to make the process a simple one. Corbett, for all the urgency of his sexual longing, also wants a woman who is interested in him for his own sake, not merely because of his Distinguished Flying Cross. Drawn to the prickly Corbett but determined to make him show that he regards her as more than a spoiled civilian and a sex object, Gilmore finally persuades the airman to talk about his traumatic experiences in the war. "You're quite a different man when you talk, open up," she tells him, even as he tries to shock her by asking if she has "ever seen one of those? A neck without a head?" Gilmore encourages him, moving closer to him and assuring him that "now I'm your friend who knows all about you and wants sincerely to help," but when she tells him, "this is my war as much as it's yours," he lashes out: "*You* feel the war? You've got nothing to feel. It doesn't touch you." Still trying to convince Corbett that empathy can bridge the gulf separating women and civilians from men who have fought, Gilmore insists that "if we'd had to, we would have" shown the same courage. "If we'd have one little bombing, it would have been different!"[51]

This remark convinces Corbett that she truly understands nothing and he unloads on her, saying that in Britain, he had seen "kids, without arms, without legs. Can't run. Can't play," adding, "I've made a few kids like that, myself." In a physical sign of what would nowadays be labeled PTSD, he starts "rubbing his thumbs, rubbing them hard, as though this time he meant to rip flesh from the bones." Unable to bear either what he is saying to her, Gilmore collapses in tears. Suddenly able to play the role of a strong man comforting a sobbing woman, Corbett puts his arms around her. In language straight out of the pulp fiction of the day, Zelda wrote, "He kissed her lips. She lay passive, not responding or rejecting. He bent down again. His hand moved over her shoulder and around the cup of her breast." But Nina Gilmore is not that kind of girl. "Stop. Don't you dare," she cries. "Perplexed and dismayed," Corbett gets to his feet and slams the door on his way out.[52]

While she was setting her love plot in motion, Zelda also elaborated the other side of her story: the panorama of American society in wartime. When he isn't in Gilmore's comfortable Pullman compartment, Corbett roams the train, looking for liquor, eyeing other women who promise to be less difficult to "make" than the elegant fashion stylist, and overhearing conversations, many of them unpleasant. His seatmate, the greasy-haired ethnic Bennie Kalchis, serves as the counterpart to Corbett: physically unattractive, he will turn out to be the murderer in the criminal subplot Popkin could not resist injecting into a story that had no need of it. Corbett sympathizes with a navy man's wife, encumbered by two small children, who is returning home after a short visit with her husband. He is troubled by a brief encounter with a war widow: "It gave him a genuine shock to come aware now that America must have many young women like this, girls, grown old overnight, putting on black, not for style but for sorrow." When he tries to get away from her, the widow says bitterly, "A woman in grief is a leper." Zelda undoubtedly identified strongly with this woman, so strongly that she put into Corbett's mind the words that had been addressed to her at Louis Popkin's funeral, to the effect that mourners should "Walk through the valley of the shadow of death. *Walk*. Not linger forever."[53]

The war widow eventually becomes the pretext for Zelda's most explicit statement of the liberal political views she wanted her novel to promote. She had already introduced those ideas through the voice of a "Doctor Kurt Frankel." Frankel's heavy German accent makes Corbett bristle, until the man tells him, "If you go over Berlin, drop one bomb for me." Frankel goes on to insist, "Make no mistake, you are not fight-ing Germans. Not Japanese. You fight an idea. That idea is effrywhere. In Europe. In Asia. In America too. . . . You must fight it right here, in your home. Your own Ku Klux Klan." Whereas Frankel, despite his foreign accent, expresses the best of American liberalism, Senator Hast-ings stands for everything Zelda despised. When Corbett briefly joins his table in the lounge car in order to cadge a drink, he is treated to an isolationist diatribe: "This futile adventure is costing enough. . . . And it's nothing, it's nothing at all to what will come after. When we're flooded with goods from Russian slave labor. When our own men come back, infected with Bolshevism. . . . Why, this country's just running with foreigners, taking the jobs that belong to our boys." After the book's publication, an interviewer told Zelda that he found it "almost unbelievable" that a United States senator would say such things. I can imagine the smirk with which she must have responded, "I took them word for word from the Congressional Record."[54]

Despite the denunciation of the Klan that Zelda put into Doctor Frankel's mouth, her novel was not a tract against racial segregation. Zelda included Black characters in her depiction of the train: anyone who had been in the South would have recognized the sights she had Corbett take in from the "Palm Queen's" windows: "the places where Negroes and 'crackers' resided, the hovels and hutches and lean-tos, shanties and shacks . . . depots with waiting rooms labelled: 'White' and 'Colored.'" She was not immune to racial clichés: her description of the sights from the "Palm Queen's" windows mentioned a "fat Negress" rocking on a porch, along with glimpses of the hard life of the region's poor whites. In a later scene in the novel, Corbett, frustrated when a Black train porter says that he can't sell him a bottle of whisky in Georgia because of the state's blue laws, tells him, "Listen, you get me that rye or I'll slit your black throat."[55]

Whereas Zelda tiptoed around the question of segregation, she was more outspoken about another form of prejudice. Opinion polls had shown American antisemitism rising to unprecedented levels during the war. A personal experience while she was researching her novel made Zelda acutely aware of this issue. In a "strictly confidential" memorandum she sent to an official at the Jewish Welfare Board in August 1944, she reported that "the soldiers and sailors who have been based at Miami and Miami Beach—and they number hundreds of thousands—are saying: 'After we finish this business, we'll come back and take care of the Jews.'" Rather than blaming this prejudice, she denounced the behavior of "Jewish shopkeepers, hotel owners and landlords," whom the military men and their families accused of profiting from the influx of soldiers and their families. She quoted an army wife whom she had heard saying,

"When we walked down Lincoln Road, and saw those fat Jewish women with their silver fox coats and their hands dripping diamonds, I said to my husband: *That's* what I'm sending you away to war to fight for," and she lamented that local Jews were complaining that they could have made even more money from vacationers if the city had not been swamped by the military. "The vulgarians and exploiters who have made Miami a dirty word among our armed forces are a festering sore that threatens to infect our entire land with racial hatred," she concluded.[56]

In her novel, Popkin accurately reflected the language she had heard from the military wives on her train ride, but then shaped her story to give her main character a chance to reject antisemitic prejudice. Midway through the story, Corbett overhears a conversation between two young women. One of them has "a sex-hungry look," despite her wedding ring, and Corbett wonders "whether she'd be worth trying for." The two of them complain about the prejudices against servicemen's wives looking for housing while their husbands are overseas, a topic that still raised many women's ire forty years later when the oral historian Studs Terkel did the interviews for his classic volume, *"The Good War."*[57] When they see Corbett listening to them, one of the women hisses, "Jews!" but her companion says, "Ah won't shush. Ef he is, Ah mean him to hear me. Ef he ain't, he'll know what Ah mean."[58] Corbett, who has been presented to readers as impeccably Gentile, loses interest in the pair after hearing this, but the women reappear a few dozen pages later.

In the interval, Corbett has had an interaction with the war widow Elaine Weston introduced earlier in the story. He recognizes that she is deeply depressed, and he gruffly tries to snap her out of her gloom. A few minutes later, he sees Weston trying to open the door to the train car's platform and realizes that she plans to throw herself off. When he rushes to stop her, she fights back, but Corbett floors her with a blow to the jaw. As the elderly doctor mentioned earlier in the story checks the widow over, the "sex-hungry" young woman from the previous scene tells him that Weston had overheard her and her companion talking about how "Jews ought to be extra careful what they did now because it was all on account of them that we were having this war." "That woman's husband was killed. On the Anzio beachhead," Corbett tells her. Then, channeling the spirit of the Friends of Democracy, he delivers a lecture: "Jews are *fighting* this war. They're dying. Like Catholics, Protestants, Mohammedans, Atheists. To make a safe world for your kids. And they've taken the beating. The very worst beating. The first. From Hitler. While you and I sat on our fannies and said it was none of our business."[59]

By putting the case against antisemitism in the mouth of a man in uniform, Zelda enlisted the men fighting the war on the side of tolerance. At the same time, she was able to sidestep the question of her own relationship to the issue. Nothing in the novel or the jacket copy alerted readers to the fact of her own Jewishness. Zelda's approach to the question of anti-Jewish prejudice in American life was not unique. In 1947, another Jewish woman author, Laura Z. Hobson, achieved even greater success with her novel *Gentleman's Agreement*, in which a Gentile American journalist disguises himself as a Jew to research a story on antisemitism. Hobson's book, made into an award-winning movie starring Gregory Peck, has often been credited with bringing about a major change in American public attitudes. Both Zelda and Hobson sensed, however, that non-Jewish readers could best be weaned away from their prejudices if the case against them was presented by impeccably "American" characters and by authors who did not identify themselves openly as Jews.[60]

Having used his denunciation of antisemitism to establish Don Corbett's fundamental decency, Zelda reunites him with Nina Gilmore. Corbett is starting on breakfast in the train's dining car, bleary-eyed after a night without sleep, when Gilmore slides into the seat across from him. To his astonishment, she apologizes to him: "I knew what you wanted, how badly you needed it, too." When I reread this episode after deciding to write about my grandmother's efforts to depict women as independent figures, this episode hit me like a punch in the gut. How could a self-proclaimed feminist author make her heroine Nina Gilmore *apologize* to a man who had drunkenly groped her? In the novel, Corbett himself is taken aback: "A hell of a note, a girl apologizing because a guy couldn't make her." He is in no hurry to accept her apology, however, even when it is accompanied with an invitation to her apartment in New York for "a symposium on whether or not it's every girl's duty—her patriotic duty—to give every soldier who asks what he seems to want," a sentence that reflected Zelda's acute awareness of the pressures on women created by the war. Brusquely, Corbett tells Gilmore, "One kick in the pants is enough." When she persists, he continues, "There are a few words in the language I hate. One of them's charity. Another one's pity."[61]

As Gilmore makes one last effort to keep Corbett from breaking off the conversation, the two are overwhelmed by "a monstrous smash of furniture, dishes and glass, of iron and steel" as Zelda re-created the experience of the "Congressional Limited" train wreck for her readers.[62] Once he pulls himself out of the wreckage of the overturned railroad car and realizes what has happened, Corbett's first thought is, inevitably, to locate Gilmore. After a panicky search, he finds her back at her Pullman compartment, washing her face. He is outraged that the first thing she can think of is her appearance. The scene was personal for Zelda: both she and my mother concurred that the first thing they themselves had done, before they fully grasped what had happened, was to clean themselves up in their own compartment, located in an undamaged car. "After that, and only then, were we aware this train was wrecked," Zelda wrote in her autobiography.[63] In the novel, Corbett realizes that Gilmore is in shock. She momentarily passes out in his arms. But once she comes to herself again, she turns to him and says, "Don, bombing's like this!" And it is Gilmore, not Corbett, who then announces, "They need us out there."[64]

As Gilmore and Corbett move among the dead and injured laid out alongside the tracks, they find the four-year-old daughter of the navy wife who had been seated next to Corbett at the start of the trip and the widowed Elaine Weston, who has taken charge of the child after realizing that her mother and baby brother are among the victims. It is she and Gilmore who have to find a way to break the news to the little girl; Corbett does not have the strength to do it. As he and Gilmore go to make arrangements for Weston and the child, Corbett suddenly collapses. "He swayed against her, steadied himself on her slender shoulder. . . . 'Too much all at once. Emotional. Physical.'" Both of them have now displayed courage and shown weakness in a crisis. The tension between them dissolves, and by the time they and the other survivors from the wreck make it back to New York, Corbett is ready to yield when Gilmore says to him, "Don, let me for once do something important. . . . Let me take care of a soldier I love." The fact that she takes him home to an elegantly decorated apartment with a Black maid emphasizes that Nina Gilmore is not an ordinary New York working girl. Had *The Journey Home* been made into a movie, there certainly would not have been a dry eye in the theater after this ending.[65]

Zelda's publisher Lippincott spent generously to promote the book; one New York bookstore consecrated its entire front window to a life-sized photograph showing the main characters posed in a crowded train car. In a 1948 interview, Zelda claimed that the book had sold a million copies. The Doubleday Dollar Book Club made it a selection, and the royalties from that deal alone amounted to over $9,000, far exceeding the $1,000 advance she had received for the book.[66] Numerous newspapers serialized it in 1946, and *Omnibook Magazine* published an abridged version, pairing it with a volume of war reportage by a male author.[67] Dell, which had put out paperback editions of Zelda's detective stories, bought the rights to *The Journey Home* and transformed the cover: whereas the jacket of the hardback edition had depicted a man's and a woman's head as seen from behind their train seats, the paperback showed a man in uniform and a young woman in a passionate clinch.

Zelda presumably appreciated hearing from her father, in his idiosyncratic English and typing, that "MOTHER and ME are very PROUD of your development in the field of writing." Oblivious to his daughter's intentions, he trusted that the book "has awakend the Rail Road Owners of what it is happening behind the Scenes" and that they would take steps to improve travel safety.[68] Press reviews of the book were mixed, with one critic finding the book too much of "a neat, shapely package with everything tied up just right," while another praised it as "a novel of character development written in the manner of the 'tough' school of Raymond Chandler."[69] But no less a personage than Eleanor Roosevelt wrote, "I like the end of the book because it leaves you with hope, the hope that tenderness and love will bridge the gaps and find the answer to the problems which will give many of us sleepless nights in the next few months."[70] By the time a young literary unknown named Saul Bellow published his evaluation in the newly founded Jewish magazine

Commentary in December 1945, his critique of what he saw as the mechanical quality of Zelda's writing could not derail the book's sales. Bellow conceded that Zelda's "subject—the guilt of civilians in the presence of soldiers—is a good one," but he lamented her "assumption that civilians *are* guilty, somehow, and need to expiate their fault in suffering before they can be reconciled with fighting men." Zeroing in on her precise descriptions of her female characters' dress and appearance, Bellow concluded, "critical of the trappings of vanity and feminine power, she is nevertheless constantly drawn to them, drawn, occasionally, a little too far."[71] (Years later, Zelda claimed, she got revenge on Bellow by beating him in Scrabble.)

Bellow's review was one of the few to comment on Zelda's treatment of her female characters. He may have been asked to review *The Journey Home* because he had written his own novel about the home front, *Dangling Man*, published in 1944, in which his protagonist, a man waiting nervously for his order to report for service, takes out his frustrations on every woman he encounters. Neither he nor any of the other reviewers, a number of whom were women, objected to the scene in which Nina Gilmore apologizes to Corbett for shoving him away when he grabs her breast, and Bellow was the only one who took exception to the idea that civilians necessarily owed deference to men in uniform. That men who risked their lives in combat were entitled to sexual privileges was not something that was said openly, but it was implicit in much of the war's culture, as shown by the willingness of both movie stars and ordinary young women to pose for the pinup "cheesecake" photos that servicemen so openly appreciated. Furthermore, it was important to Zelda's plot that Gilmore not come off as a prude. In the apology scene, when the resentful Corbett snarls, "Don't tell me I picked New York's only virgin," she responds with virtually the same words used by a defiant young woman in the first of Zelda's detective novels: "I'm a grown woman. I can do what I please with myself."[72] Soon, Zelda would be urging the female readers of her articles on widowhood to adopt the same attitude, and it was doubtless the credo she tried to follow herself. For my grandmother, and perhaps for her readers, what was most important in *The Journey Home* was the message that women could show as much courage in the

Figure 3.1. Zelda Popkin and World War II servicemen (1945): A publicity picture shows Zelda discussing her bestselling novel *The Journey Home* with servicemen like the central character in her story.

face of death and suffering as men. Fortified with that conviction, they could form egalitarian relationships with men, even men whose chests were covered with medals.

The majority of the readers' letters about *The Journey Home* that Zelda saved in her files were from men, many of them servicemen. Summarizing their contents, a Lippincott press release claimed that these readers "see in her book a description of their own emotions and experiences when they themselves came home after lonely years in the combat zones." The *New York Times* reviewer concurred that "Zelda Popkin has been very successful in telling just how a soldier comes home." Her servicemen readers were apparently not troubled by her depiction of one of them as a traumatized personality who breaks down under the stress of a calamity on the home front. Responding to one reviewer who objected that "no one who has not undergone a shocking experience can possibly understand what it was like," Zelda admitted that "I haven't been to war—and the fault lies with the American Red Cross, not with me," since they had hesitated "about sending grandmothers over while the shooting was on." In her opinion, however, she had met the challenge of proving that "a lady novelist could know what returned soldiers think and feel." She cited a letter from an Air Force captain who had told her "that wounded comrades had read it and said 'But how *did* you know?'"[73]

In addition to giving women confidence about their worthiness, Zelda was convinced that she had made the point that the privilege of writing about the war, the greatest historical event of the time, was not reserved only for men. She had unquestionably succeeded in writing a book that expressed liberal American values and that, in her mind, refuted antisemitic prejudice without indulging in special pleading. She had created an independent female protagonist who could stand up for herself, even against a war hero, and who could also envisage a sexual relationship outside of marriage. Above all, however, Zelda had satisfied the ambition she had cultivated since childhood. She had established herself as a recognized writer, one who could take on serious subjects and also reach the bestseller list. Necessity would drive her to do other things in the years that followed, but she never abandoned the conviction that she was, above all, an author. Disappointingly for her, however, she would never write another book that would enjoy the commercial success of *The Journey Home*.

CHAPTER 4

Facing Personal Loss and Jewish Catastrophe

IN A PHOTOGRAPH TAKEN AT BILLY ROSE'S NEW YORK NIGHTCLUB IN 1946, Zelda Popkin looks as though she is enjoying her status as a literary celebrity. The picture shows a group of two women and four men, odds that my grandmother probably considered favorable, although the woman with whom she had to compete for the men's attention was considerably younger than herself.

Figure 4.1. Zelda Popkin at Billy Rose's nightclub (1946): The success of her 1945 novel *The Journey Home* made Zelda a minor celebrity. Gossip columnists reported on her activities, and she was photographed in New York nightclubs.

The paperback edition of her wartime novel, *The Journey Home*, was still selling well. She had discovered, she told one interviewer, that "writing fiction is much easier than straight reporting," and she thought she had found the secret of presenting serious themes in ways that would attract ordinary readers. Her next book, she promised, "is going to have a lot of sex and excitement and a lot of social ideas presented in the vernacular." Zelda's career as a publicist had given her connections with the era's leading gossip columnists, such as Walter Winchell, Leonard Lyons, and Drew Pearson, who reported on her activities. Since her younger son had married in June 1944 and moved out, she had the apartment at 12 Gramercy Park, one of Manhattan's most attractive neighborhoods, all to herself; for the rest of her life, she would fondly remember evenings at her favorite restaurant in the Gramercy Park Hotel. Zelda "was really at her prime during those early years," my mother later wrote. "After recovering from her husband's death, a loss that had left her angry and bewildered, but then had spurred her on to a renewed and more brilliant career as a single woman and a novelist, Zelda seemed to flourish professionally and socially. She was probably better looking at that time . . . and more compelling as a personality than she had ever been before."[1]

The picture of Zelda's nightclub outing and my mother's recollection tell only half the story of the life Zelda was leading in the months immediately after the end of the Second World War. The woman in the fashionable hat who looks out of the photograph had not spent the months after the release of *The Journey Home* partying and promoting her book. Instead, she had left New York in October 1945 and spent three months in rubble-strewn Europe, where she had confronted the aftermath of war and genocide. Just before she flew across the Atlantic, she had also published a major article in one of the leading magazines of the day about the experience of widowhood, a trauma that she had experienced personally two years earlier. Her trip to Europe would lead her to become one of the earliest American writers to incorporate the events we now know as the Holocaust into American fiction; after a long period in which she had avoided writing on "Jewish" themes, she suddenly returned to being a "Jewish" author consciously attempting to attract Jewish readers as she had in her days at the *American Hebrew*. Her translation of her personal experience of loss into words launched her on a career as what she her-self called "a professional widow," culminating in the publication of one of the first novels to seriously explore that theme. With good reason, Zelda could tell an interviewer from the *Gramercy Graphic*, a neighbor-hood newspaper, that her experiences in 1945 and 1946 had made "the concoction of mystery stories seem rather trivial. There are bigger issues with which she would prefer to deal henceforth."[2] Up to 1945, my grand-mother's writing had aimed to inform or entertain readers and, perhaps, in some cases, to reflect about the situations she was describing. Now, she became focused on making her readers "protagonists," as she put in an author's note to her 1947 novel *Small Victory*: people who would work to change things, such as widowed women's attitudes toward their lives and American policy in occupied Germany.

My effort to imagine my grandmother's life in these years is both facilitated and complicated by the multiple self-portraits of herself that she created. For the period up to 1945, my main source of information about her life is her autobiography, supplemented by her numerous magazine articles and a few scattered personal documents. Her detective stories and *The Journey Home* drew on her own experiences for local color and, in the case of her wartime novel, for the drama of the train wreck she had survived, but their plots did not closely follow her own life. Her next four books, however—four novels published in 1947, 1949, and 1951, and her 1956 autobiography—were all unmistakably drawn from that life. Episodes transformed into fiction in her novels all had their coun-terparts in her personal memoir; in many cases, sentences and even whole paragraphs from the novels appear almost unaltered in the autobiography. Often, however, the versions of these experiences in her novel are given quite a different significance in the autobiography. Sometimes it is hard to avoid concluding that fiction gave Zelda the freedom to express certain truths in ways she chose not to do in her autobiography.

The challenge of understanding my grandmother's life after 1945 is further complicated by the existence of another source: the letters she wrote to my parents, which begin in this period, when my parents married and moved away from New York City, and continue until a few weeks before her death in 1983. In some cases, particularly for her novel about the aftermath of the Holocaust and her book about the creation of Israel in 1948, these letters served as rough drafts for her novels and her autobiography: stories and wording from her correspondence sometimes went into her books virtually unchanged. My historian's training would incline me to assume that the versions of her experiences given in her letters, intended only for an intimate audience, are closer to "the truth" than either her novel or her autobiographies, but this is not always the case. Perhaps surprisingly, the letters often minimize Zelda's emotional reactions to situations she encountered. There is no reason to assume that the dry, factual paragraphs about her encounters with Holocaust survivors in the letters from her 1945 trip to Europe are necessarily "truer" than the more extended and emotionally charged versions of the same stories in her 1947 novel, *Small Victory*, or her autobiography. Some facets of her personal experience that are discussed at length in her books, such as her unhappy involvement with a married man in the years after her husband's death, go completely unmentioned in her letters: presumably she did not feel comfortable writing to her son about a possible replacement for his father. My parents were certainly aware of this affair: when I began writing about my grandmother's life, my mother happily told me her version of it, and a 1947 letter from my father assured Zelda that he had no objection to a possible remarriage.[3] Valuable as these letters are for my purposes, I read this family correspondence as one more example of Zelda Popkin's talent for self-fashioning, not as a uniquely authentic source.

Zelda first drew on her personal experience to grapple with the theme of widowhood in one of the subplots of *The Journey Home*, through the character of the depressed young war widow Elaine Weston whom the hero, Don Corbett, saves from suicide. Bereaved servicemen's wives were all too common during World War II, and readers of that novel would have had no clue that the gloss on the 23rd Psalm that Corbett formulates in that novel were words that had been spoken to the book's author when her husband died. Zelda first wrote openly about her own experience in an extended article in *McCall's Magazine* titled "A Widow's Way," published in October 1945. Although Louis Popkin had died in his bed in the Bronx, Zelda conflated her loss with that of the thousands of American women whose husbands had died in the just-concluded war. In a forecast that was soon invalidated by a tidal wave of postwar marriages, she predicted that an unprecedented number of American women would never find partners and would have to face life alone. The magazine's editors reinforced the point with a chart demonstrating the long odds facing single women: widows of my grandmother's age, according to these statistics, had fewer than two chances in ten of finding a new husband.[4]

Zelda's magazine article began with a recollection of something the "clergyman" who had conducted Louis Popkin's funeral service had said to her. (Only when she repeated the story in her 1956 autobiography would she identify the clergyman as a rabbi.) "Tomorrow I shall read the Twenty-third Psalm," he had told her. "I want to repeat one line of it now, 'Yea, though I walk through the valley of the shadow of death.' The words are '*walk through*.' Not remain. Not stay forever." Popkin acknowledged that this was hard advice to follow. "Grief is a sickness of body and spirit. . . . Time itself will not cure it," she wrote. Noting that "the mortality rate for widows is nearly twice that for married women," she warned that bereaved women often failed to eat regularly, drank too much, and became dependent on sleeping pills. In her own case, she claimed, it had been helpful to recognize that she was not alone. Because of the war, "there has been no single time in our history when such large numbers of women have found themselves faced with the identical problems of enduring the illness of grief, making homes without men, supporting themselves and their children." Even so, Zelda could not help adding that young war widows had better prospects of making new lives than "the middle-aged woman who faces the prospect of two decades alone."

Zelda used the authority provided by her own experience to outline for her readers a program that she claimed would allow them to overcome their personal tragedy. They should face the challenge of living on their own with a determination to avoid "dependence and idleness." At a time when government agencies were urging women to leave the job market in order to make place for men returning from the military, Popkin insisted that widows do just the opposite. If they could not get themselves hired, she recommended that they establish a "business of their own." Recalling how she had lived with "five o'clock panic" after her husband's death, Zelda told her readers that, rather than sitting home alone in the evenings, single women should summon up their courage and go out on their own or invite friends to their homes, and they should not feel ashamed to have a sex life outside of marriage. "If love or the illusion of love is essential to your sex relations . . . then it's all or nothing," she wrote. But "if you look upon sex as diversion or physical need or ego fulfillment, casual romance will satisfy you. It is a personal decision, between you and your conscience and nobody's affair but your own," a variant on the words spoken by a character in her first detective story in 1938 and then by Nina Gilmore in *The Journey Home* that she now repurposed as real-life advice.

Zelda was probably wise not to tell her readers what she herself had done in the two years following her husband's death: few of them would have been in a position to write a best-selling novel, as she had done. She was also careful not to mention her love affair with a married man. The tone of her article might have been less optimistic if she had known in 1945 that she would not publish another commercially successful book until 1968 and that she would never find another husband. In her autobiography, published eleven years later, she recounted a relationship with a man she called "Paul," the husband of one of her friends, whom she claimed had actively pursued her after Louis Popkin's death, "as if he had long been waiting to come to me." But, she wrote, "this was a family whom I could not hurt, whom I was sure he would not hurt," and so she decided to break off the affair. Was she telling the truth, or giving herself moral credit she did not really deserve? According to my mother, my grandmother had done all she could to get her friend's husband for herself, and it was he who ended her hopes.[5]

Zelda's advocacy of female independence plunged her into the middle of a raging cultural debate. Historians have shown that she was not the only writer in the postwar period to emphasize what women could achieve through individual effort, although few authors challenged traditional gender roles and the social structures that maintained them as feminists would do after 1960.[6] Nevertheless, most public discourse in the 1940s pointed in the other direction. "A Widow's Way" shared a page in the October 1945 issue of *McCall's* with an article entitled "Women and Wives" by one Marynia Farnham, MD, who argued that biology and history made it a man's responsibility to work and provide for his family, while "the woman's biologically determined role" was to make a home for her man and care for his children. Farnham later denounced Simone de Beauvoir's *The Second Sex* as "one woman's outcry against her nature"; she also coauthored an influential best-seller, *Modern Woman: The Lost Sex,* which classified feminism as a "deep illness" and remained a standard reference in discussions about women's psychology until the 1960s.[7]

As the issue of *McCall's* featuring these two discordant articles was going on sale, Zelda was following her own advice about taking an active role in the world. She had persuaded the Red Cross to send her to report on the organization's efforts to assist the thousands of "displaced persons" living in camps in Europe. For three months, she crisscrossed the continent, observing and taking notes. Thanks to her status with the Red Cross, the American military provided her with free transportation, lodging, and meals. Except for a Caribbean cruise with her husband in the early 1930s, this was Zelda's first trip outside the United States. Her first stop was Paris, and she was immediately smitten with the city she had fantasized about in some of her articles in the 1920s but never seen. "I kept pinching myself all evening to convince myself it was me and Bob at a concert in Paris," she wrote in her first letter to my parents. She observed French politics and the prickly behavior of the man she called "Charlie de Gaulle" with a certain detached amusement, but she was upset to hear many American military men express a preference for their former enemies over their ostensible allies. "The hate the French love the Germans line is so omnipresent that I am ready to haul off and sock the next G.I. who pulls it," Zelda wrote to my parents.[8]

Zelda's next letters to my parents, written from Frankfurt, had a very different tone. "I am on German soil and it is indescribable. The blackened ruins of the railroad station, with D.P.s in rags crawling around. It is horrible. I am billeted at a hotel without windowpanes. As the German hotel clerk said to me: 'Alles ist Kaputt.'" The Germans she saw in the street "look like zombies, pale, lifeless, ragged and mean. Children and young boys dog your footsteps, hoping you'll tip them a stick of gum or at least your cigarette butt. Many a G.I. grinds his under his heel. The railroad station across the way is crowded with Germans with all their worldly goods on their backs, moving somewhere anywhere nowhere. They look thoroughly whipped. Only in the young boys is there any defiance. You live in a graveyard—the graveyard of a great city—surrounded by the bare bones of what was once a city. Skeletons are not pretty. Certainly not skeletons of houses and hotels and office buildings. The devastation is simply incredible." Like many Americans who found themselves in Germany, she wrestled with conflicting feelings of hatred toward an enemy who had committed bestial crimes and recognition of the hardships the population was now facing. "It is sometimes hard to stay stony, especially when a child begs you for something, but you can do it," she wrote. "No effort is being made by us to get the wreckage cleaned up—except for our own needs. We want them to look and keep looking. They asked for it, Bud & they got it."[9]

In the same letter in which she described her first glimpse of the defeated "master race," Zelda also condensed into a few lines her first encounter with Jewish survivors of the horror that was not yet known as the Holocaust: "Last night, I went to a wedding at a D.P. camp. Two Jewish D.P.'s—who met at Dachau. I gave the bride my amethyst earrings. I wanted her to have one good and pretty thing to start a new life with. I suppose Max has told you or will tell you of the extraordinary circumstance by which I found out what he asked me to about the sons of his relative." The gift of earrings to a survivor bride, a gesture only a woman could have made, was one of many incidents first described in her letters that she would reuse, in *Small Victory*, the novel which was probably already beginning to take shape in her mind, and again in her autobiography, *Open Every Door*.[10]

In her autobiography, Zelda identified the "Max" referred to in her letter as the prominent lawyer and political activist Max Lowenthal, a close family friend, and made it clear that discovering the answer to the question he had asked her had been an experience that, even more than the wedding, seared into her mind an understanding of what the Jews had suffered. When she was preparing to leave for Europe, Lowenthal had given her a photograph showing the two sons of one of his cousins, who had last been heard of in Lithuania in 1944; he hoped that she might meet someone who knew their ultimate fate. "That picture was to change my life," Zelda wrote in 1956. According to her account, among the first survivors she met were two men from the boys' home town who told her they had witnessed the brutal deportation of its children. "When they had finished we who had not seen sat horror-frozen," my grandmother recalled. "It had been done to Max's cousins . . . but for the grace of the Atlantic Ocean, those boys in the carts might have been Sandy and Dick. No longer could I think or speak of *they*. Now there was only *we*."[11]

Zelda's letters to my parents do not reflect such a deep emotional reaction to her first encounters with the Jewish survivors. Aside from the mention of the wedding, she described only one other episode involving them, a visit to a camp outside of Salzburg. "I got angry at the D.P. camp," she wrote. "When they found I spoke Yiddish, they deluged me with their complaints—some serious—one that an American soldier had come to the camp ostensibly hunting for 'contraband'—G.I. clothing which they are forbidden to wear, cigarettes, American money—and had locked the door and demanded that the wife of one of the men get into bed with him—'like the S.S.'—another complaint came from an orthodox Jew, after we had waded in the sticky mud up to our knees outside the Kosher kitchen. He complained because the Army hadn't cleaned that up—said it was because they were Orthodox they were being discriminated against. I turned on him and said: 'Well, why don't you fix it yourself.' It caught him off base. The people in the camps, for a large part, are not yet willing to do anything to maintain themselves and if they are to really get over their experiences and to achieve rehabilitation, they must begin to work for themselves."[12] Having just surmounted her own personal crisis of widowhood by dint of personal effort, she evidently thought that Jewish survivors also needed to pull themselves up by their own bootstraps.

Zelda's attitude toward the survivors she met was not unique: many of the other Americans who encountered the DPs (displaced persons) had trouble understanding how traumatized they were and how difficult the conditions confronting them were. In a letter from Berlin that Zelda passed along to my parents, her former public relations partner Morty

Zerwick had written, "The other night I met fifteen Jews who had just arrived from Cracow [Krakow] Poland. They fled to Berlin from Cracow to escape the pogrom. They told me scores of Jews were slaughtered there and in Lodz and that the Poles had fired the only remaining synagogue in Cracow. . . . My own idea is that they were wrong to flee, that they ought to stay put and fight with sticks and even get killed." Zelda did not see herself as unsympathetic to the survivors; in fact, she wrote that she was "nursing the idea of finding a little girl to bring home. . . . I feel I should like to give at least one of them a break." Even so, she added that the child would have to be "one who looks as if she might be the right kind of daughter."[13]

Zelda's confidence that she could do something helpful for the Jewish survivors reached a high point after an incident in Vienna gave her the opportunity to "become the Jewish Joan of Arc." During her visit, she had overheard a Red Cross representative refusing to provide milk for the children in a DP camp, even though the organization was distributing it to "every Nazi child in the town." Outraged, she "spat tacks all over the place," a friend recalled. Back in Paris, Zelda complained to a representative of the Civilian War Relief organization, who arranged for her to meet the agency's top administrators. My grandmother's plan was to threaten to use her connections to put the story "in Drew Pearson's or Walter Winchell's hands! And on their radio programs! Holding all the aces, I'm going to press for game and rubber now—see if I can't make the price of my silence a relief priority for the Jews of Europe. If I can convince them—or scare them—into giving real help to the Jews, then I will have more than justified my trip over here."[14] Rather than seeking to understand the experiences of the DPs, she was more concerned to make a practical intervention on their behalf.

Our present-day perspective, in which the enormity of the Holocaust has come to dwarf all other aspects of the period, makes one as impatient with my grandmother as she was with the survivors she encountered in Salzburg. In her letters to my parents, those encounters occupied less space than her interactions with the members of the American occupying force in Germany and the staffers of the numerous international organizations working to aid refugees and "displaced persons." "I wish I could convey to you some sense of the strange life I lead—that thousands of civilians are leading in Europe today," she wrote to my parents from Frankfurt. "I mean the civilians attached in some way to the war or post-war activities who are gypsying over Europe as guests of the Adjutant General." The luxury of General Eisenhower's headquarters, situated in the former I. G. Farben factory complex, which had survived the bombing unscathed, showed her "how conquerors live." The Army mess there was "something like a Hollywood dream." From Berlin, Zelda wrote, "Meeting the wealthy army here has been quite an experience. Everybody from Generals on down has been peddling watches to the Russians. Everybody's pockets are now crammed with marks. The Army won't let them send any more money home & there's nothing to spend it on. So they pay $100 a bottle for Scotch and cable home orchids. . . . Berlin is now the rumor capital of the world and most of the rumors concern the Russians and are peddled by Germans. Everyone here is all set for the war against Russia. No one knows why, however, except they don't like the Russians."[15]

Most of the encounters Zelda mentioned in her letters were with members of the American military, but it was her contacts with representatives of the Joint Distribution Committee and other relief organizations, many of them Jewish women like herself, that provided the opportunities for her to learn about the situation of the DPs.[16] The Red Cross may have been dissatisfied with the results of Zelda's trip: she published only one short article about that organization's relief efforts. In August 1946, however, the *Ladies' Home Journal* featured a much longer piece, "Europe's Children," based on her experiences. The article makes it clear that her encounters in the DP camps had had a much stronger emotional impact on her than her letters to my parents reveal. Speaking of European children in general, she wrote that "the quality which sentimentalists call the innocence of childhood is gone. They are 'wise cookies': wise in a terrible fashion, aged in a world where lies and cunning, even desperate violence, were ways of survival." Anxious to avoid appearing to be giving special treatment to Jewish survivor children, she mentioned youth in Britain who had learned to think of what they had endured as "good, clean bombing," and she appreciated that, for children in bombed-out German cities, "the schoolroom is a refuge for part of the day from the cellar, the hovel which is now home, from the depression of rubble-filled streets."[17]

The heart of Zelda's article, however, consisted of anecdotes about Jewish children like the Hungarian survivors in Vienna. "In their eyes and their manner I sensed such hate of the whole adult world which had let dreadful things happen to them that I was actually afraid they would haul off and strike me, if I were to ask an intimate question, make a heedless unsympathetic gesture," she reported. She wrote empathetically about a group of Jewish boys, determined to go to Palestine together and found a kibbutz which they wanted to call "Kibbutz Buchenwald" because "'there we suffered and almost died together. Under that name we wish to live together.' . . . Their families are gone. One another is all they have in the world," Zelda told readers. "Working with them calls for infinite patience and understanding, for a love that can measure the insecurity behind their defiance, comprehend and soothe the waves of hysteria that sweep them when something in the present awakens the past."[18] In this article, perhaps more than in any of the other things she wrote about her encounters with survivors, my grandmother managed to convey both a real sense of the trauma they had endured and of the spirit that would enable many of them to forge new lives in spite of their losses. Her insights into child psychology may have owed something to the conversation on the subject she had had with Anna Freud during her stop in London.[19] The gulf in comprehension that her words struggled to overcome was driven home by the fact that part of her article appeared on a page that also featured an advertisement showing a bride in her gown, admiring the set of sterling silver her new husband had just presented her.

Zelda returned home in January 1946 with ideas, not just for articles but for a novel based on her experiences. Awareness of the fate of the Jews in Europe was widespread by then, but American Jewish writers were hesitant about integrating it into their fiction. As a result, Saul Bellow admitted in 1987, they "missed what should have been for them the central event of their time." The exceptions were Jewish men who had served in the military in Europe, such as Irwin Shaw in *The Young Lions*, who often had their characters participate in the liberation of the camps in Germany, but none of their books had appeared at the time when Zelda's novel was published. Instead of writing about events in Europe, "home front" Jewish authors took on the once taboo theme of antisemitism in American life. Playwright Arthur Miller published a novel, *Focus*, on the theme, and the most successful of these "problem novels," Laura Z. Hobson's *Gentleman's Agreement*, in which a non-Jewish reporter disguises himself as a Jew to uncover the depth of prejudice in the country, was on the best-seller lists and would be made into an Oscar-winning movie in 1947. Hobson, who, like Zelda, was the daughter of Jewish immigrants, had deliberately decided not to mention the fate of Jews in Europe; according to Hobson's son, she did not want to suggest "that it was European Jewish victimhood and vulnerability that earned Jews pity and tolerance."[20]

The originality of Zelda's *Small Victory* was that she transposed the American confrontation with antisemitism to European soil, making her one of the earliest American authors to introduce Holocaust survivors as characters in a work of fiction, while also directly identifying American military and government policies, and not merely the diffuse prejudice of the population, as antisemitic. She did this by constructing a story set in Germany but in which the main characters were Americans like the ones she had met during her trip: members of the military government established after the country's occupation and workers for the relief organizations that dealt with displaced persons. At the same time, however, Zelda wove into her plot another, more personal theme. Her two main characters were Randolph Barlow, an idealistic American college professor separated from his wife by his decision to volunteer for the mission of implanting democratic values abroad, and Helen Kimball, a middle-aged American social worker whose great love died "long ago." Zelda's friend Ruth Gruber, an activist dealing with Jewish refugees, had no doubt that the character of Kimball, despite the impeccably Protestant ancestry ascribed to her, "was you, with all your wisdom and beauty," as she wrote to my grandmother; in the novel, another character refers to Kimball as someone who might well "go home, write a book."[21] One can hardly doubt that the love affair between Barlow and Kimball represents a happier version of the relationship with a married man that had ended just before Zelda traveled to Europe.

The love plot in *Small Victory* may have been intimately connected to Zelda's own life, but her main purpose in writing the book was to play the role of a "Jewish Joan of Arc" that she had claimed for herself in one of her letters to my parents. Like many critics of American policy toward the surviving European Jews, she objected that American policy in occupied Germany was shaped more by concern not to offend the defeated enemy than by a determination to achieve justice for Jewish survivors.[22] In particular, she was outraged by the American occupation authorities' decision, taken at the end of 1945, to impose a numerical quota on the number of Jews from the refugee camps in Germany who could be admitted to study in universities there. In the customary author's note disavowing any similarity between her fictional characters and actual persons, she made it clear that the policy denounced in the book was one the American military government had actually adopted in November 1945. To articulate her message, she had her character Randolph Barlow write to a friend, "The terrible thing is that here, where we are the masters, where we can do as we will, we are making discrimination official American policy. We are giving the undemocratic, anti-Semitic *Numerus clausus* our sanction and blessing." Although Popkin wanted her book "to make protagonists of its readers" and rouse them to protest against their government's policy, she was careful to avoid identifying herself as Jewish and she put the case against antisemitism into the mouth of a Gentile character.[23]

In her August 1946 article in the *Ladies' Home Journal*, Zelda had talked about the "astounding achievement" of military government, but, as the *New York Times* reviewer noted, *Small Victory* followed an already established pattern for postwar novels in its disillusioned view of the American crusade to de-Nazify Germany.[24] Aside from the well-meaning but naïve Barlow, the book's American military characters have given up any hope that their efforts might have any serious impact on German society. Instead, they devote themselves to enjoying the company of their *Fräuleins* and accumulating war loot. Zelda allowed herself to create one potentially sympathetic German character, a man who tells Barlow that he joined the Nazi party to protect his half-Jewish daughter, but Barlow dismisses him as just another *"Muss Nazi"* ("Nazi out of necessity") who lacked the courage to stand up for what was right. The other Germans in the story are either cynical opportunists, kowtowing to the Americans in exchange for cigarettes and chocolate, or unreconstructed antisemites who have learned that many of the occupiers share their prejudices.

What was original about Zelda's book, and new in her own work, was the introduction, in important secondary roles, of Jewish characters: Pincus Gold, a camp survivor, and Jimmy Ahrens, a captain in the American army. My grandmother's hardboiled view of humanity, already evident in her detective novels, and her determination not to engage in special pleading for her coreligionists led her to create Jewish personages who were anything but idealized. Gold has no patience with the naïve American Barlow's crusade to overturn the *numerus clausus* policy; what matters to him is securing his own medical-school admission. He tells Barlow, "Do not forget who we are. Some of us took bread from the other, that we might live. Some of us took off the shirt from the dying, that we might not be cold." A young woman who survived the camps is depicted as a shattered wreck, fearful that the groom at her own wedding might try to poison her; a wedding guest pathetically shows every American he meets an outdated letter from a cousin in Brooklyn, hoping it will be his ticket to the United States. *Small Victory's* depiction of Holocaust survivors appears to bear out the judgment put in the mouth of one of the story's prejudiced American characters: "Now, I don't go as far as those who insist that only the worst have survived. That's going a little too far. What I say is just this and I think it makes sense: treat people like animals, burn them and beat them, enslave them, degrade them—what do you expect?" Zelda's emphasis on the survivors' damaged psyches was not unique—a number of other American Jews who dealt with the DPs in the first months after the war reacted in similar ways—but it probably did not sit well with readers.[25]

Zelda's American Jewish character, army captain Jimmy Ahrens, presented readers with other problems. The author's intent was to portray a deeply troubled man, but one driven by easily understandable and all-too-human impulses. Ahrens was intended to demonstrate her point that a Jew "was what all the world was. He was good; he was bad; he was weak; he was strong; he was brilliant or boorish; he was noble or cheap. . . . He was, in fact, everyman," a sentiment she put in the mouth of her central character, Randolph Barlow. Ahrens was portrayed as an idealist who had signed up for an additional tour of duty to participate in the crusade to purify German life, but also a man who had lost his bearings on receiving the news that his wife, at home in the United States, had filed for divorce. The pure-minded Barlow is shocked when he stumbles on Ahrens in bed with a German *Fräulein* and discovers that he has filled his room with looted treasures. Like Barlow, Ahrens is appalled by the *numerus clausus* policy, to the point where he despairs of the possibility of a decent life for Jews in the United States. In a heated exchange with Barlow, he voices the Zionist position that Palestine is the only place where a Jew "can live like a man, work like a man, fight like a man, even die like a man."[26] Although her book was published in the month in which the United Nations voted for the partition plan that would create the Jewish state of Israel, Zelda did not mean to endorse this argument, which Barlow immediately tries to refute, but she clearly wanted to challenge readers to make America live up to its egalitarian principles.

In any event, the Jewish army captain was not a character with whom readers, Jewish or not, were invited to identify. Demoralized by the discovery that his German girlfriend has given him VD, he ends up shooting the woman and then himself. Barlow, who finds the two bodies, has no doubt that Ahrens is, in the last analysis, a victim of the world's hostility to Jews. By this point, the idealistic university professor has been put through a lengthy course of moral education by the sensitive female social worker Helen Kimball. The process starts when Kimball describes the liberation of Buchenwald, which she saw "with my own eyes" as a Red Cross nurse. Later, she takes Barlow to a Jewish wedding in a DP camp, a scene based on the personal experience Zelda had described to my parents in two lines but that she now expanded into a major episode in her novel. As the two arrive to observe the ceremony, Kimball warns Barlow that the survivors have been denigrated as people who have lost all sense of moral values. "'You can't take away dignity, decency, and then hope to find it. That's why this wedding—the first—means so much.

The beginning of healing,' she tells him. As the two Americans enter the camp, they hear the crowd assembled for the wedding weeping and wailing. 'The *El Mole Rachamim*,' Kimball explains. 'Jews always remember. In their most festal moments, they remember their dead.'"[27]

As he watches the ceremony, Barlow thinks to himself, "This was the whole last decade. Why, this was all Jewish history, five thousand years. . . . These were the ones who had lived, stronger than fire, than whips, than starvation. The chosen. Six dead for each living." This thought leads him to reflect on his relations with Jews in America, concluding that "you knew Jews at home, yet you never knew Jews because the face they presented was so much like yours. . . . Yet, save for the grace of an ocean, what had happened to everyone in this room, might have happened to all those you knew." The tone of the passage changes sharply as the wedding ceremony ends and food is brought in. "All at once the room was the Zoo. Over the benches and tables, the wedding guests swarmed, climbing and pushing and giggling and screaming. Why, these weren't people; they were ravening beasts." When the groom tries to feed the bride the traditional piece of challah, she has a flashback to an incident in which she saw her mother die from eating food given to her by a German and collapses in hysterics. She calms down only when Kimball presents her with a set of earrings and tells her, "Let them be the first. Of the good things you will have," the wish Zelda expressed in the letter in which she described herself making this gesture. As the young woman in her fictional version of the story raises her arms to put on the earrings, the numbers tattooed on her arm are clearly visible.[28]

Trying to reconcile his conviction that a Jew is simply a human being—"in fact, everyman"—with the bizarre behavior he witnesses at this wedding and the even more shocking discovery of Captain Ahrens's liaison with a German woman drives Barlow to develop a theory of the origins of antisemitism that reflected Zelda's own secularist revolt against the religion of her parents. "Why, the Hebrews themselves started it," he tells himself. "Abraham when he smashed the idols. . . . Father Moses who . . . laid down rigid rules for his all-too-human flock." In reaction, Gentiles had turned the Jews' "separate rites, their stubborn, unwilling self-discipline . . . into bludgeon and sword, transformed by a million shameless lies." As a result, "men like Ahrens must always walk frightened, looking like Gentiles, living like Gentiles, knowing themselves nowise different, yet aware that the world did not know and terrified always that it one day would mistake them for that other, that mythical ogre Jew."[29]

Fortified by this insight, Barlow decides to oppose the American military government's policy of setting a quota on the number of Jews allowed to study at German universities, which he compares to Ulysses Grant's notorious Order Number 11 expelling Jews from the area under his command during the Civil War. Like Zelda herself in her letters to my parents, he threatens to go to the press, although he quickly discovers that a touring journalist whom he encounters does not want to hear about the matter. Kimball, however, takes Barlow in hand, patiently explaining to him that the members of the military "learned about quotas in the land of the free. . . . They're average Americans. All the ignorance, prejudice, fears, and benevolent impulses of the rest of the folks." "'When you've been here as long as I have,' she concludes, 'you learn to take a little, whenever you get it, before someone changes his mind.'" Pincus Gold reinforces her message, telling Barlow, "We have sometimes to fear . . . our friends as much as our foes." In her autobiography, Zelda recounted a conversation about the quotas that she had during her trip with Simon Rifkind, the American jurist appointed as General Eisenhower's advisor on Jewish affairs. "This was the best I could do," Rifkind supposedly told her. "'When you have nothing,' I found myself replying, 'I suppose 10 percent is very good.'"[30]

For Barlow, the hopelessness of expecting anything more from the American occupying forces is driven home when he learns that a military policeman has confiscated the earrings Helen gave to the Jewish bride in the DP camp as illegal contraband. "'They were searching the place—you know, black market stuff, schnapps, cigarettes, uniforms, and damned if he doesn't find these,' an officer tells him. The woman from whom the M.P. had confiscated the pair of earrings 'put up a holler,' the officer adds. 'Said they were hers. Given to her for a present.'" Outraged, Barlow storms out of the room. "'A fräulein will wear Helen's earrings,' he thinks to himself. 'Helen's earrings, given with love, stolen, in cruel, callous search. Good God, do you let these things happen? Haven't you hurt them enough? Must there still be terror, insult, *from us?*"[31]

Small Victory was certainly, as Zelda had intended, a "serious" novel that tackled large themes. The staff at Lippincott, her publisher, were optimistic: "It deals with the most vital subject of this day and year, and you will not be surprised to know that all hands were completely enthusiastic concerning its prospects during Sales Conference discussions," the company's promotion manager told her. *Small Victory* was widely reviewed in the daily press. A number of reviews, it is true, damned the book with tepid praise, although some, like the *Washington Star* book critic Fletcher Isbell, were strongly positive: "The book is that rara avis, fiction with a racial theme which can stand on its own feet as entertainment." The *Saint Louis Post-Dispatch*, a major regional paper, called it the "most effective and accurate picture" American readers had yet been given of occupied Germany. The *New York Times* reviewer admitted that "the problems it presents are ours and will be ours for a long time to come," but he patronizingly categorized the book as being written "on the level of a popular women's magazine," as if women's magazines were an inherently inferior form of journalism.[32] Rediscovered by scholars exploring the evolution of American images of postwar Germany, *Small Victory* is now recognized as one of the more serious depictions of the country in the immediate aftermath of the war.[33]

Although Zelda did not identify herself as a Jewish author and Barlow and Kimball, the main characters in her book, were Gentiles, she put her publicity experience and her knowledge of the American Jewish scene to work to help the Lippincott market staff promote the book to Jewish readers. Lippincott's in-house knowledge in this area was so scanty that they were using an article published in *Life* magazine that listed various Jewish organizations to guide them. Zelda gave them additional names, including those of community leaders like Abba Hillel Silver, and pointed them to the numerous Jewish community newspapers published around the country. The correspondence and reviews in her files show that this outreach produced results. Her old friend Stephen Wise wrote that he liked the book "immensely," another New York rabbi based several sermons on it, and the critic for the *Detroit Jewish News* called it "a modern *J'Accuse* and one of the [more] effective appeals for justice that I have ever read."[34]

Jewish reviewers zeroed in on specifically Jewish elements in the story that reviews in the general press usually ignored. In *The Day*, an English-language daily in New York City, Abraham Duker contrasted it favorably to the latest effort of Saul Bellow, praising Popkin's accessibility and dismissing Bellow as "essentially a writer for the intellectual crowd." Zelda's depiction of Jewish survivors did divide reviewers. In *Jewish Bookland*'s critic thought that "the Jewish D.P.'s are treated with understanding that is not weakened by soft sentimentalism," whereas the anonymous reviewer for the *Palestine Post* opined that "in her picture of the D.P. camps and the GI attitude to their inhabitants the author tends to lose herself in emotion; but then she has seen their horrible reality. If she lacks the genius to make the inmates seem human she is honest enough to admit in a postscript that the purpose of such a book must be to make protagonists of a cause." The Zionist paper *The Answer* called the suicide of the Jewish army captain Jimmy Ahrens a "bit of melodrama" that was "the only weak spot in an otherwise tightknit and fast-moving story. And yet it is only in Ahrens, the American Jew, that the true nature of the Jewish dilemma is really presented," the reviewer concluded.[35]

Despite the generally favorable reviews in the press and particularly in Jewish publications, none of which remarked on Zelda's reliance on non-Jewish characters to deliver her message or on her reticence about her own Jewish background, *Small Victory* was not the commercial success that *The Journey Home* had been. In part, my grandmother was a victim of a changing political situation. In 1945, when she visited Germany, Allied governments and relief organizations had assumed that most Jewish survivors would either return to their former homes or perhaps remain in Germany. By late 1947, when the book appeared, it had become clear that the majority of them were determined to leave Europe, either for Palestine or for the United States and other overseas destinations, and American treatment of them had improved, although it would not be until 1948 that legislation was passed allowing many of them to enter the country.[36] Lippincott quickly decided to abandon efforts to push the book. It was, an editor told Zelda, "a very good and honest piece of work," but "present advices of his own sources of information indicated that conditions mentioned in your book have changed since you were there."[37]

This setback was certainly discouraging for my grandmother. Eventually, after several more unsuccessful publications with Lippincott, she would develop a full-scale case of paranoia about her publisher. Nevertheless, it has to be said that, aside from the unfortunate timing that rendered the book's details out of date by the time they appeared, there were real weaknesses in *Small Victory*. One correspondent wrote to her soon after the book appeared commenting that she had missed a chance to give readers "a fuller view of the D.P.s and what they lived through." If she had made them, rather than the American occupiers, her main subject, the significance of the *numerus clausus* policy she denounced would have been clearer, and she might later have been recognized as the author of the first real American novel about the Holocaust.[38] Zelda's decision to interweave a love affair between her two main characters into her story also muddled the clarity of her messages about the Jewish catastrophe in Europe and the contradiction between democratic values and American policy in Germany. Most reviewers ignored this aspect of the book, but the *New York Times* critic targeted it. "Her love story fails to come to life," he wrote. "Their affair seems more like that of two inexperienced college freshmen than of two mature people. At the end, the whole thing is left hanging in the air."[39]

A similar romance plot had worked effectively in *The Journey Home*, and Zelda probably also wanted to include it in *Small Victory* because, as she later wrote in her autobiography, the trip to Europe on which the book was based had given her a way to disentangle herself from the love affair that she had been engaged in after her husband's death. Clearly, however, she was unable to decide exactly what message she wanted this part of the book to deliver. At the outset of the story, Randolph Barlow is portrayed as a loving husband and father, troubled by his separation from his family. He ignores the taunts of the other Americans who can't understand why he rejects the easily available German *Fräuleins* and the persistent advances of a young American woman lieutenant with "lips red as holly berries and a pert little nose." By the time the novel ends, Barlow has planted a passionate kiss on Helen Kimball's lips and told her that he now realizes that "a good marriage shuts you away from the world." Zelda immediately pulled her punches, however: rather than falling into bed, Barlow and Kimball separate, albeit with a clear intention of meeting again. Barlow "loved her, of that he was sure, and she loved him . . . But the end or the midpoint of love between grown man and grown woman need not be getting to bed," she wrote. "There could be the friendship, deep, tender; the rich comradeship, the giving and taking of gifts of the spirit and mind."[40] Some readers were no doubt left wondering whether Barlow could really remain loyal to his wife while loving another woman, and how his willingness to admit that love could be reconciled with his principled moral convictions. Others may have been disappointed that two characters so obviously meant for each other were not brought together in a happy ending.

Not only was the significance of Barlow and Kimball's personal relationship left unresolved at the book's end but so was its moral and political message. Throughout most of the book, Barlow speaks for a universalistic liberal idealism; he is determined to have no truck with the antisemitic *numerus clausus* policy, and to stir up American public opinion against this outrage. Kimball, however, represents pragmatism and a willingness to settle for "small victories"; she tries to impress upon Barlow that getting 10 percent of the spaces in German medical schools opened to refugees will alter the lives of Pincus Gold and many others. When he fights back, she does not hesitate to ask him "how many Negroes" attend his college in North Carolina. "Don't be absurd. You know how it is in our part of the country," he tells her. "Yet you stay," she replies, forcing him to recognize that he already lives with moral compromises.[41] The book ends with Barlow deciding to stay in his post and do what modest good he can rather than resigning in protest; not coincidentally, of course, this guarantees that he will have further opportunities to see Kimball. How this conclusion fits with Barlow's ringing declamations, which reviewers in the Jewish press took to be the author's sentiments, and with Zelda's claim that she wanted to motivate her readers to become "protagonists" who would take some kind of action was hard to see.

A few years later, after the commercial failure of her second Jewish-themed novel, Zelda would lash out in print at Jewish readers who didn't support novelists like her, but at the beginning of 1948, she was busy with too many other matters to dwell on the disappointing sales figures for *Small Victory*. Even before that book appeared, her sister Helen, a journalist for the *Palestine Post* in Jerusalem, was urging her to write a book about the struggle for the creation of a Jewish state. "Your next great book is here and the faster you come out to get it the happier you will be. The story needs to be put down now and you're one of the persons who could do it."[42] Throughout the early months of 1948, events in Palestine affected Zelda directly. When the *Palestine Post*'s building was bombed, a phone call from Helen allowed Zelda to relay the first account of the event to the American press. After the Israeli declaration of independence on May 15, she began making plans for a trip that would place her in the center of events; arriving in October, she spent two months in the new country and came home at the end of December with material for a new novel.

Before Zelda began to write what would be the first novel in any language to depict the Israeli war of independence, however, she turned her attention back to another theme that had preoccupied her since Louis Popkin's death in 1943: the drama of a middle-aged woman suddenly left without a husband. Whereas she had previously been determined not to be classified as a "women's author," she now told her publishers that "it's a woman's book, about love and marriage, life and death." She was conscious of taking on something of a taboo topic: "Its subject matter has been seldom, if ever, honestly touched on in fiction: the reconstruction of a woman's life, in the middle years, after the death of a beloved husband." She was nevertheless confident that she would find readers. Her *McCall's* article "aroused much interest and comment and brought much mail," she wrote. "It was, as far as I was concerned, the starting point for this book." The closeness of the story to her own experience made it different for her from any of her earlier writing projects, however. "For obvious reasons, I do not want personal publicity in connection with this book. It is subjective and I would necessarily shrink from saying, 'This is my story.' Katherine [the book's central character] is a woman for whom I personally did the research. Let it go at that." Lippincott's editors were enthusiastic about the manuscript. "It is going to be a swell book, and you are in line for every kind of encouragement and congratulations," one of them wrote to her.[43]

The title of *Walk Through the Valley* came from the clergyman's admonition she had quoted in her *McCall's* article and it summed up the story of her heroine, Katherine Brewer, whose husband, John, dies suddenly after uttering the words, "I'm cold. I'm freezing," that Louis Popkin had said just before he expired. The novel follows Katherine as she struggles with grief and depression, wrestles with the practical problems of finding a new place to live and selling the family home, strives to build a new social life, comes to terms with the fact that her two children are starting lives of their own, and decides to restart her career as an actress. Defying the odds cited in her *McCall's* article, the story ends with Katherine finding a new love. Closely as the novel follows events in Zelda's life, she did make some effort to distinguish herself from the fictional Katherine Brewer. Zelda was a physically unprepossessing writer; the fictional Katherine Brewer is an attractive former stage performer. Zelda had been an active professional woman before her husband's death; Katherine has forsaken her career to care for her husband and children. Zelda never said a critical word about her former husband; the fictional Katherine discovers that her husband had been involved in a corrupt political deal and had let another man suffer the consequences for it, a discovery that allows her to avoid glorifying him excessively in her memory. Most significantly, Zelda was a secular Jew, but she made Katherine a Gentile, although a nonreligious one, and married her to a man who, according to the backstory she provided, had worked his way up from dire poverty in New York's immigrant neighborhoods and through City College, just as Louis Popkin had, but who nevertheless, improbably enough, came from good Protestant stock.[44]

Of all of Zelda's novels, *Walk Through the Valley* was the one that most closely adhered to the standards of what the influential literary historian Janice Radway defined as "middlebrow fiction" that would permit readers to experience things "with greater force and fervor than one might be permitted in ordinary daily life" while at the same time not being asked to identify with "people thought to be too different from the white middle class."[45] In reworking her own experiences into a story that she hoped would appeal to a wide audience, Zelda airbrushed out those aspects of herself that might have hindered readers' identification with her heroine, such as Jewishness or excessive female assertiveness. As long as her husband is alive, Katherine happily accepts her position as a wife and mother; it is only her husband's death that propels her back into the job market. Was Zelda pleased with the gushing letter she received from one male fan who wrote that "I read aloud while my wife does fancy work" and congratulated her on being "the fortunate possessor of a strong religious conviction"?[46] Ensconced in his easy chair while his wife did her embroidery, this man apparently did not realize that, despite its biblical title, *Walk Through the Valley* was a defense of women's autonomy written by a Jewish secularist.

The heroine of *Walk Through the Valley* emerges in the end as a strong, independent woman, living in her own apartment, earning her living by reviving her acting career, and, on the last page, ready to embark on a love affair with a man she finds attractive. Nevertheless, it would be an exaggeration to hail my grandmother as a precursor of post-1960s feminism, even though a gushing interview published when the novel appeared called her a "feminist."[47] Katherine Brewer becomes an independent woman only when fate leaves her no other choice: nothing in Zelda's characterization of her suggests that she would have embarked on such a course if her husband had not died. Furthermore, she displays no particular sense of solidarity with other women. In the novel, she does join a circle of middle-aged single women for a time, but she finds their company unsatisfying. Intelligent, skillful at maintaining their physical attractiveness despite advancing age and wartime shortages, they remain obsessed with one thing: finding a man, even at the price of betraying each other. "They stayed in the game, grimly gallant, these brainy, substantial, good-looking women, who were prayerfully eager to imitate tramps," Zelda wrote, drawing one more time on the language she had first used in depicting single career women in her second Mary Carner mystery novel, *Time Off for Murder*.[48] Even the one member of the group who occupies an important professional position as a judge puts herself at the mercy of a married man who leads her on but finally dumps her.

The plot of *Walk Through the Valley* gave Zelda another opportunity to work through the experience of her abortive affair with a married man, this time without the distraction of the political themes that dominated her novel about postwar Germany. Although the heroine of *Walk Through the Valley* is unwilling to submit herself to one-night stands with men who do not appeal to her, she does find herself strongly attracted to a married man who had been part of her and her husband's circle of friends, just as Zelda later admitted she had been when she wrote her autobiography. Observing the evident strain between the man and his wife, Katherine Brewer allows herself to wonder, "Would it be mercy to set Jo free?" by declaring her love for the other woman's husband and breaking up their unhappy marriage. In the end, she renounces the possibility, recognizing that her friend's husband is too indecisive for her to count on him and that the price of fracturing his family would be too high. "It was time again, time to break up this drift, this hopeless closeness to Carl," she tells herself.[49] As she would in her autobiography, Zelda took the opportunity to transform what must have been a bitter disappointment into a praiseworthy instance of self-denial.

More coherent in plot and content than *Small Victory*, *Walk Through the Valley* was more commercially successful than its predecessor. For once, Zelda expressed satisfaction with her publisher's promotion efforts. "*The Valley* is doing very well. In its second printing and maybe getting on to its third. Reorders are coming in well, Lippincott have been doing good and consistent advertising and last week the orders topped Betty McDonald's 'Plague & I,' which is sensational for Lippincott's," she told my parents.[50] She received a number of heartfelt letters from female readers, many of them widows, who strongly identified with the main character. "The letters which Mrs. Popkin has received about her novel are a book in themselves and all bear witness to the accuracy of her portrayal of the loneliness, the dreams, the difficult decisions, the unintentional thoughtlessness of friends and family, the intolerable sense of being suddenly withdrawn from life," a journalist with whom Zelda shared her correspondence wrote.[51] Some women readers begged her for personal advice. "Realizing the knowledge which you have of all things pertaining to 'relicts,' I felt you might know of an arrow which points 'this way,'" a Missouri woman wrote to her. Others hoped my grandmother might help them learn how to become writers. "Aside from admiration, I am feeling a little jealousy too. I've had, so far, exactly one story published, and my thought right now is: I wish I could write as well as you," Irma Pharylles Torem told Popkin. Less impressed with Zelda's literary skills, another reader took her to task for spoiling "a good book with so many tiresome clichés. . . . 'Hold your horses.' 'Ships that passed in the night.' . . . 'Stand on one's own two feet' . . . and hundreds more."[52]

Professional reviewers, both male and female, were less taken with the book. The *Herald Tribune*'s critic praised its "excellent form, pace and clarity" but complained that "that third dimension, so necessary to the creation of a really significant novel, depth, is curiously, inexplicably missing." In the *Saturday Review*, Margery Stoneman Douglas, now celebrated as one of the pioneers of environmentalism for her 1947 book that launched the movement to save the Florida Everglades, thought that Katherine Brewer, with her good looks and skills, was an unrealistic character: "Afterward one remembers that there are widows who look their age and have no special talents and no such elegant way of healing what was so deeply broken." Zelda's publisher sent an advance copy of the book to the prominent psychologist Karen Horney, who opined that "it surely might have a consoling and encouraging quality for people in similar situations; but the book lacks, in my opinion, a clear, uniform and constructive idea which would put it above the level of an average good novel."[53]

The book may have had special meaning for one particular reader. My mother must have realized that she had inspired the character of the young bride of the fictitious Katherine Brewer's son, who found herself living "in a Quonset hut on a Midwestern campus" exactly like the one on the University of Iowa campus in which my parents conceived me in early 1948.[54] When I first read this novel, I wondered how my mother ever managed to forgive Zelda for portraying her as a ditsy dame infatuated with her own sex appeal. In the first months of 1949, when *Walk Through the Valley* appeared, however, my mother was suffering from a severe case of postpartum depression. In a letter in which she took pains to assure her mother-in-law that her novel was "prominently displayed in the bookshop, a fact I attribute to my spade work," my mother, who received little support from her own mentally unstable mother, pleaded that "what I need is someone to mother me a little." Zelda replied sympathetically, assuring her that "What's happening to you isn't mysterious or strange. It's merely what being human means. . . . Strong women like you and me get to telling ourselves we're emotional superwomen. We're not. Inside, there's this unfulfilled craving of the child—the child who never had the security of knowing he was loved. (I knew that, too, remember. I was a middle child, whipped when I didn't behave.) It took me long to find my emotional feet—and even now, there are long periods of depression and the sense of rejection and despair." Even so, however, she added that the speaking tour she was making, lecturing on her recent visit to Israel, made it impossible for her to come for a visit.[55]

Had Zelda been willing to embrace the role of counselor and guide that my mother and many of her readers longed for her to play, she might have had a very different life in the years that followed the publication of *Walk Through the Valley*. Just a few years later, the twin sisters Pauline and Esther Friedman, two Jewish women a few years younger than Popkin, began their long careers as the advice columnists "Dear Abby" and "Ann Landers," dealing with the kinds of issues my mother and Zelda's readers wrote to her about. As she worked to promote her novel, Zelda flirted with such a role. She gave lectures telling women, "You really can have a whole, wide world if you want it enough to work at it," and she jumped at the opportunity to publish an article in *Harper's Magazine* protesting the way in which "the words 'helpless' and 'female' have been so long hitched together that even women believe in the notion." Like her earlier piece on widowhood in *McCall's*, the article provoked reactions, including a commentary by Norman Thomas, the longtime leader of the American Socialist Party.[56] If she had been willing to delve more deeply into the substance of women's lives along these lines, Zelda, whose novel appeared in the same year as Simone de Beauvoir's *The Second Sex*, might have been remembered as a true pioneer in writing about women's issues. *Walk Through the Valley* was ahead of its time in tackling the issue of a widow's personal life so directly. Although it was a work of fiction, it prefigured the "widowhood memoirs" that American scholar Jeffrey

Berman, writing in 2015, would see as one of characteristic forms of women's writing after the feminist movement validated women's intimate experiences as legitimate subjects for literature.[57]

Zelda certainly did not intend to abandon writing about women, as her subsequent books, which all featured female protagonists, show. Nevertheless, even though they were deeply personal for her, the kinds of purely private issues that made up the plot of *Walk Through the Valley* did not offer enough scope for her literary ambitions. In 1955, a male Jewish novelist, Herman Wouk, would publish the period's signature American novel about women's domestic lives, *Marjorie Morningstar*. Just as she had seen the importance of the Holocaust for both Jews and Americans in *Small Victory* but missed the opportunity to foreground the experience of survivors in her novel, so my grandmother, by narrowing the focus of her serious "women's novel" to the issue of middle-aged widows and then by abandoning the subject, deprived herself of the chance to make a greater contribution to American women's literature. At the time, however, she was satisfied that she had demonstrated the ability to write about serious subjects, and she already had a new one in mind: the story of the creation of the new Jewish state of Israel.

CHAPTER 5

Zelda Popkin and the Women of Israel

"IT WAS VERY SWEET OF YOU TO HOPE I WAS 'SAFELY LOCATED IN JERU-salem when the shooting broke out.' Jerusalem is a front line city, honey children, and the bullets whistle through the trees." So began one of the letters Zelda Popkin wrote to her children during her two-month visit to the newly created state of Israel at the end of 1948. But nothing, certainly not sporadic sniper fire, could spoil her exuberance about her experiences. Summing up her thoughts at the end of her trip, she wrote, "I've been wondering how what I have been with for two months was going to hit me. The state of Israel is a very real thing. I have never felt as safe and secure in my life as I do here—in spite of the war, in spite of the barrier of language—a sense that here I can't be hurt. But at the same time, being as I am, I know that this is the first thing in my life I've gotten, without having worked for it. Israel is here, to offer me security—not just in the physical sense—for that I don't need—but in the much deeper sense that only Jews know. But I've not lifted even a little finger to get it."

This was a remarkable statement for a woman who had always considered herself as nothing more and nothing less than an American. Her encounters with Jewish survivors in Germany had shaken her sense of security, but Zelda's status as an American had allowed her to imagine herself as "the Jewish Joan of Arc," able to persuade other Americans to live up to their principles and protect endangered Jews. In meetings with Israelis, she felt that she was the one being protected. In her autobiography, she recalled a conversation with a young Israeli woman on the voyage over that underlined this sense that Israelis had taken on tasks that

American Jews were not fully sharing. The woman remarked to her that she was jealous of the young Americans she had met: "They have so much and so little responsibility. We have so little and so much responsibility. We were born, you must understand, with a state on our backs."[1]

Zelda would repay the debt she felt to the Jews who created Israel by writing *Quiet Street*, the first novel in any language about the dramatic struggle that had led to their success. As her letters to my parents show, she was deeply moved by her 1948 sojourn, but she never seriously contemplated moving to Israel; she made only two other short trips to the country, in 1951 and 1975, and never wrote another book with an Israeli setting. Nevertheless, she recognized that the existence of a Jewish state had implications even for American Jews who had no intention of leaving their native country. As my father would put it some years later, in a letter to his good friend the Jewish-studies scholar Judah Goldin, "the very existence of the political state of Israel changes the meaning and purpose of those who live their lives in terms of the stream of Jewish history. So what does one do???"[2]

Even if she did not think of transplanting herself from New York to Jerusalem, Zelda had to decide what responsibilities writing a book about Israel imposed on an American Jewish author. As the project proceeded, her editor challenged her: Did she want to promote a cause, recount a historical episode, or was she writing "a novel about people," with all their individual complexities, even if her story might raise questions about some aspects of Israel? As she labored on her manuscript in 1949 and 1950, Zelda was truly a pioneer. Journalists and eyewitnesses, including other writers whom Popkin knew, such as I. F. "Izzy" Stone and Ruth Gruber, had described the public events of the 1948 war, but no one had yet tried to take readers into the inner thoughts and emotions of its Israeli participants.[3] Her novel would be her most substantial contribution to American and Jewish literary history.

That Zelda Popkin would become the author of the first work of fiction about Israel was hardly a given. Like the vast majority of the children of East European Jewish immigrants, she considered herself an American, without any qualifications. Even after Israel gained its independence, many American Jewish novelists took the attitude of Bernard Malamud, who told an interviewer, "I'd rather write about Israel if I knew the country. I don't, so I leave it to the Israeli writers."[4] The articles Zelda wrote for Jewish magazines in the 1920s celebrated Jewish life in America, not the *chalutzim* who were founding settlements in the British mandate territory of Palestine. As her participation in campaigns against antisemitism in the 1930s showed, she was aware of the existence of anti-Jewish prejudice in her native country, but she regarded it as a relic of attitudes brought over from Europe and confidently assumed that it was contrary to true American values. Zionism—the movement to create a Jewish state in the land of Palestine—had never attracted her. To be sure, she was familiar with the ideas of the Zionist movement. In the early 1920s, the Popkins worked with Stephen Wise, then the head of the American Zionist movement, and they made the publicity arrangements for one of Albert Einstein's lecture tours on behalf of the American Palestine Committee, an ancestor of the United Jewish Appeal.

Zelda's only personal connection with the Zionist enterprise was the fact that she had a close relative who had made *aliyah* and settled in prewar Palestine. Her sister Helen, eight years younger than my grandmother, had gone to the Soviet Union in 1928 with her first husband, hoping to be involved in the avant-garde theater scene there. She quickly recognized that the country was not the socialist paradise she had expected. Returning on a ship that sailed from Odessa into the Mediterranean, Helen stopped in Palestine and fell in love with the country, even though, as she told my mother in an interview in the early 1980s, "I knew nothing about it when I arrived here." She did have a grandfather living in Jerusalem with his fifth wife, but he died during the Arab riots in 1929, so it was not a family connection that brought Helen back permanently in 1934. After a stay on a kibbutz, Helen left her first husband for another man, found a job on the *Palestine Post*, the English-language newspaper later known as the *Jerusalem Post*, and eventually became a fixture in Israeli life, famous as the founder of the newspaper's annual holiday toy drive.[5] Helen's move to Palestine did not convert the rest of the family to the Zionist cause. From Chapel Hill, where he was a freshman in the fall of 1938, Zelda's older son, Roy, gleefully described how he and his fellow members of the Communist-influenced American

Student Union had heckled a speaker who "slung a line of Zionist crap a mile long." As the Second World War spread to the Middle East in 1940, Harry Feinberg fretted about his youngest daughter's situation and asked Zelda "if there is a way or passobility and desire on their part that we try to transplant them to America."[6]

Like many American Jews, Zelda began to see the Jewish settlement in Palestine differently after the end of World War II. In an interview during her Israeli trip, she told the *Palestine Post* that her meetings with Jewish Holocaust survivors had "shocked her into Zionism," and in her 1947 novel, *Small Victory*, she allowed her American Jewish character, Jimmy Ahrens, to voice the Zionist sentiment that Palestine was the only place where a Jew "can live like a man, work like a man, fight like a man, even die like a man."[7] While she was in Europe at the end of 1945, she toyed with the idea of accompanying a shipload of DPs who were trying to run the British blockade. She did not pursue the idea; her friends I. F. Stone and Ruth Gruber would be the ones to publicize the experiences of the survivors who tried desperately to make their way to Palestine in the face of British opposition.[8]

At the end of 1946, Zelda's sister and her son Donny visited her in New York, and Helen began a campaign to persuade the family author to make the trip that would permit her to "write the book about Palestine that we need so badly." Zelda resisted at first, but Helen soon began to draw her into a supporting role in the intensifying crisis there. In October 1947, she wrote asking Zelda to assist a visitor from the Yishuv, the commercial artist Ismar David; thanks to her help, he returned to Palestine with ink and materials that were later used to produce the first Israeli civil defense posters.[9] When the British expelled 2,500 Jewish families from their homes to make room for personnel being transferred from Cairo, Helen begged Zelda to launch a campaign to get American state and local governments to protest the move. At the beginning of February 1948, a bomb destroyed the offices of the *Palestine Post*, the English-language newspaper for which her sister worked. Helen sent a cable to Zelda in New York: "Urgent produce goodwill advertising now no issue missed. Emphasize copy appeal musnt tearjerk." Although the British authorities blamed Arab terrorists for the explosion, Jewish groups were convinced that the British themselves had attempted to silence the paper, which was strongly critical of their policies. At her sister's behest, Zelda succeeded in getting the *New York Post* to publish a short article under the headline "Says British Planted Bomb. Girl Reporter Charges Plot on Zion Editor." Shortly afterward, the *Palestine Post* dispatched Helen to New York to drum up paid advertising from American firms, giving her further opportunities to lobby her sister to make a visit.[10]

Helen was back in Israel by the night of 14 May 1948, when David Ben-Gurion proclaimed the country's independence, but she had been unable to return to her home in Jerusalem because the road from the coast had been cut. On 15 May 1948, she wrote an emotional letter to her sister from Tel Aviv describing the scene. "I wept with joy yesterday . . . when I walked thru the blackout streets at about 10:30 and found a crowd of people at one of the main intersections standing motionless and singing the Hatikvah—it was a warm cry of happiness that escaped from everyone's throat." She wept again at 3:00 a.m. when she and the left-wing journalist I. F. Stone, who had gone to a bar to celebrate, learned that President Truman had announced American recognition of Israel. "Izzy Stone kept jumping up and down shouting that lousy bastard, so he did do it—Jesus the bastard really did it." In mid-August, at that year's Republican presidential convention, Zelda talked to Stone, who had just returned from Israel, and to her friend Ruth Gruber, who was about to set out, and finally made up her mind. "We all certainly do hope that you really get aboard that boat sailing on the 15th of September," Helen wrote. "For Christ's sake don't miss it for anything." She added requests for a long list of dried and powdered food products and "a refill for my Revlon lipstick."[11]

Even before she set out on her trip, Zelda was already thinking about the book she would write. Unlike Stone and Gruber, she did not want to simply be a reporter, and she had not yet been completely won over to unquestioning enthusiasm for the new Jewish state. In a memorandum to her Lippincott editors she explained that her theme would be "human growth." "In thinking about that little corner of the globe, where a handful of men and women are just ending twenty centuries of defeat, I am thinking about human stature," she continued. "I should like to write a novel about people who traveled through despair, disillusion, and defiance, won a victory over incalculable enemies, and found themselves faced with the greatest of all tests, the assumption of adult responsibility." With notable foresight, she singled out "Israel's relation with 300,000 dispossessed Arabs" as the issue that would define the nature of the new state, "a focal point of spiritual values comparable to the Numerus Clausus of Small Victory. . . . When one gains a miraculous victory, does one become arrogant, hard, proud? Here, too, will idealism go by the board, before the practical realities?" When Zelda described the real-life people who would serve as inspirations for her characters, however, she spoke only in admiring terms, mentioning her sister Helen, the "pampered, petted soft youngest child of our family . . . who changed into a woman as tough and unyielding as the stones of her own Jerusalem"; the young artist Ismar David, "who said when he returned to bomb-torn Jerusalem this winter: 'I know I am not a fighter but when I come back my friends will say: "David was safe. He was in America yet he returned to us!" and that will give them strength and courage'"; Gershon Agronsky, the publisher of the *Palestine Post*, "one of the fabulous heroes of journalism"; and her nephew Donny, who "at nine lived alone in a bullet-riddled street, ran Haganah errands, whistling 'Oh, What a Beautiful Morning!'" "Obviously, my ideas may change drastically on the scene," she concluded, "but here, I feel, I have something to shoot at."[12]

Zelda debarked in Haifa on 9 October 1948 and her sister's connections allowed her to hitch a ride to Jerusalem in the *Jerusalem Post's* truck via the "Burma Road," the tenuous track through the Judean hills that the Israelis had carved out earlier in the year to break the siege of the city's Jewish neighborhoods. The main phase of the war between the newly proclaimed Jewish state and the five Arab countries that had invaded after its proclamation of independence had been ended by an uneasy truce in June 1948 that left both Palestine as a whole and the city of Jerusalem divided, but there was still no agreement on definitive cease-fire lines and everyone expected more fighting. By the end of the twentieth century, so-called "revisionist" Israeli historians had used their country's own archives to demolish the myth that the Jews had ever been in real danger of annihilation in 1948, in spite of their enemies' apparent numerical advantage, but, as she listened to shells whistling over her sister's apartment on Abarbanel Street in Jerusalem's Rehavia neighborhood and soaked up stories from Haganah fighters, Zelda could hardly doubt that the situation was still critical.

Zelda's letters to her children back home—she addressed them to my uncle and his wife, with instructions to forward them to my parents, in whose files I found them decades later—reflected the mixture of exhilaration and anxiety that American Jewish visitors to Israel regularly experience. "Here, in Rechavia, in a small house circled by pines, looking out on a sunny tennis court, it is hard to realize that you are at battle-front. Yet, just beyond the courts is King George Avenue, soon to be officially King David Avenue, and there a tall cement wall protects pedestrians from snipers on the walls of the Old City just down the hill. A few days ago, bullets ricocheted off the walls of the Synagogue around the corner during Yom Kippur services," she wrote a week after she arrived. "That night Jerusalem was blacked out, but a moon drenched the streets and we walked through ineffable beauty to the Edison cinema where Leonard Bernstein was to conduct an all-Beethoven concert of the Israel Philharmonic Orchestra. During the Leonore overture there was some heavy shelling and everyone marked it but no one remarked it. The ovation at the end of the concert was long and thunderous, unusual for a Jerusalem audience which is usually reserved and dignified, and the woman who sat next to me said: 'We are so grateful when anyone comes to us now. We have been so isolated.'"[13]

Armed with an Israeli press card identifying her as a correspondent for the *New Republic* magazine, Zelda spent ten weeks in the country. After a second truce ended the active fighting that had been going on when she arrived, she and Helen visited northern Israel and the Jordan Valley. "It was a wonderful trip—the mountains of Galilee—soft, subtle in evening—are beautiful beyond words and you must come to see," she told her children. Later, she spent time in Tel Aviv, where she heard Bernstein conduct again, and she concluded her trip with a tour of the Negev desert, which allowed her to attend another of his concerts in Beersheba. "Before the Negev, I had been seeing Israel with my mind, now for the first time, I saw it with my guts. That land is so barren, so ugly

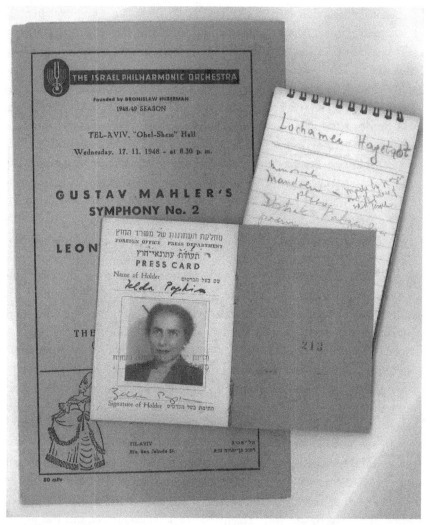

Figure 5.1. Zelda Popkin in Israel: Her press pass allowed Zelda to interview participants in Israel's war of independence in 1948. She filled several small notebooks with her observations. A program from one of Leonard Bernstein's concerts was one of her souvenirs from her trip.

and forbidding that to come down to it even in times of peace took more than ordinary courage. And to live a half year in bunkers underground and fight back the Egyptian invaders was an epic of courage," she wrote.[14]

Like most visitors to Israel, Zelda was impressed by the heroism of the outnumbered Israelis. In the miniature spiral notebooks she used to record her impressions, she jotted down details of suffering and endurance and comments such as "The Jews' secret weapon Ain Brairah—one choice [sic]." She began shaping her material into stories even before her trip ended. Interviewed for a New York radio station, she faithfully reproduced the elements that were to become the clichés of the Israeli myth in the American mind. "High courage is a commonplace in Israel where men and women carved a nation with bare hands," she announced, and she gave special praise to the young kibbutzniks of the Negev, where "men and women lived like moles in bunkers underground dug by frantic hands while shell fire rained." In an interview with the *Palestine Post* just before she left, she gave Israeli policy toward the Arabs a positive gloss. "Mrs. Popkin had gone to Nazareth to see what the town looked like under Israeli occupation," the paper reported. "Before going, in her mind's eye she had the picture of Frankfurt under American military occupation in 1945, and of Athens. But in Israel-held Nazareth, she said, she was amazed to find that the Army of Occupation stayed in the background, laying down policy, but tactful, discreet and careful."[15]

On her return to the United States, Zelda made a quick trip to Iowa City to meet her newest grandchild—me—and then set out to exploit her Israeli experiences. "The week has been terrific—so much to do! Saw the New Yorker—they want the Jerusalem Reporter at Large—Saw Colliers—they'd like a piece on the Negev, if I can do it. Am seeing Ladies Home Journal tomorrow. If you don't hear from me for ages and ages, you'll know I'm snowed under," she wrote excitedly to my parents. None of these journalistic prospects seem to have panned out, and the *New Republic*, which had provided her press credentials in Israel, never published anything by her, but she did give a number of lectures and interviews. "Zelda Popkin's whole being lights up when she speaks of Eretz Yisrael," the local synagogue bulletin in Wilkes-Barre told readers. At a fundraiser in Montreal, she told her audience that it was a privilege "to be your brother's keeper," although she admitted that Jews overseas were as tired of receiving charity "as people on this continent may be of campaigns."[16]

Zelda briefly thought of working first on what she called "the Weit-zenkorn book," a story based on an antisemitic incident in Wilkes-Barre that she would eventually incorporate into her most ambitious novel about American Jewish life, *Herman Had Two Daughters*, in 1968.[17] She quickly decided to give priority to a story based on her experiences in Israel, however, and by the beginning of May 1949, she had a contract from Lippincott and a $2,000 advance, twice what she had received for *The Journey Home* in 1945, but not enough to keep her from complaining about her financial situation in her letters to her children, as she would continue to do regularly for the next two decades. The book she planned differed in several important ways from her three previous novels. In the prospectus she submitted to Lippincott, she remarked that "formerly, I have written from the viewpoint of a single central character. This time I want to try writing from the objective viewpoint of the omniscient author. . . . It's a new approach to literary material for me." Her story would involve multiple characters. "I hope to make them believable and identifiable in American terms," she told her editors.[18] She did not point out one obvious challenge: for the first time, she would be writing a novel in which all the main characters would necessarily be Jews, and in which the author's identification with Jewish concerns would be unmistakable. Her decision to write such a book was one of the first indications of how the establishment of Israel would change life for American Jews like her, who had previously defined themselves as nothing but Americans.

The story Zelda eventually told wove together the experiences of many different people, mostly characters based on friends of her sister Helen. The irrepressible but goodhearted ten-year-old character Teddy was unmistakably modeled after Helen's son Donny, while the motherly Edith Hirsch was a composite figure based partly on "Sabta," Helen's mother-in-law, who had kept the household going during the siege of Jerusalem, and partly on the Canadian-born Goldie Joseph, the Israeli liaison with the International Red Cross, whose kibbutznik daughter had been killed in the Negev in an incident that furnished the climax for Zelda's book. If Zelda had no trouble gathering material for her portrait of everyday life in embattled Jerusalem, she had considerable difficulty in deciding how to shape her story after she returned to New York to begin writing.

One result of her determination to write a novel rather than a journalistic report was that she needed more time to complete her book than many of the other authors who were rushing to write about Israel.[19] Zelda's prospectus shows that she had three distinct themes in her mind as she started writing. All were to be present in the final work, but in very different proportions from those suggested in her first thoughts. The basic story line with which she started was, unsurprisingly, the struggle for Israel's independence, both the heroism of the front-line fighters like the young kibbutzniks and that of the civilians whose endurance assured the survival of an Israeli presence in Jerusalem. As she had indicated in the version of her book proposal written before her trip to Israel, however, my grandmother also wanted to highlight the question of whether the state of Israel would remain true to universal values of justice. In her initial prospectus, she had made the treatment of the displaced Palestinian Arabs the test of this, but after her return from her trip, she dropped her concern with the issue. "I wasn't too greatly concerned about the other side. The Arab legions were the aggressors," she told a newspaper interviewer, and she explained to her Lippincott editors that "there are at present only about 170,000 Arabs within the land of Israel (and despite the hullabaloo in many places, there aren't likely to be many more in the near future)."[20] Instead, she chose an entirely different issue to serve as the "catalyst" that would pose the question of the Israeli state's commitment to justice: the story of a Haganah officer named Mischa (Meir) Tubiansky, the only Israeli executed for treason during the fighting in 1948.

The Tubiansky affair, which Zelda called "the main thread of my story," occupied more than half of her six-page outline. To Zelda, the fact that the Israelis had dealt so sternly with a traitor from their own ranks, while acquitting his supposed British accomplice on grounds of "inconclusive evidence," demonstrated that "the Jewish state is a state of integrity and justice. We no longer believe in 'An eye for an eye; a tooth for a tooth.'" Tubiansky also interested her because, as she claimed that her brother-in-law had said, he demonstrated Israel's right "to have our sons of bitches. . . . That's one of the reasons we fought for our State—to

have the right to be human, good and bad, as everyone else in the world."
As we have seen, this insistence that Jews were no different from anyone
else had been an element of Zelda's writing on Jewish themes throughout her work; it was a conviction she shared with many other American
Jewish writers of the period.[21]

The third theme occupying her mind was reflected in the book's
tentative title, "The Silver Salver," and in the character of the young
woman Dinah, whose death in combat became the climax of the novel.
As Zelda explained, the reference to a salver or serving platter had been
introduced by Israel's first president, Chaim Weizmann, who used the
image to emphasize that the country had not been handed to its people
on a silver platter. Weizmann's words inspired the Hebrew poet Natan
Alterman, who had called the young Jewish soldiers killed in the fighting
"the silver salver on which the Jewish State is handed you." Alterman's
poem and the question it raises have continued to echo in Israeli culture
down to the present day. In 2007, on the sixtieth anniversary of the
November 1947 United Nations vote to create a Jewish state in Palestine,
Israeli prime minister Ehud Olmert quoted the poem in his address to
the Knesset, and in the Israeli novelist Amos Oz's 2014 novel *Judas*, one
of the main characters, a woman whose young husband was killed during
the fighting, makes it clear that, for her, the achievement of statehood
was not worth the sacrifice it required.[22] Had Lippincott accepted Zelda's
proposed title, her book would be remembered as one of the first testimo-
nies to the Alterman poem's resonance.

The ambivalences that were to run through the finished novel were
thus present from the earliest stages of Zelda's thinking about it. My
grandmother, who had insisted throughout her writing career on exam-
ining the darker and more painful aspects of human life, was too honest
to write a simple-minded celebration of Jewish courage, like her friend
Ruth Gruber's *Israel Without Tears*. Her fascination with what she took
to be a case of Jewish criminality harked back to her detective-novel days,
but she set herself a major challenge by deciding to put the Tubiansky
affair in the center of a book whose readers would expect a positive portrait of the new Jewish state. Finally, the perspective suggested by her
original title raised a much more fundamental difficulty. In another early

draft of the book's prospectus, Zelda elaborated on her thought, which had clearly been inspired by the story of Goldie Joseph's daughter's death: "Its basic theme is the relationship between parents and children in time of war, and the problem with which it concerns itself chiefly is one which has obsessed every parent of a grown child in the country which is now Israel during the dramatic months in which the state was established: The all-but-unanswerable question, Which do I want more, the Jewish state which has been my life-long ideal or my living child? It was precisely the same question which disturbed every parent who sent a son to fight against Hitler." Her sister Helen found Zelda's framing of this question problematic. "The particular quirk that Israel presents is that our children believed in exactly what their parents did—they did not die for what their parents believed in," she wrote.[23] But Zelda clung to her perspective, even in the book's published version.

Curiously, in view of the strong statement about women's autonomy that Zelda had just made in *Walk Through the Valley*, her first ideas for what became *Quiet Street* gave little importance to women characters or their points of view. Her prospectus identified Jacob Hirsch, a doctor, and the character based on Tubiansky as the principal protagonists. Ilona Hirsch, Jacob's wife (renamed Edith in the published book), was mentioned but there was no hint that she would become the story's focal point. Zelda had already decided to represent Israel's heroic sabra youth through the Hirsch couple's daughter, Dinah, but, aside from this iconic role, she initially had no clear idea what part women would play in her story. Zelda's editors at Lippincott seem to have recognized earlier than she did that the mother was the character who truly tied the story together and with whom readers were most likely to identify. Tay Hohoff, now celebrated as the editor who helped Harper Lee turn *To Kill a Mockingbird* into an American literary classic, told her, "The great, serious weakness lies in Edith's lack of development. . . . A strong central figure—Edith presumably—is essential to tie together all elements." She advised Zelda to make her "more attractive. . . . It is said that she used to be very pretty, but the impression of her now is of a dowdy, be-spectacled, ineffectual-seeming creature who is not an appealing heroine with whom to identify." Zelda, whose nerves at this moment were frayed to the breaking point by the stress of having to move her elderly parents into a retirement home, was unhappy about this criticism, and George Stevens, Hohoff's boss, had to reassure her that "you have got it in you to make this by far the best novel you have yet done." The final shape of the book shows that she paid attention to many of Hohoff's ideas, although she rejected the suggestion that she eliminate the climactic scene in which Edith Hirsch's daughter, Dinah, is killed.[24]

A popular novel without a love story was hardly conceivable, and Zelda invented one that allowed her to create a bridge between Israelis and American Jews by introducing an American air force veteran who volunteers to fly for the new country. Shuttling back and forth between the small airfield outside Jerusalem—where, in real life, Helen's husband Sasha had been stationed during the fighting—and the Negev, Al Brody meets Dinah Hirsch and a romance develops. In *The Journey Home*, it had been the young woman who had to prove to a combat veteran that she was his equal; in *Quiet Street*, it is the man who has to convince a female Israeli fighter that his wartime flights over Germany and the ten months he spent in a German POW camp make him a match for her. Through her depiction of Brody as the son of poor Jews in New York, shocked into volunteering for the fight in Palestine after the United States officially withdrew its support for the UN partition plan in March 1948, Zelda tried to combat the notion that American Jews were all children of privilege, unwilling to share the burdens of the Israelis. Unlike Dinah, Al Brody has ample sexual experience, but it is only during the chaste night he spends watching the stars in the Negev with his arms around her that he realizes, "This may be it." Like Nina Gilmore in *The Journey Home*, Dinah stops Brody when he touches her breast, but she promises him, "you will come back and we will be together and there will be time and you will teach me love."[25] Readers would soon discover that this particular coming together of American and Israeli Jews was doomed, but Al Brody would not be the last American Jew to fall in love with Israel.

The romance plot in *Quiet Street* remained essentially as Zelda outlined it in her original plan for the book, but the espionage story she had intended to put in the center of the narrative soon took a turn that she had not anticipated. By the summer of 1949, the "traitor" Tubiansky had been rehabilitated as the "Israeli Dreyfus." Prime Minister David Ben-Gurion announced that his execution had been "a tragic mistake" and ordered a state funeral for him. Zelda's papers include a newspaper clipping about his widow's campaign to clear his name in the face of the ostracism she had suffered in Israeli society after his arrest.[26] The spy story, which Zelda had originally seen as posing the problem of how an individual could go wrong, now took on broader implications: it raised the question of the collective responsibility of Israeli society for persecuting an innocent person. Zelda's decision to keep the Tubiansky affair as a major subplot in the finished book and to insist on how easily the majority of the population accepted the false accusations and turned on Tubiansky's family meant that her novel would be something more than just a triumphant celebration of the new country. Furthermore, by incorporating a character based on Tubiansky's widow into the story, and by making her a close neighbor of Edith Hirsch, Zelda both enlarged the part of the story devoted to her female characters and confronted her central personage with a real moral dilemma, thus giving her role more depth and complexity.

Although she had decided from the outset to stress some of the difficult questions posed by the war, Zelda certainly had no desire to be read as a critic of Israel. As in the case of *The Journey Home*, where she had imagined the thoughts of wartime soldiers, she wanted the approval of the people she was writing about. In the fall of 1950, Zelda showed a draft of the manuscript to Avraham Harman, Director of Information at the Israeli consulate in New York, who corrected some minor factual details and gave her what she regarded as "an official 'clearance'" for the text. According to her report on the conversation, Harman thanked her for "treating us as human beings" and applauded the accuracy of her re-creation of people's thoughts and feelings during the siege. With regard to the Tubiansky story, Harman purportedly said, "Some people may say it was a pity to bring that up, but I think you handled it very well."[27] In February 1951, Zelda made a brief trip to Israel in order to show the galley proofs to her sister and other Israeli acquaintances. "This is a quite different Jerusalem to which I've come. Busy, bustling, like Tel Aviv—and without the barbed wire and sandbags and constant shelling," she wrote to my parents. She had hewed so closely to reality that readers in the close-knit Rehavia community could easily identify individual characters and sometimes protest about her treatment of them, as the *Jerusalem Post*'s book reviewer Z. Kloetzel did with respect to her carica-ture of Dr. Prinz, her representative "Yecke" (German Jew). In her autobi-ography, however, Zelda claimed that the friends with whom Helen and Sasha had shared her galley proofs had said that it was "'Biddyuk—right on the button.' . . . Exactly how it was."[28] Like the letters she received from GIs after the publication of *The Journey Home*, these reactions con-firmed my grandmother's sense that she had achieved her goal of giving an accurate and convincing picture of history in the making.

Lippincott timed the release of the book, now titled *Quiet Street*, for 14 May 1951, the third anniversary of Israel's independence. Despite the disappointment she had suffered with her earlier novel on a Jew-ish theme, Zelda had high hopes for the new book and anticipated an immediate movie contract. In the case of *Small Victory*, Lippincott had been uncertain about the best way to reach Jewish readers, but this time Zelda and the firm had come up with a lengthy list of organizations and publications to receive copies. As befitted a former public relations pro-fessional, she actively sought out speaking engagements to promote the book, addressing students at the Jewish Theological Seminary, the New York chapter of Hadassah, and any other groups that would listen to her. Israeli prime minister David Ben-Gurion was touring the United States in honor of the third anniversary of independence; Lippincott sent him a copy, and his staff responded diplomatically that "he was extremely inter-ested in it and is carrying it with him on the rest of the trip in the hope that some time or other in a free hour he will be able to dip into it."[29]

Quiet Street was widely reviewed, both in the general press and in Jewish publications, and most judgments were favorable. The *San Fran-cisco Chronicle*'s critic wrote, "This warm, human account of the struggles and sacrifices involved in the building of a new democracy is well worth reading not only for its dramatic narrative but for its vivid documentary picture," and a reviewer for *Middle Eastern Affairs* noted that "she . . . avoids the pitfall of black-and-white characterization which one often finds in a story written with such passion." Not surprisingly, since her sister Helen was on their staff, the *Jerusalem Post* printed a favorable review: "Its main value is not to be found in documentary exactness but in the warmth and inherent truthfulness with which the human story behind the bitter facts is told."[30]

Quiet Street received an unexpected burst of publicity in July, when Frank Frisch, manager of the Chicago Cubs, hurled his copy at umpire Lee Ballanfant's head, narrowly missing him. "I felt ashamed of my aim and my arm, but, then, you know, the Old Flash is getting old," Frisch told a reporter. Although her beloved Dodgers were the other team involved, Zelda endorsed Frisch's use of her book, quipping, "The man has a vigorous approach and an average reviewer's attitude."[31] The incident earned her an on-air interview with the nationally known sports broadcaster Red Barber. She also appeared on Eleanor Roosevelt's nationally syndicated radio show. Roosevelt, who had known Zelda since the Popkins had persuaded her to buy her inaugural gown from Arnold Constable, one of the main clients of their publicity firm, was one of the few interlocutors to ask her explicitly about the status of women in Israeli society. Zelda noted that "in the farm settlements, and in the army, women have always had equality of work, responsibility and risk. They sit in the Knesset, the parliament, and there is a woman in the cabinet, Golda Meir. Yet in their personal lives, they are still burdened by medieval religious disabilities." In May 1952, the Jewish Book Council gave *Quiet Street* its Samuel H. Daroff Fiction Award. "She writes as a Jewish author should write—not with vulgarity, sensationalism or a bid for monetary success—but with a majesty and humaneness in keeping with a majestic and humane theme," the prominent New York Reform rabbi Louis J. Newman wrote in the Council's publication.[32]

In spite of this recognition, *Quiet Street*, like *Small Victory*, was not a commercial success. Zelda suffered one blow a week after the book appeared, when the *New York Times* printed a distinctly negative review. Other reviewers mixed gentle criticisms of the book's literary quality with praise for its evocation of the Israelis' courage and sacrifices, but Gertrude Samuels honed in on its weaknesses: "rarely allows the characters to be flesh and blood . . . a shapelessness to the whole book. . . . A great book has yet to be written on the great siege."[33] Zelda's friends urged her not to take this "unfair and shallow" critique to heart, but she knew that the "bitchy" review was a "dreadful break" for her. Four months after the book's release, Marie Syrkin, whose own life may have inspired some elements of the fictional Edith Hirsch's biography, told Zelda, "I am not surprised at the failure of *Quiet Street* to sell. We know that the 'market' apparently has nothing to do with merit or significance. And the 'Jews' are apparently fed up with the themes that should be closest to their hearts. . . . I think you should still be happy in the knowledge that you have contributed something genuine to our understanding of Israel's struggle."[34] Zelda had hoped that sales in Israel would supplement those in the United States, but there, too, she encountered frustration. Lippincott's agent reported that Israeli publishers would not pursue a translation, citing the shortage of paper, and that currency controls kept booksellers from importing the American edition.[35]

For Zelda, the book's failure was hard to accept. Like many other unhappy authors, she blamed readers who rejected her work. At the end of 1951, she told the American Jewish journalist Harold Ribalow that "I simply cannot afford to write another book concerning Jews or Jewish matters. As an independent writer, I must earn my living with my typewriter. Jewish books do not sell. And I find that books dealing with Zionism or Israel sell too poorly for me to continue writing them." In a contribution to a Jewish authors' forum organized by Ribalow, she complained that "the 'Jewish audience' prefers to read books written by Gentiles about Jews . . . it will not support a 'Jewish theme' book unless that book has earned the accolades of the Gentile world. . . . American Jews, like American Gentiles, limit their reading to the sex and sensationalism which tops the best-seller list. The writer who tackles a Jewish theme may be a happier man for having returned to his times a bit of understanding and compassion or having cleansed his own emotional closets, but the chances are that, financially, he will be a poorer man." Zelda's claim was not entirely accurate—several novels on such topics had been best-sellers since 1945—but her views were shared by several other contributors to Ribalow's forum.[36] Just a few years after the failure of *Quiet Street*, Leon Uris published *Exodus* and resoundingly demonstrated that it was indeed possible to write a best-selling novel about the Israeli war for independence. I have a childhood memory of my grandmother holding up her copy of *Exodus* and asking plaintively, "What did he put in there that I didn't have in my book?" Uris had a flair for drama that my grandmother lacked, but *Exodus* has never been regarded as a literary classic and has been criticized for its one-dimensional characters, wooden dialogue, and preachiness.[37]

Comparison of the two books suggests that the difference in their fates was not just a matter of authorial skill: Uris did a better job of judging what approach to the story of Israel's creation would sell with both Jewish and non-Jewish readers in the late 1950s and early 1960s. Even the two books' titles are indicative of their two very different perspectives. For reasons not indicated in her papers, the title of my grandmother's novel was changed prior to publication. Instead of *The Silver Salver*, with its evocation of Natan Alterman's poem about the human price paid for Israeli statehood, the book became *Quiet Street*. The new title was ironic, in the same way as *Small Victory*, the title of Zelda's novel about postwar Germany; it also emphasized the way in which the book stressed the experience of ordinary people and a view of history rooted in the private sphere of domestic life as opposed to the public world of politics and history. In contrast to Uris's *Exodus*, the title of *Quiet Street* gave no hint of the book's theme and certainly did not link it to a founding moment of the Jewish religious tradition.

At 382 pages, *Quiet Street* was considerably longer and more complex than any of Zelda's previous novels, but the story lacked the tight structure of her previous books, as Gertrude Samuels's damaging review in the *New York Times* noted. Although Zelda had made the Hirsch family and especially Edith Hirsch central to the story, the book swarmed with other characters and jumped from one setting to another without transitions. Most of the action took place in the New City of Jerusalem, but Zelda also took readers to Dinah Hirsch's kibbutz in the Negev, to Tel Aviv and even, for background on the American flyer Al Brody, to New York. Her plot followed the sequence of events that had made the headlines in 1948 and had already solidified into episodes of the Israeli Iliad: the bombings of the *Palestine Post* and Ben Yehuda Street, the defeat of the Kfar Etzion convoy, the ambush of the medical convoy to Mount Scopus, the declaration of statehood on 14 May, the opening of the "Burma Road" that secured the Jewish claim to at least part of Jerusalem, and the truce of June 1948. Against this background, she wove the personal stories of her own characters and her fictionalized version of the Tubiansky affair.

The setting of *Quiet Street* dictated that Zelda would for the first time have to let Jewish characters fill the leading roles in one of her novels and convey her message. Although the story was unmistakably a Jewish one, she did not go out of her way, as Leon Uris did in *Exodus*, to situate it in the larger context of Jewish history. *Exodus* incorporates a heart-tugging history of Jewish suffering in Europe, from Tsarist Russia to the Holocaust, and a popularized account of the entire Zionist movement, so that the battle for a homeland becomes a true struggle for survival and redemption, comprehensible both to Jewish and non-Jewish readers. Zelda's procedure was less pedagogic, but somewhat contradictory. On the one hand, she wrote as if her readers would know the history of Jews around the world; on the other hand, she deliberately underplayed the "otherness" of her characters and of Israel in an effort to make them easily assimilable by general American readers. Although the characters in her novel had come to Israel from all over the world, she made only brief allusions to the experiences that shaped them; for example, she let a simple reference to the tattoo on a young Holocaust survivor's arm speak for itself. One effect of Uris's decision to make his characters embody the full sweep of modern Jewish history was to emphasize the exotic nature of their identities: Ari Ben Canaan and his comrades were not like ordinary Americans. Zelda's strategy was just the reverse. As she told Eleanor Roosevelt, "There's a tendency to speak and write of Israelis as though they were strange and exotic people. They're not. They're people like us, with standards of living like ours," a claim that the repeated requests for small luxuries like lipstick in her sister Helen's letters disproved.[38]

Even though she now proclaimed herself something of a Zionist, Zelda's determination to downplay the otherness of Israelis reflected her continuing commitment to the prevailing American Jewish ideology of assimilation, according to which the best way to state the Jewish case was to emphasize that Jews were just like other people, and specifically that they resembled middle-class Americans. *Quiet Street* had forced Zelda to abandon the protective coloration she had deployed in her earlier books, in which she used experiences from her own American Jewish milieu but made her characters Gentiles, but her instincts told her to make her Jewish characters conform to Gentile expectations. Although *Quiet Street*'s Jerusalem milieu was described in greater and more accurate detail than the settings of *Exodus*, there was little about it that was distinctively Jewish or Middle Eastern. Zelda evacuated almost all references to Jewish culture, religion, and ritual from her story: numerous characters die in her book, but no one ever recites the *Kaddish*. She confined her tale to Jerusalem's New City, with its Western architecture—the Hirschs' apartment block was, she noted, built in the Bauhaus style—and to a bleak segment of the Negev, and she hardly ever evoked the biblical resonances of the landscape. My grandmother was a classic example of an author who had internalized the pressures on authors aiming at the "middle-brow" audience of the period to avoid depicting "people thought to be too different from the white middle class" that Janice Radway noted in her study of the Book-of-the-Month Club.[39]

Zelda's novel also differed from Uris's *Exodus* in the way it depicted its characters' connection to the historical events they lived through. Her people experienced events but were never in control of them. She eschewed the portrayal of Jewish supermen that is one of the easily criticized features of *Exodus*: even her youthful kibbutzniks were shown grimly holding out in their battered pillboxes, rather than taking the offensive. In *Quiet Street*, Jews do not liberate comrades from British prisons or use their ingenuity to improvise weapons and stratagems that will overcome overwhelming numbers of Arabs. Jacob Hirsch, the principal male character, sums up the Jewish achievement by saying, "Jerusalem was saved, not by the Davidka, not by arms—we had none—not by an enemy's cowardice. . . . But by discipline and by stubbornness. By the drivers of the food convoys, the bakers, the water carts . . . and the housewives."[40] Zelda's depiction of war rings truer than Uris's, and it contrasts sharply with the tone of I. F. Stone's 1948 articles for the *New Republic*, which had rhapsodized about the military genius of the Jewish forces, but readers of the book could be pardoned for wondering how her characters managed to win a war, since they were shown fighting only defensive battles.

Comparison with *Exodus* thus suggests several reasons why Uris's novel became a popular success whereas *Quiet Street* did not. The same comparison also suggests that Zelda's book is not without its virtues, which are more evident now than they were in the 1950s. In one respect, admittedly, both books remain rooted in that period: neither made any serious effort to understand or to humanize the Arabs. Except as anonymous enemy soldiers, Arab characters make only fleeting appearances in *Quiet Street*. Zelda's earliest proposal for the book had suggested that the Palestinian issue would play a major role in her story, and her notes from her trip to Israel in 1948 show that she was aware of complexities in the relationship between Jews and Arabs that never made it into her book. She tried to get permission to visit a camp for Arab prisoners of war, but was told that women were not admitted. She also interviewed a German Jewish woman who had married an Arab. Her jotted notes read, "Wore the veil—Jewish girls were bargains, cost you nothing. Arabs made wonderful lovers—charm, knowledge of all the arts of sex." The prospectus for her book mentioned a character based on this woman, but the published version omitted any reference to such transgressing of boundaries.[41]

The longest scene involving Arabs is an unpleasantly caricatural episode, in which the Nassair family, patients of Jacob Hirsch, arrive for an appointment, speaking dreadful English and allowing their undisciplined children to cause havoc in his office. They announce that they have received orders to leave the city while the Arab armies crush the Jews, and drive off for Cairo in their limousine. Later, the Hirschs' young son, Teddy, sees the Arab survivors of the Deir Yassin massacre being driven through the city "like animals" and asks his mother, "Imma, was that a fair thing to do?" Edith Hirsch responds with an appropriate moral lesson: "When you are cruel, you hurt your own self, down deep, where no enemy can possibly reach."[42] In the novel, however, there is no follow-up to this mention of Deir Yassin, and, unlike Uris, Zelda did not accord herself the luxury of creating a "good" Arab character to suggest at least the possibility of a constructive relationship between the two peoples.

If Zelda ended up saying little about the problem of relations between Jews and Arabs, she was nevertheless sensitive to some realities of Israel that Uris's more propagandistic novel glossed over. She was determined not to depict the Israelis as a nation of superheroes. The military virtues of unthinking courage and unreflexive action lead, in her story, to Dinah Hirsch's unnecessary death and to the Haganah officer Yora Levine's unjust execution. Furthermore, she saw that courage was not just a matter of taking up a gun. Like historians of the Holocaust-era ghettoes who have argued that simply keeping up the routines of everyday life in the face of an enemy bent on destruction constituted a form a resistance to the Germans, Zelda was sensitive to the bravery and determination required to maintain daily life in the face of danger and privation. For her, the heroes of the siege of Jerusalem were not only the Haganah soldiers—she wrote no scenes about the fighting in the city—but the drivers of the water trucks, the doctors in the clinics, and the housewives like Edith Hirsch, feeding their families on maggot-ridden *kvacker* oatmeal while somehow keeping up their spirits.

This sensitivity to the unspectacular forms of courage in everyday life allowed Zelda to give full credit to the contributions and the concerns of women. This was an issue that had preoccupied her for many years. *The Journey Home*, set in the context of the Second World War, had raised the question of whether and how women could demonstrate the courage and toughness that would allow them to face the men who had served in combat as equals. *Small Victory* depicted American women army officers and relief workers holding their own with the men, albeit not in a combat situation, and *Walk Through the Valley* featured a woman heroine coping with another form of disaster. It was *Quiet Street* that gave Zelda the greatest scope to explore the issue of women's bravery, however. Like so many American Jewish writers about Israel in the decades since, such as Philip Roth in *Portnoy's Complaint*, she highlighted the phenomenon of Israeli women soldiers. In Dinah Hirsch, she created a stereotypical representation of them, and she wrote one of the first versions of that cliché moment in which an American Jewish male finds himself unnerved by Israel's gun-toting "bosomy babes with the sparkling eyes . . . with their Stens."[43]

Dinah and her comrades were set off against an array of civilian women, however, particularly Dinah's mother, Edith, and Carmela Levine, the wife of the unjustly accused Haganah officer. In some respects, the women of Rehavia portrayed in *Quiet Street* were a retreat from the energetic female characters in Zelda's earlier novels. The love scene between Dinah and the American pilot Al Brody is so inhibited—it supposedly deals with two healthy young combat veterans!—that it is positively embarrassing to read. If one wanted to be literal-minded, one could describe Edith Hirsch's life during the siege as a caricature of the domesticated existence middle-class American women were being groomed to lead during this period, focused entirely on shopping, cooking, maintaining her home, and worrying about her husband and her children. But Hirsch has to do this in a context where snipers take aim at the lines outside grocers' doors; where food, water, and fuel are lacking; and where the main housekeeping problems are posed by soldiers occupying her bedrooms and shells exploding on the roof. The husband whose return she awaits every day is risking death to cross the city to his clinic, and the children she agonizes over are dodging grenades in the streets of Jerusalem and defending an isolated settlement against enemy soldiers. Zelda showed that, in these circumstances, keeping a household together was indeed a heroic achievement.

As American scholar Emily Alice Katz has shown, several other American Jewish women, particularly the *Hadassah Newsletter* columnist Molly Lyons Bar-David, had already stressed the quiet heroism of Jerusalem housewives during the siege of Jerusalem.[44] The plot of her novel allowed Zelda to go further by making her women characters the moral compass of the community, the custodians of the values that would make the state of Israel worth having. There are, to be sure, positive male characters in the story, particularly Edith Hirsch's husband, Jacob, and Dinah Hirsch's heroic comrades on the kibbutz, and there are female characters who are shown in a negative light, but it is women—Dinah Hirsch, Carmela Levine, and above all Edith Hirsch—who exemplify most strongly the book's positive messages. Dinah Hirsch is the Jew without complexes, the one who has dedicated herself to "the straight line. . . . Build the Land. Defend the Land," and who dies because, when an Egyptian plane approached, "the men ran for the ditch. She did not. . . . [H]er last words were . . . 'Drive straight ahead. Keep going. Don't stop,'" a scene which, for all its melodrama, is actually a toned-down version of Zelda's sister's description of the death of Goldie Joseph's daughter.[45] Carmela Levine, widow of the unjustly executed Haganah officer, is both the loyal wife and the person who shows the book's other characters why her husband's death cannot be ignored if the new state is to be worth having. As she says to a judge who is debating whether to respond to her demand for justice, "I ask this not only for us. . . . I ask what I ask for the State. . . . Our State is young, like a small child. It, too, must be punished when it does wrong. Otherwise how will it learn what is right?"[46]

Finally, it is Edith Hirsch who experiences most fully and painfully the dilemma underlined by the Alterman poem that provided the original title for Zelda's novel: the fact that the country's independence had to be purchased at such a high cost. Unlike her daughter, Edith is a divided soul. She joins her neighbors in shunning a Rehavia couple whose son has decided to remain safely in Canada rather than returning to fight, but she understands their feelings. She admires her daughter's courage but is in agony every minute that Dinah is out of sight. When the rest of the book's characters turn their backs on Carmela Levine after her husband's execution, Edith instinctively reacts against their cruelty and brings food to the "traitor's" family. Dedicated to the ideal of the Jewish state—we are told that she is the granddaughter of one of Herzl's earliest associates— Edith Hirsch nevertheless never loses her concern for the concrete needs of those around her. In the book's final lines, when Hirsch's husband breaks down and cries over their daughter's death, it is Edith who finds the strength to rise above her own grief and comfort him.

Zelda Popkin's novel thus offers a human-scale and feminized vision of the events of 1948, in contrast to Leon Uris's testosterone-filled epic. Although *Quiet Street* undoubtedly has its weaknesses as a work of literature, it seems clear that its commercial failure represented a reluctance to accept the idea of a woman author depicting a great historical event through stories of women's experiences. That a woman like Katherine Brewer, the protagonist of Zelda's *Walk Through the Valley*, could surmount the personal trauma of widowhood was one thing; that women could win a war and establish a nation was another. Discovering the reprint edition of *Quiet Street* in 2006, *Jerusalem Post* columnist Suzanne Selengut wrote that "Popkin preserves a dignity for its Jewish women characters, without turning them into models of perfection. Notable is the lack of stereotyping so favored by Uris or the bitter vitriol so often released by Roth and Saul Bellow."[47]

It is true that several decades of feminist literary criticism have taught us to recognize the ambiguities lurking in Zelda's presentation of her Israeli women. The assumptions that women are more sensitive to other people's pain and more concerned with moral issues than men are ultimately rooted in notions about women's "nature" that perpetuate old stereotypes. Zelda had challenged some of these assumptions herself in her Mary Carner detective novels and in *Walk Through the Valley*, and she would do so again in her autobiography and some of her subsequent novels. In *Quiet Street*, however, her desire to raise questions about the balance between public and private concerns in a wartime context led her to create a main character who lives essentially in the private sphere, for only such a character could really offer the implicit critique of the demands of statehood that Popkin wanted to make. Edith Hirsch is not entirely a conventional "unliberated woman"—she is saddened rather than relieved when her daughter's American boyfriend assures her that they did not have sex during the one night they spent together before the daughter's death—but she is the embodiment of the private concerns and private virtues that the American culture of the late 1940s and 1950s assigned to middle-class women.

The main difficulty with *Quiet Street* grows directly out of this decision to cast the war for independence as a conflict between public and private interests, however, because Popkin had no intention of undermining enthusiasm for Israel, unlike several other Jewish novelists of the period who wrote books in which the central figures reject Zionism.[48] Consciously, at least, her goal was to make readers more sympathetic to the new Jewish state by making them fully aware of the price that had been paid for its establishment and of the determination with which its people would correct even their worst mistakes. Unfortunately, her plot was less effective at making the passion for a Jewish homeland understandable than it was at emphasizing the human cost of achieving it. Zelda's fascination with the Tubiansky affair reflected a commendable concern for justice, but it also highlighted an episode that Israel and its friends were undoubtedly eager to forget. By the time she came to describe the writing of *Quiet Street* in her autobiography, Zelda dropped all mention of this subplot, perhaps a sign that she recognized how awkwardly it fit with the rest of her story. At the time, her decision to tell the story of the Israeli war from a civilian woman's point of view almost certainly worked against her as well. Had she written something like *Exodus* with a woman "freedom fighter" as its heroine, she would have produced a much less realistic story but the novelty of the idea might have attracted more readers. The housewife-heroine she created was a more genuine human being, but too passive and too entirely kind and good to hold the interest of readers who turned to the book thinking that extraordinary circumstances must surely have produced extraordinary people.

Regardless of the book's shortcomings and the internal ambivalences it displayed, *Quiet Street* undoubtedly also suffered because neither the general American public nor American Jewish readers, who had been spared the disasters of the Old World, were ready for a novel that portrayed Jews caught in the great historical dramas of the Holocaust or the Israeli war in a less than idealized manner. In the 1950s, the books on these themes that American readers welcomed were stories in which Jews seized control of their own fates, such as John Hersey's earnest celebration of the heroes of the Warsaw Ghetto uprising, *The Wall*, and Uris's *Exodus*. Only long after readers had come to accept complex and ironic characters in fiction about American Jews, such as those created by Saul Bellow and Philip Roth, or by Zelda herself in her "comeback novel," *Herman Had Two Daughters*, which she published in 1968 after a seventeen-year hiatus following the failure of *Quiet Street*, would they be ready to embrace books about flawed and unheroic Holocaust victims or Israelis.

In 1961, ten years after it appeared, *Quiet Street* found a new reader: me. I was preparing for my bar mitzvah and I was soaking up everything I could find about the Jewish past. I didn't tell my grandmother, of course, but I liked Leon Uris's *Exodus* better: it was full of the kind of action that preadolescent boys crave. Just as Zelda felt she owed something to the Israelis who had furnished her the material for her novel, I eventually developed a sense of a debt to my grandmother. When I realized that Andrew Furman's standard work on *Israel Through the American-Jewish Imagination* omitted any mention of *Quiet Street*, treating *Exodus* as the first serious American novel on the subject, I worked with my mother, who was at that time running a small literary agency, to get the book back in print.[49] Revisiting the matter twenty years later, in the context of this biography, I am still convinced that it is not just family loyalty that justifies giving attention to *Quiet Street*. To recognize that the first American work of fiction about the making of Israel was written by a woman and that its central figure was not a heroic freedom fighter but a middle-class housewife requires us to revise our notions of how the image of Israel developed in American literature. In an age when Israel has come to be identified with military toughness, it is worth remembering that there was a time when even a reviewer in the *Jerusalem Post* could praise a depiction of his country that emphasized its feminine side.

CHAPTER 6

Left Behind in the Golden Age

ZELDA POPKIN'S NOVEL ABOUT THE CREATION OF ISRAEL WAS NOT AS complete a failure as she made it out to be in her contribution to Harold Ribalow's forum for Jewish authors. *Quiet Street* went through at least three printings and, in May 1953, it was adapted as a radio play on the Jewish Theological Seminary's weekly *Eternal Light* broadcast.[1]

She was invited as a headliner at a major United Jewish Appeal fundraising dinner in Pennsylvania in 1952, where she told the audience that "what is happening in Israel is one of the greatest human adventures in the history of man."[2] Nevertheless, my grandmother's life definitely took a downward turn after *Quiet Street*'s appearance. From 1938, when her first Mary Carner mystery appeared, until 1951, when *Quiet Street* was published, she had written ten book-length works of fiction, one of which had been a genuine best-seller. In her four "serious" novels, *The Journey Home, Small Victory, Walk Through the Valley*, and *Quiet Street*, she had tackled major themes that more celebrated authors avoided: the place of women in a wartime society, the aftermath of the Holocaust and the issue of American antisemitism, the fate of widowed women, and the creation of an independent Jewish state. After 1951, however, Zelda would not publish another novel for seventeen years. Her hopes of finding another husband slowly faded, her confidence that she could show other single women how to make careers for themselves dissolved, and her conviction that she had her finger on the pulse of her times gave way to a sense of alienation from the world around her. Although I did not realize it at the time, the grandmother I was coming to know in the 1950s and 1960s

Figure 6.1. Zelda Popkin at her typewriter (1940s?): Although she never had a success like *The Journey Home* again, Zelda considered herself as a writer above all else. Her heavy-duty typewriter dominated the small New York apartments where she lived for the second half of her life.

was a frustrated and unhappy woman who was, at times, truly living in poverty almost as dire as that her immigrant family had experienced during her childhood.

Ironically, the most difficult years of Zelda's adult life were a time of prosperity for American society in general and a "golden age" for American Jews in particular. After 1945, the United States was the world's most powerful nation. For more than two decades, a growing economy provided a rising standard of living for most of the population. The antisemitism that Zelda had denounced in *The Journey Home* and *Small Victory* seemed to have disappeared, and most American Jews became comfortable members of the middle class, concerned at most that affluence might be diminishing their ethnic and religious distinctiveness.[3] While Zelda lived in a succession of small Manhattan apartments, her Bronx-reared sons joined the American Jewish migration to suburbia—my uncle Roy to Long Island and the Maryland suburbs of Washington, DC, my father and our family to academic communities in Iowa and Southern California. Neither of them became rich, but my uncle, a "disaster specialist" for the American Red Cross, and my father, a university philosophy professor, became members of the country's professional class, distanced from the marketplace pressures that Zelda had known so well in her public relations days.

As her trajectory separated her from the mainstream of postwar American Jewish experience, Zelda also found herself leading a very different life from the majority of middle-class American women. Marriage rates rose to an all-time high in the years after 1945, but Zelda no longer had a partner. Until the mid-1950s, her letters to my parents make occasional references to hopeful prospects, but none of them seem to have resulted in a significant relationship. Unwilling to settle for the role of grandmother—she determinedly taught her grandchildren to call her by her first name—she was not particularly close to her sons' families. In her own mind, she was still an author, but her efforts to support herself with her typewriter proved less and less successful. The expanding world of Jewish organizations offered her an alternative: during the 1950s, three of them hired her, at relatively impressive salaries, to do public relations work. On her own, without her more outgoing husband, Louis, to offset her increasingly difficult personality, she was unable to make a success of any of these jobs. Rather than vindicating the assertions about the possibilities of women's independence she had made in her writing about the experience of widowhood, her own life in the 1950s and 1960s showed how even a prosperous society could leave single women in a precarious situation.

During these years, I was growing into a bookish youngster, prepared to idolize a grandmother whose productions filled a shelf in our house. Raised in the small college town of Iowa City and then in southern Californian suburbia, I could not imagine anything more glamorous than life in Manhattan. To my parents, however, Zelda was a constant source of worry. As they struggled to meet their own financial needs, she badgered them for money, and at times they feared that she was developing signs of mental instability. By the early 1960s, I was old enough to actually read her books and conclude, with the snobbishness of a teenage sophisticate, that they did not meet my exacting literary standards. On a visit to New York City during my freshman year in college, I committed the ultimate sin: I stayed in the dorm room of a friend at Columbia University instead of accepting her invitation to sleep on her couch.

In the early 1950s, as she pondered how to keep her writing career alive after her disappointment with the reception of *Quiet Street*, Zelda was in no mood to embark on another novel about Jewish life. Harold Ribalow, a New York Jewish journalist who befriended her during these years, kept her from abandoning her Jewish identity entirely by including her in several forums of "middle-brow" Jewish writers that he organized; it was one of those opportunities that allowed her to vent her spleen toward Jewish readers who, in her opinion, were responsible for the failure of her books. A story she published in *Commentary* about "Antek" (Yitzhak Zuckerman), one of the few survivors of the Warsaw Ghetto uprising, based on an interview she did with him during her brief trip to Israel in 1951, was her last attempt to deal with the Holocaust or the new Jewish state. By this time, Zelda's 1947 Holocaust novel, *Small Victory*, had been overshadowed by a number of other books about the catastrophe of European Jewry. Zelda had read some of this literature, including John Hersey's novel about the Warsaw Ghetto uprising, *The*

Wall, and one of the early memoirs by a woman survivor, Olga Lengyel's *Five Chimneys*, but one senses from her *Commentary* article that she had not succeeded in comprehending the mentality of the survivors who were struggling to make a new life for themselves in Israel. Antek fended off Zelda's questions with monosyllabic answers and kept trying to send her away to tour the Ghetto Fighters' Museum his kibbutz had established and leave him alone. When he showed her the children's house on the kibbutz and told her, "I have a son sleeping there," Zelda felt obliged to remind readers that the fictional character modeled on Antek in Hersey's novel had smothered a baby in one of the ghetto bunkers so that its cries would not betray the group's location. Zelda's article reinforced the image of Holocaust survivors as psychologically damaged that had dominated her letters and her postwar novel.[4]

Persuaded that she had nothing to gain from writing about Jewish issues, Zelda thought she might have better luck exploiting the growing market for literature offering advice on personal problems, drawing on ideas she had developed in some of her post-widowhood publications. Already in 1946, the rabbi Joshua Liebman had found a wide audience for his volume, *Peace of Mind*, demonstrating that a non-Jewish audience would welcome a psychological advice book rooted in secularized versions of Jewish moral traditions. Liebman died unexpectedly in 1948, before he could consolidate his position as America's first Jewish psychological guru, but he had set a precedent.[5] In 1952, Norman Vincent Peale's *The Power of Positive Thinking* reinforced the message that self-help was a hot subject. By early 1953, Zelda was writing excitedly to my parents about the prospect of becoming "the poor man's Sigmund Freud—a two-bit Freud." *Coronet*, a woman's magazine, offered her a contract for a monthly column. "Some of us can see possibilities of Popkin's Gramercy-Park-spun philosophy reaching out to the multitudes."[6]

Zelda's ambition was not implausible. In his survey of American Jews' contributions to popular psychology in the 1950s, Andrew Heinze lists "six Jewish women [who] were on their way to achieving positions of authority over public attitudes about how to live in the suburban age": Ayn Rand; the sisters Esther Pauline and Pauline Esther Friedman, who became better known as the advice columnists Ann Landers and

Abigail van Buren; Betty Friedan; Gertrude Berg; and Joyce Brothers.[7] Unfortunately, my grandmother lacked the ideological persuasiveness of Rand and Friedan, the sense of humor of Gertrude Berg, and the ability to relate to individuals that made Ann Landers, Abigail van Buren, and Joyce Brothers successful. In her retrospective character sketch of her mother-in-law, my mother commented, "She had no patience for women who were primarily housewives and mothers, middle class women who went to beauty parlors and played bridge," or, in other words, for the main audience for 1950s advice literature. "In her mind, there was a vast category of women who did nothing but 'sit around on their cans yakking and playing cards.'" Zelda's columns in *Coronet*, drawn heavily from her own personal experiences, abounded in clichés: "courage is not a rare commodity, but something which we all possess"; "every experience has its own values for growth"; love means "caring for another person as a person"; "everyone has his own way of behavior and everyone has the right to be himself"; "middle age is no handicap. It can be an asset." Before long, even Zelda became bored grinding out such commonplaces. "Trying now to get up energy enough to write off my debt to Coronet," she wrote to my parents in October 1953.[8]

Zelda tried to find her way back to novel-writing with a book about the Molly Maguires, the Irish coalminers who had been tried and executed in the 1870s on charges of having formed a terrorist group that murdered several mine owners in eastern Pennsylvania. Having concluded that stories with Jewish themes were unprofitable, she hoped to be able to make something out of a piece of the "Americana" that she had exploited in many of her magazine articles in the 1930s. "The anthracite region is my home terrain. I grew up, surrounded by the breakers and mine patches, intimate with the miners and their families," she wrote in one of the many proposals she drafted for her project. "I have climbed the steeply pitching streets of Pottsville, to the mansions of the coal and iron kings and the unmarked graveyards of those who died as Mollies. I have seen the dungeon cells where they were chained to wait for death, and also the patch and union hall in St. Clair where John Siney's union was conceived with so much hope. I have talked with many people who remembered or who knew, from family folklore, bits and pieces of the tragic drama of the eighteen-seventies yet cannot, even now, be named in quotation since the fear and shame of those days endures." In her mind, the trial and execution of the "Mollies" was the first of a long series of episodes that included the prosecution of the "Haymarket Martyrs," the Sacco and Vanzetti case, and the conviction of Julius and Ethel Rosenberg, which was fresh in her mind as she drafted her prospectus. "The general framework and implications of the story are similar to the later 'miscarriages' of justice on the American scene," she insisted.[9]

Although the publishers she approached about her project recognized the drama of her material, they were unconvinced by her plan to tell the story through the experiences of a descendant of one of the executed men who wrestles with deciding whether to think of his grandfather as a murderer or as a martyr.[10] Zelda would eventually recast her novel in response to these criticisms, but at the time, she concluded that the political atmosphere of the early 1950s stood in her way. The Republican election triumph in 1952 made her aware that the liberal values she had committed herself to in the 1930s were now passé. "The landslide surprised me but not the Eisenhower victory," she wrote to my parents. "I'd been afraid for a long while that it was certain to happen. One reason I was sure was the defection of people in my own circle—persons whom I knew to be liberal and intelligent—old-time Roosevelt supporters—who were supporting Eisenhower. 'The mess in Washington—corruption' chiefly disturbed them. Some of them worried about the Communist issue—Alger Hiss, etc.—others about taxes. But mainly, it was the feeling that the time had come to 'turn the rascals out.'" When her longtime publisher Lippincott turned down the Molly Maguires proposal, Zelda was sure that she had become a victim of the new conservative atmosphere. "The heat is on in the publishing field now, exactly as it has been in the entertainment and education fields and no publisher is going to stick his neck out for a book with a background of injustice to labor," she told my parents. "To me, the American climate is now so nasty and threatening that I'm considering that this may well be the time for Zelda to pick herself up and move to Jerusalem, where there's only good clean war and hunger." Like many American Jews, she feared that the 1953 conviction of Julius and Ethel Rosenberg for spying portended a return to the antisemitism of the

1930s, and she worried that her son Roy might lose his job with the Red Cross because of his youthful connection with the *Daily Worker*.[11]

Unlike most Americans who complained about the McCarthy period's political climate, Zelda really did leave the country—not for Jerusalem, but for Montreal. In late 1953, she was hired as the publicity director for the Canadian Hadassah organization. Initially, she was confident that the job was "an opportunity to serve a cause which I am very close to, and to enjoy the love and respect of the whole Canadian community," and her first impression was that Montreal was "a big city, charming and colorful, where I have the dearest of friends." To my knowledge, my grandmother had never been an active member of Hadassah in the United States, but the job took her back into the world of Jewish organizations in which she had begun her professional career more than three decades earlier and with which she and Louis had always had ties. Within a few months, however, she decided that she had made a serious mistake. The Hadassah milieu was uncongenial for her. "What I most dislike, aside from the fact that I have to work for a living," she told my parents, "is the fact that I move in a women's world. . . . Hundreds of women, and if anyone invites me to another afternoon tea, with the silver tea service, I shall scream." According to her, the Hadassah organization was "a snake pit. I had never met anything quite like it before, or dreamed it existed—all these years of being a free woman quite spoiled me. . . . The back-biting and gossip here is murderous! You whisper in Montreal. Ten minutes later it is repeated in Vancouver."[12]

Zelda did have enough self-awareness to "wonder if the fault of independence is not now so deeply rooted in me that I'll find it most difficult to function in any job anywhere," but after less than a year, she decided to return to New York. "The job has become so hateful to me that my stomach turns every time I see the Winnipeg post-mark," she wrote to my parents. (Winnipeg was the home of the Hadassah president under whom she worked.)[13] Two years later, after Zelda's autobiography appeared, a Canadian newspaper picked out the choicest passages from her 19-page denunciation of her country's neighbor to the north. Canadian writing, in her opinion, was "imitative, self-conscious, barely breathing." Canadians needed to loosen up: "A people, full of muscle, won't laugh out loud, lest someone criticize." Quebec's metropolis did not please her: "Does spring ever come to Montreal? Eternally, it snowed." Toronto was no better: "As ugly as though ugliness had been decreed by civic ordinance." Rather than finding Canada a refuge from her native country's political excesses, she complained about Canadians' "almost malicious glee when they discussed the States, as if they were glad we were having trouble because it made them feel superior."[14]

Zelda was able to quit her Hadassah job in 1954 because she had signed a contract for another book—not a novel, but the autobiography in which she delivered her devastating critique of Canada. Her relatives were unhappy that she was giving up an assured income. "Now she puts all her faith in this book. I wish that I shared her faith in her writing ability," her older sister, Pauline, wrote to my parents. Having given up her Gramercy Park apartment when she went to Montreal, Zelda needed a new place to live. It took her almost a year, but she eventually found a one-bedroom apartment on Lexington Avenue, a few blocks from her previous residence. "It is exactly right and a joy to be back in the old neighborhood," she reported to my parents.[15] The address is still engraved in my mind, thanks to all the envelopes on which I carefully block-printed it in order to mail letters and birthday cards to her.

According to my mother, Zelda had originally intended to write a book about her husband, Louis, but in my grandmother's mind, the project seems to have truly been born as "the book about Zelda Popkin that you've always been wanting to do," as she claimed.[16] The "memoir boom" of the late twentieth century was still far in the future, but America's democratic culture has always welcomed such enterprises—Benjamin Franklin's *Autobiography* is often called the first American literary classic—and American Jews had quickly taken advantage of this openness. "Either the mental and spiritual processes of all human beings rate scrutiny, or no one's processes are worth the telling," the popular Jewish author Fannie Hurst wrote in her memoir.[17] Hurst's memoir appeared two years after Zelda's, but my grandmother may have known of earlier examples by Jewish women authors, such as Mary Antin's *The Promised Land*, a popular account of the immigrant experience, and Edna Ferber's *A Peculiar Treasure*, a writer's life story. In 1951, Alfred Kazin published

A Walker in the City, one of the earliest memoirs by a member of the first generation of East European Jews born in America, the cohort to which Zelda belonged. The "Broadway Madam" Polly Adler's scandalous *A House Is Not a Home* came out in 1953 and Ben Hecht's *A Child of the Century* appeared in 1954. In any event, for years, much of Zelda's writing had been thinly veiled or even open autobiography. Her articles on child-rearing, her pieces about Wilkes-Barre in the *New Yorker*, and many of the scenes in *The Journey Home*, *Small Victory*, and *Walk Through the Valley* had come directly out of her own experiences, and she incorporated many passages from these earlier publications in the memoir she called *Open Every Door*, a phrase close to a line in one of her earnest *Coronet* advice columns, which had urged readers to overcome grief and depression by "opening the doors" to new experiences.[18]

At one point in my own career, I became fascinated with autobiographies as an academic subject; I even wrote a book about the relations between autobiographies and works of history as ways of telling stories about the past.[19] Zelda's autobiography was probably one of the first examples of such writing that I had read when I was growing up; as a fact-oriented youngster, it interested me more than her novels, and I generously told her it was a "good book."[20] My explorations in the theoretical literature in what was, in the 1990s, the fast-growing subdiscipline of "autobiography studies" taught me that the difference between autobiography and fiction was not as clear as I originally thought. Paul John Eakin, one of the founders of the field, announced "that autobiographical truth is not a fixed but an evolving content in an intricate process of self-discovery and self-creation." Patricia Meyer Spacks, another of the scholars of the subject, contended that both novelists and autobiographers "necessarily depend upon artifice—shaping, inventing, selecting, omitting—to achieve their effects . . . [and] both communicate vital truths through falsifications."[21]

Zelda was no literary theorist, but she was conscious that the challenges she was taking on in writing *Open Every Door* were different from those she had faced in composing her novels. "It looks strange to see 'Autobiography of Zelda Popkin' on a contract," she wrote to my parents. Lippincott, her long-time publisher, was unwilling to take a chance on a project so different from the kind of writing they were used to seeing from her, so she wound up working with a new firm, E. P. Dutton. Any illusions she might have had that such a project would be easier than writing a novel were quickly dispelled as she got down to work. "I've been plowing ahead on the book and it's been rugged. I'd forgotten how hard it is to write a book," she commented in the fall of 1954. Friends' encouraging words buoyed her spirits; she did not take into account how difficult it would have been for any of them to criticize such a personal project. It was only in the course of her work on the book that she discovered that her father was also trying to write the story of his own life. She immediately grabbed his typed sheets for herself. Her remark to my parents about how "the man was out peddling needles and pins in the blizzard of '88" reflected a clear awareness of how different her parents' lives had been from hers.[22]

The proposal with which Zelda secured her contract with Dutton showed the ambitious scope of the project she had in mind. It was to be "my autobiography, and a biography of the first half of this century," she wrote, and it was to take in all the experiences she had written about separately over the years. "It will be a story which might have been any- one's," she admitted, but she claimed that it would stand out because she was a person "who had the good fortune to find and open infinite doors of human interest. . . . Since I belong to the century of Sigmund Freud, I'll try to write with insight about people and events, and with candor about myself," she added. She was confident in the accuracy of her rec- ollections because "I was born with what Somerset Maugham declares is basic equipment for writers, a small detached lobe of the brain, a third eye, which sees and records everything. . . . I need no reporter's pencil. It takes my notes." As she thought about the meaning of her experiences, Zelda divided her life into three parts. "On Another Planet, Far Away," would "deal with the pastoral years of this century, those before the First World War"; she would emphasize how, even when she became a reporter for the local paper, she and the whole town "lived and worked in a vacuum," oblivious to the forces that were about to transform the world. The second section of her book, "'Life with Popkin,' will be both intimately subjective and reportorial," she wrote. She would tell the story of "a twenty-four hour a day marriage and a unique partnership in a public relations business which lasted nearly a quarter of a century," and brought her into contact with "every avenue of contemporary life. This will be a section warm with laughter and human interest," she assured her publisher.[23]

The concluding portion of her book, "Yes, There Is a Second Chance," pulled together themes from the writing she had done after Louis Popkin's death, "when I came out of the walled city of a good marriage, to find a wide world, with no strangers anywhere. . . . It will include the shambles of Europe after the war and the excitement of Israel's war for independence." As a whole, she promised, her book would deal with dramatic topics such as war—"I have lived with many wars and have seen and smelled war and so war must necessarily be part of my book"—but also with "ordinary things—the meaning, the terms of a good marriage, the warmth, the pity, the kindness one finds in neighbors and strangers, the frustrations of rearing children in the so-called 'Age of the Child,' the many levels of love, the conquest of loneliness and the slow process of human growth." Still engaged with her experiment in advice writing for *Coronet* as she prepared her prospectus, she thought that "*Open Every Door* may well come within the category of 'inspirational' books, for frankly and deliberately, I intend to urge men and women to welcome all of life, to trust it, to open all of its doors and to live less afraid."[24]

Zelda chose to emphasize the importance of writing in her life by starting her story, not with her family and childhood, but with her arrival in the Wilkes-Barre *Times Leader*'s newsroom at the age of sixteen. She then told readers that she could still "remember the day on which I knew I would be a writer." She was just seven when she committed herself to composing a poem every day, lying on the kitchen floor where the rest of the family could not avoid observing her dedication to her craft.[25] Other Jewish memoirists, such as Fannie Hurst, Alfred Kazin, and Irving Howe, turned their experiences writing for magazines and interacting with editors into rich material, but Zelda said little about her twenty-year journalistic career, a form of writing which she had come to regard as too simple to be considered as a serious achievement.[26] "A journalist amasses facts, anecdotes and interviews with top brass. Enough of these add up to a book," she wrote. Fiction writing was more challenging. Lest anyone think authorship was easy, she repeatedly emphasized the intense concentration it required: "When I am doing a book, I know the loneliness of lighthouse keepers. I worked alone all day." Thinking of how she had written her novels about postwar Germany and widowhood, she concluded, "You write at each time what you must, what you are filled with. Fiction is autobiography. It represents your heart, your attitudes, as well as what you have experienced." Recalling how she put together her story about Israel led her to muse that "a novelist . . . has to find himself in his materials, to know for sure how he would feel and act in the events he writes about. In addition, he requires a catalyst—a person, idea, or emotion which coalesces his ingredients and makes them jell into a solid purpose."[27]

"Writer" was just one of the identities Zelda stressed in her book. "Some will say it's a women's book," she told one interviewer, "since it details the various aspects of a modern woman's existence—wife, mother, grandmother, mistress, and career woman."[28] She shaped her narrative to show herself as someone who had had an egalitarian marriage, a family, and a career, but who had then made herself into an independent woman when circumstances required her to do so. Published at a moment when Herman Wouk's cautionary tale of the dangers of female professional aspirations, *Marjorie Morningstar*, was topping the best-seller lists, *Open Every Door*'s message that a woman's concerns and ambitions could be the same as a man's was unusual for its day.[29] Some 1950s readers were put off by Zelda's unembarrassed evocation of the pleasures of sex and her open discussion of her longing for male companionship after her husband's death. Her description of her life as a working woman contrasted sharply with that of her fellow public relations pioneer Doris Fleischman Bernays, the wife of Edward Bernays, who published her own memoir almost simultaneously with Zelda's. Bernays titled her book *A Wife Is Many Women*, making her relationship with her husband the center of her story, and included chapters on housekeeping, child-rearing, and shopping, but very little about her professional career or the public events that had taken place during her lifetime.[30]

Another major difference between Zelda's memoir and that of Doris Bernays was that Bernays never explicitly acknowledged her Jewish origins. By contrast, Zelda emphasized her father's religiosity and her memories of Sabbath meals at home, although she also made it clear that, even as a child, she had felt constrained by "so many inconvenient admonitions in the minor aspects of piety." She did not polemicize on the subject, but she made it clear that she had quickly decided not to let her "daily existence in the twentieth century" be shaped by "medieval dogmas."[31] With the exception of a few references to her and Louis's involvement in combatting antisemitism, Jewish concerns were largely absent from the middle section of her book. She did not mention her involvement with the *American Hebrew*, even though it had been the launching pad for her writing career, nor did she say much about the publicity work she and Louis had done for the Joint Distribution Committee and other Jewish organizations during the 1920s and 1930s, or about the way in which relationships with her parents and her sisters kept her connected to Jewish life. Her narrative of those decades was a portrait of the author as a thoroughly secularized American Jew with no concern about transmitting her heritage to her own children.

Jewish issues became more salient in the chapters she devoted to her postwar trip to Germany and her visit to Israel. In her letters to my parents from her 1945 Europe trip, Zelda had written much more about her interactions with American military personnel and relief workers than about Jewish survivors, and in the novel she constructed from those experiences, the central characters were Gentiles. In her autobiography, however, she began the chapter devoted to her trip by recalling how the photograph of two young Jewish boys that her friend Max Lowenthal had given her, in the hope that she might learn their fate, had "change[d] her life." She mentioned this incident in passing in one of her letters, and omitted it entirely in *Small Victory*, but she now insisted on the impact it had had on her. Her autobiographical account of her trip to Israel began with an evocation of how, thanks to her sister Helen and her nephew Donny, "a country, a city moved from the history books, the *Times* front page, into the family circle" and finally drew her to visit the newborn Jewish state.[32]

Although readers of *Open Every Door* were thus left in no doubt about Zelda's Jewish origins and the effect the Holocaust and the birth of Israel had had on her, the book did not document what the historian of Jewish American women Joyce Antler, unwittingly borrowing the title of Zelda Popkin's best-selling novel, has called "The Journey Home," a "return to heritage" after an initial rebellion against it.[33] The emotional impact of her discovery of Max Lowenthal's relatives' murder, Zelda claimed, was that it made her realize that she had "joined the human race"—that she had learned a universal, rather than a specifically Jewish, lesson about evil and intolerance. She paired that story with another episode involving children that she called "my crisis": the day when she visited a German elementary school and found herself "putting my arms around a child, hugging her fast," even as she realized that "I have embraced one of *them*." Similarly, when Zelda explained how she had found the central thread that, in her mind, constituted the meaning of her story about Israel, it was when Goldie Joseph told her the story of her young daughter's death that she turned into *Quiet Street*'s climax. "When I heard this, I no longer had an Israel story," Zelda wrote in her autobiography, "but rather the story of every mother whose child is summoned to war." On the closing page of her autobiography, she reaffirmed her belief in the unity of humanity by describing how, on Christmas Day, her son Roy's children "left their Christmas tree and crossed the room to light their Chanukah candles. This is good, I told myself. This is how our world should be. These grand-children of mine are fortunate. Two religions belong to them."[34]

If the great lesson Zelda drew from her postwar experiences was that human beings were the same everywhere, she made a partial exception in her final chapter, devoted to her unhappy year in Canada. She was careful not to reveal that the "dominion-wide philanthropic organiza-tion" whose administration she was hired to head was the Jewish group Hadassah, saying only that "the cause for which I labored here was noble and important," but she was unsparing in her criticism of the women members who "gabbled, gossiped, fought each other with tooth and claw for the petty, momentary advantage of a picture in the daily paper, a seat at a head table, a name engraved on a silver presentation dish." Taken in its entirety, her judgment on the country was not as harsh as the passages excerpted in the *Montreal Star* made it sound. She praised the beauty and variety of the Canadian landscape, she enjoyed the mixture of French and English spoken in the streets of Montreal, and she compared the country's "modest, high-principled, clear-eyed" politicians, "mindful of the needs of average citizens," favorably to their American counterparts. She created a lasting connection with Canada for herself by joining my father in investing in Canadian penny mining stocks, whose fortunes became one of the regular themes of their letters for a number of years.[35]

Nevertheless, Zelda's pages about her stay in Canada served primarily to provide her the opportunity to end her autobiography by affirming her identity as an American. Critical as she was of the excesses of McCarthyism, she reacted against the "almost malicious glee" with which Canadians talked about it. Her arguments with Canadians reminded her that Israelis, too, had made what she regarded as unjustified criticisms of the United States. "As I talked with [Canadians] and listened to them," she wrote, "each day I felt myself becoming more and more . . . American. My roots pulled back, to the brawling, strutting country in which the family rows were held in public, under klieg lights, in which you climbed the walls in violent arguments with friends over issues, over world concerns. . . . With all its rows, its jitters, faults, I knew I loved my country best. Whatever it was, all it was, that was myself." Concluding with a final reference to her authorial vocation, she closed her story by recounting how she had moved into her new Manhattan apartment "and, with the stirring essence of New York before me, sat down to write a book."[36]

Zelda's book, with its assertion of its author's Americanness, appeared just a few months after the publication of Will Herberg's *Protestant, Catholic, Jew*, which argued that members of all three faiths had come to share what amounted to a common civic religion. Zelda might have dissented from Herberg's emphasis on religious affiliation—other than Passover Seders, she does not seem to have taken part in any Jewish rituals during her adult life—but she clearly shared Herberg's conviction that Jews like herself were as thoroughly American as anyone else. Her attitude was quite different from that of Alfred Kazin, whose *A Walker in the City*, one of the earliest of what is now a large corpus of memoirs by second-generation American Jewish authors to which Zelda's book belongs, portrayed himself as "standing outside America"; in a later volume, *Starting Out in the Thirties*, he would recount how he, like the other "New York Jewish intellectuals" of his generation, consciously adopted political and literary positions at odds with the mainstream of the country's culture.[37]

As always, Zelda kept files of the correspondence she received in response to her book and the published reviews of it. Autobiographies often provoke strong reactions from family members of the author. I would love to know what Zelda's parents thought about her depiction of her childhood, but her father's only response was "that so far I have reached up to part seven of the book 'Open Every Door' and will not offer any comment about it until I have finished the entire volume." From Jerusalem, her sister Helen wrote, "I think it's good—better written than any of your others—and I'm so sorry that there isn't anything in it I can sue you for." My father, who in later years referred to *Open Every Door* as "Zelda's greatest work of fiction," avoided saying anything substantive about the book in his letters to his mother. He did assure her that she had one enthusiastic reader in Iowa City, who was "buttonholing people everywhere raving about it. . . . So, if the nation goes the way Iowa City does, you'll be living in a hacienda in Florida ere long."[38]

As Zelda herself said in an interview, "people will find different things in this book." Some commentators emphasized her remarks on politics, which the Associated Press reviewer said revealed her to be "a soft-hearted, hard-headed, open-minded liberal pretty consistently right on the burning questions of our time." The more conservative reviewer for the *World-Telegram and Sun* remarked that "to say that I frequently disagree with her logic or subscribe to her causes would be an understatement. She has been uncomfortably liberal on a number of occasions, though currently she appears to be a middle-of-the-roader who is highly articulate in defense of her country," and another commentator regretted that she "seems to be soft on Communists." That reviewer was one of several who focused on her attitude toward Judaism. "She had no objection to her child intermarrying . . . adores Christmas, likes the Pharisees," he noted suspiciously. Her Jewish journalist friend Harold Ribalow wrote two reviews of the book. In the *Hadassah Newsletter*, he called it "a bit more lively" than Zelda's friend Marie Syrkin's recently published biography of Golda Meir, but thought that there had been "more of her Judaism, her talents and her heart" in her novel about Israel. In a South African Jewish periodical, Ribalow added that Zelda "writes of internal Jewish organizational life after a fashion usually unknown in American Jewish literature."[39]

Reactions to what Zelda had revealed about her personal life were as varied as those to her political views and her passages about Jewish identity. Ribalow found that she "emphasizes her personal problems more than the reader might desire. Of course, in an autobiography one expects the personal touch. Yet Mrs. Popkin's moving account of her sudden widowhood takes a curious turn when she permits the reader to learn of her physical demands after her husband's death." Sterling North warned that "many conservative readers will be a trifle startled by the author's utter frankness on every conceivable subject, from sex to politics and from childbearing to international relations." The *Herald Tribune*'s reviewer was less critical but had a similar reaction: "Without a trace of self-consciousness Mrs. Popkin illumines the inner being of a woman who, in her own phraseology, has not been afraid 'to open every door and let the world move in.'"[40] By the standards of subsequent Jewish women's memoirs, such as Kate Simon's *A Wider World*, published thirty years later, or even in comparison with the depictions of sex in Herman Wouk's *Marjorie Morningstar*, *Open Every Door* was relatively restrained, but in the mid-1950s, the mere acknowledgment that a respectable woman might have enjoyed the physical aspects of love and missed them after her husband's death was still controversial.[41]

At first, the reviews, which Zelda told my parents were "coming in high, wide and handsome," made her hopeful for the book's sales. She even hoped to use the book as the springboard for a television program that would help middle-class housewives escape from the boredom of their lives. "Vicariously, they play Cinderella, following the details of the glamour wedding in Monaco, while they lean against the vacuum cleaner," she wrote in a prospectus. Her program would be "Mrs. America's own guide to better living. It aims to meet her problems in stimulating, down-to-earth discussion, give her the comfort of knowing she is not alone, the assurance that others have met and conquered similar problems." More clearly than in any of her published writings, Zelda foreshadowed some of the themes that would be taken up a few years later in Betty Friedan's *The Feminine Mystique* and other feminist manifestoes. She anticipated programs titled "I'd Like to Take a Job Again"; "Why Not a Day Off for Mom?"; "Are Sports for Men Only?"; and "Must Women Dread Middle Age?" The television series never materialized, but a few months later, *McCall's* magazine negotiated with her about doing regular columns of sex advice—"what every bride wants to know," as she described it to my parents—and once again Zelda thought her luck was about to turn.[42]

Unfortunately, these hopes were premised on the belief that *Open Every Door* was going to make her a household word. Like most of her novels, however, her autobiography did not sell well, and she concluded that, once again, her publisher had deliberately sabotaged her. "My agent learned on last Monday what has gone on at Duttons. Elliot MacRae, the top boss came back from Europe soured on the book, just at publication time and announced, 'This book is not going anywhere' and all promotion was stopped at once. Literally, nothing was done," she complained to my parents.[43] *Open Every Door* had been Zelda's chance to portray herself as she wanted to be seen: as a writer, as a successful independent woman, and as a Jew who also represented the best of American life. The book's commercial failure put all of these convictions in jeopardy. "There are some years which just aren't your year and this one is apparently turning out to be *my* year when everything adds up to nothing and you keep climbing the mountain only to find you're just where you started—only a little more tired," she wrote to my parents. "I know there's a law of averages—and when you're down, eventually, you go up, but, as you know, too, the periods of frustration leave scars." Rather than inspiring others through her life story, she found herself seeking inspiration from a fellow memoirist. "This spring I read Ellen Glasgow's autobiography. One refrain ran through the book, '*I will not be defeated.*' That's me, too," she concluded.[44]

Sadly, however, Zelda was defeated in many ways during the years that followed. At first, she returned to her Molly Maguires novel, but she soon had to recognize that she was not going to find a publisher. "A year and a half of the hardest kind of work is over. It was a gamble and for the moment I seem to have lost," she told my parents. She decided that she needed to find some other way besides writing to support herself. "I'll start hunting a job, for I want no more of sitting alone and writing for a long, long while. The isolation has been as critical as the financial situation," she wrote. Considering what Zelda had published about them, Canadian Hadassah officials provided her with generous letters of reference and, in the late 1950s, she was able to obtain employment first with the America-Israel Cultural Foundation and then with the American Friends of the Hebrew University, the latter for a quite respectable salary of $13,000 a year, but she quickly gave up both of these positions. Since whatever letters Zelda wrote to my parents during these years are missing, I have only the formulaic letters in which her employers thanked her for her services and tried to help her qualify for unemployment benefits. I can only guess at the reasons why she left these jobs.[45]

Unable to find support for her writing or to hold an office job, and depressed, among other things, by her parents' deaths in 1959, Zelda fell into increasing difficulties. She was beset with health problems, and she began borrowing money from friends and relatives, piling up debts that in most cases she could not repay until many years later. Her constant pleas for money strained her relationships with her sons. After one difficult visit with her, my father told my mother, "As usual what's behind it all is that she wants a husband and no one can supply one."[46] Her letters to my parents regularly included complaints about my uncle, whom Zelda claimed had borrowed money from her years earlier and was now unwilling to pay her back; my uncle maintained that the money in question had been a gift, not a loan. My parents did what they could to help her out, but, like my uncle, they had growing children to raise and aspirations for a middle-class lifestyle, as well as obligations to support my mother's parents, who were as poor as Zelda.

In 1961, after my father had traded his professorship at Iowa for one at the Claremont Colleges, Zelda came to southern California for six months to help out after the birth of my younger sister and to see if she could adjust to life away from New York City. It was a chance for me and my sister Maggi, a year and a half younger than me, to get to know her better, but Zelda was bored in Claremont. At the end of her stay, she was tasked with chaperoning the two of us on the three-day train trip to the East Coast, while my parents and my new baby sister drove across the country. As soon as the Santa Fe "El Capitan" pulled out of the station in Los Angeles, Zelda disappeared into the bar car, emerging at mealtimes to make sure we got something to eat. When the train was delayed, she shared with me a sample of her philosophy as she prepared to go get herself another drink: "When you're going to be raped, you might as well enjoy it."

At the end of that year, Zelda thanked me for the gift of a *Peanuts* cartoon calendar and quoted a line from Charlie Brown included in it: "'Last year I was the only person I know who had 365 bad days.' It daren't happen this year," she added, but things were still far from turning around for her. In response to her demands for money, my uncle told her firmly, "You will have to take a hard look at your living situation." He urged her to consider moving in with her sister Pauline, who had a large house in Paterson, New Jersey, a solution Zelda was unwilling to consider.[47] In 1964, she found a less expensive apartment in Stuyvesant Town, a large apartment complex on First Avenue, not far from the Lower East Side where some of her relatives had lived a half-century earlier. "The apartment is lovely. . . . I moved here primarily for economy and never expected this much beauty and comfort," she told my parents; she would remain there for the rest of her life, and over the years I would make use of her spare couch many times. Nevertheless, she was still trying to cover her expenses from unemployment benefits, the minimal Social Security payments she began to receive when she turned sixty-five, and very occasional free-lance jobs and speaking fees. "Worst of all, is my loss of confidence in my writing ability," she wrote a few months before she moved. "'Washed-up' is the word I think of most often. I wish I didn't need to write any longer. I wish I could sit in the sun awhile . . . just sit. The old guts have taken a terrible beating in the last two years. Hell, I've worked for 50 years."[48]

The repetitious complaints in Zelda's letters undoubtedly strained my parents' patience, but the same letters did provide evidence that her mind was still sharp and that she continued to be engaged with the world. John Kennedy's election victory in 1960 was a triumph for the liberal political values she had always espoused, and a few free-lance assignments from the Anti-Defamation League gave her a chance to denounce the period's new crop of right-wing extremists, who reminded her of the antisemites and Nazi sympathizers she and Louis had combatted in the 1930s. They were not the only targets of her disdain. Commenting to my parents about the launching of the *New York Review of Books*, during a strike that silenced the city's daily newspapers, she wrote, "It's being gotten up by the Partisan Review crowd, whom I hate, lock-stock-and-barrel, finding them a supercilious and sterile crowd." (My parents promptly became lifelong subscribers.)[49] In August 1963, she went to Washington to participate in the civil rights march organized by Martin Luther King Jr. It was "probably the most moving experience of all my years of watching the making of history," she wrote. "A quarter of a million people (about one third white) knowing why they were there, being firm and dignified and gentle and courteous with one another, the Negroes and whites alike . . . no tension, not even among those who had traveled all night in buses great distances to get there." I still have the souvenir badge she sent me as a present.[50]

The great civil rights demonstration was perhaps the last time Zelda felt confident that the liberal political values she had long espoused were secure. The assassination of John F. Kennedy, just three months later, inspired her with "real fear for the future. I'm one who fears a wave of repression which will make the McCarthy days seem like a Sunday School picnic," she told my parents. "The relaxation in relations with the Soviet Union, the live-and-let live which extended to liberal and even leftist causes, may be over. And if a crazy man could pull that trigger, another crazy man might press that nuclear-war button." The optimism she had felt about race relations evaporated after riots broke out in Harlem in the summer of 1964. "Cab drivers now carry revolvers and no white person goes to Harlem if he can help it," she claimed. Two highly publicized mass murders in the summer of 1966, forerunners of the episodes that have become sadly familiar in recent decades, prompted her to comment, "the white Christian—not the Negro—is apparently the wild man on rampage this long, hot summer. . . . Had the murderer in either of these cases been Negro or Jewish, there would have been a general racial outcry. . . . What appalls me is that we haven't yet begun to look into our national selves—to ask what is it in our affluent society that turns our young men into murderers?"[51]

Zelda's pessimism about American society did not make her sympathetic to the radical protest movements of the period. "I don't like the war in Viet Nam. I don't like war. Period. But one thing I didn't like about the Viet Nam war protests was the burning of draft cards. Protest the war, yes, but service is a universal responsibility," she wrote to my father in October 1965, at a time when he and I were both helping to organize anti-war demonstrations in San Diego. Earlier in 1965, she had taken note of one of the first public manifestations of the new wave of militant feminism, but not in friendly terms. "As you may be aware we have a tizzy here over the Women's House of Detention," she wrote. "One Andrea Dworkin, a very homely Bennington freshman, got herself involved with the cops in a demonstration outside the U.N. building. . . . A stupid magistrate sent this girl off to the House of Detention when she couldn't post bail. . . . Dworkin made the sensational discovery that a women's prison isn't like the Bennington campus. . . . She hollered to the press and television, mentioning such awful words as lesbianism (sure there's some . . . like in the WAC and at Bennington), and mice and vermin (like at 12 Gramercy Park) and a brutal vaginal examination in which her virginity was discussed by the M.D.s. Nobody's bothered to point out that the prison doctors invariably ask whether the female is a virgin . . . the examination's different if she is. . . . Miss D. was not." She was particularly upset because the furor about the women's prison reflected badly on her old friend Anna Kross. "Anna is not corrupt and it would be a pity if after her years of outstanding public service, she'd be forced out of office in disgrace, which may happen."[52]

Once Zelda was able to collect Social Security, which gave her a dependable, if minimal, income, she made one last effort to salvage something from the years she had invested in her Molly Maguires book project. She tried to rewrite the book as nonfiction instead of as a novel. "Doing it straight, as a definitive historical work, is exceedingly hard for me, since I'm not a scholar or professional historian . . . merely an old reporter and ex-novelist. But I'm breaking my back on it, the seven-day-a week bit," she told my parents. Arthur Wang, co-owner of the Hill and Wang publishing company, saw promise in the idea, and for more than two years, Zelda struggled to meet his demands. In the end, however, she could not satisfy his exacting standards for precise documentation. "I will not do a book with ibids and footnotes and little numbers after sentences," she told her professor son, whose own publications consisted of nothing else. Her exasperating confrontations with Wang dragged on and on. "I want this book off my back, it has cost me too much, in time, energy, emotion, and cold cash, and I need to cut my losses," she told my father. The ordeal finally came to an end in early 1966, when Wang agreed to release her from her contract.[53]

As she filed away the last version of her Molly Maguires manuscript, Zelda had every reason to feel defeated. Ten years had passed since the appearance of her last book. She had had paying jobs for only two of those years. Estranged from her older sister, Pauline, in New Jersey and separated from her younger sister, Helen, in Israel, she had barely avoided a total break with her son Roy, and distance kept her from seeing much of our family. She did follow with interest the development of my father's critique of the official inquiry into the assassination of President Kennedy, which led to the publication of his only mass-market book, *The Second Oswald*, in 1966, and she showered him with advice about how to promote it.[54] The Brooklyn Dodgers had broken her heart when they moved to Los Angeles in 1958; the debut of the New York Mets in 1962 was one of the few bright spots in her life, along with the election of the dynamic liberal Republican John Lindsay as mayor of the city in 1965. But she no longer had the energy to take herself to ball games or to take an active part in political campaigns. The ambitious young woman who had thrown herself into the midst of New York City life a half-century earlier seemed fated to spend her final years alone and unhappy in her one-bedroom apartment, a few blocks from where some of her ancestors had started their American lives.

CHAPTER 7

"Yes, There Is a Second Chance"

EVEN AS THE FAMILY WAS IN DESPAIR ABOUT ZELDA'S SITUATION, SHE was preparing a surprise for us. She may have lost touch with the American Jewish *zeitgeist* in the 1950s, but by the mid-1960s, she was ready to channel the anger and frustration she had built up over the years into a fresh look at the issues that had shaped her earlier writing. Her autobiographical novel, *Herman Had Two Daughters*, published in 1968, the year my grandmother turned seventy, combined the tide of nostalgia for the Jewish life of the early twentieth century with the more critical view of the middle-class community that Jews had forged in subsequent decades. Although Zelda had little sympathy for the new wave of feminism that was beginning to build, her book also dramatized the difficulties that independent-minded women had faced in twentieth-century America. She followed *Herman* with two more commercially successful novels. *A Death of Innocence*, which appeared in 1971, gave her view of the youth culture of the 1960s; four years later, her final novel, *Dear Once*, revisited the saga of East European immigration to North America with a new honesty about relations between the sexes that echoed some concerns of the 1970s feminist movement. These books provided my grandmother financial security for the last years of her life. They also vindicated the conviction that she had cherished all her life: that she was smart enough and tough enough to make her own way in the world.

Zelda's rebound from her decade of disappointment owed something to a rare stroke of luck: in 1965, the Yaddo writers' colony in Saratoga Springs, New York, awarded her a short-term fellowship. The Yaddo evaluators were not enthusiastic about her application (they split about whether she deserved a grade of "B" as a novelist or merely a "B–"), but she was grateful for the opportunity. She spent most of her time at Yaddo arguing at long distance with Arthur Wang about her Molly Maguires book, but she did manage to start a new novel. She was one of two Yaddo visitors that summer who were writing books on the same theme: the battle of children from American Jewish families to escape their parents' influence. The other writer wrestling with that theme was the rising young male star Philip Roth, at work on *Portnoy's Complaint*, the breakout novel that would propel him into the first rank of American authors. Zelda's own novel, *Herman Had Two Daughters*, would be published in April 1968, a few months before Roth's. To compare a literary classic like *Portnoy's Complaint* with a now-forgotten work of middlebrow fiction may seem absurd, and even family loyalty cannot blind me to the difference in literary talent that separates Roth from my grandmother. Nevertheless, the two books have some significant elements in common. Both emphasize intergenerational conflicts, both evoke the reactions of American Jews to the Holocaust and the creation of Israel, and both strive for an outspoken frankness about sexuality. As she completed her manuscript, Popkin even dared to hope that the author of *Goodbye, Columbus* might deign to endorse her book. "Alfred Kazin and Philip Roth were both at Yaddo the summer of 1965, when I was there, and one or both of might come across with a pre-publication blurb," she told her publisher. "I believe they both thought well of me." (She would put her own opinion of *Portnoy* into the mouth of a fictional character in her 1971 novel *A Death of Innocence*: "Very funny, very dirty.")[1]

Herman Had Two Daughters gave Zelda the opportunity to express new thoughts about American Jewish life that she had been formulating for a number of years. Even when she thought of herself as having definitively renounced any ambition to write fiction about Jewish subjects, Zelda had never lost her interest in Jewish affairs. Aside from her unhappy stints working for Jewish fundraising institutions, she was still in regular touch with her sister Helen in Israel. In the spring of 1963, she told my father she was thinking of starting "a serious research project of the failure of the democracies to save or even help the Jews during the Hitler era," or else trying to put together "a paper-back anthology of 'The Jews in America,' a collection of first-rate fiction (and some nonfiction) telling the running story of Jewish life in America, as seen by leading authors." In the same letter, she reported that she had held a "pseudo-Seder" with a few friends, who, like her, "find it very pleasant to be Jews and feel a bit sorry for those Jewish neuters who have no frame of reference in Jewish life." A year later, she was still thinking about the new perspectives on the Holocaust provoked by Hannah Arendt's controversial *Eichmann in Jerusalem* and Rolf Hochhuch's equally controversial play, *The Deputy*, which accused Pope Pius XII of complicity with the Nazis. "Coming so soon after the dreadful Arendt book, it has stirred up the whole theme of guilt for the tragedy of the Hitler era and perhaps it may even stir an examination of the American conscience. I am hoping that somehow there may be a way to remind a paperback house that I once wrote a book called 'Small Victory,' which dealt with a particular failure of the American conscience," she wrote.[2]

Zelda knew she could count on my father's interest in what she had to say about Jewish issues because, after turning away from his Jewish heritage for a number of years, he, like so many Jews of the "third generation," had begun to rebel against his own parents' rejection of their Jewish heritage. This process started in the late 1950s, when our family began celebrating Passover for the first time and my sister and I found ourselves being enrolled for Hebrew lessons. Zelda's own sons had not had bar mitzvahs, but her stay in Claremont in 1962 had allowed her to be present for my ceremony. By that time, my father, a historian of philosophy, had begun doing serious research on the role of exiled Spanish and Portuguese Jews in the development of European thought during the sixteenth and seventeenth centuries, a topic on which he would continue to work for the next four decades. In 1963, we moved to the San Diego suburb of La Jolla, where he became the founding chair of the UCSD philosophy department. Jews had long been excluded from that beachfront community by a restrictive real estate covenant. The opening of the university campus brought an end to the covenant, but there were no existing Jewish institutions in the area. My father took the initiative to organize a community Seder and then to help found a permanent congregation. "The news that you're starting a shul in La Jolla amuses and intrigues me and in my spare moments I speculate on whether you are beginning to run true to Harry Feinberg's genes. Your grandfather, remember, was a kind of Jewish Johnny Appleseed, scattering new synagogues and Jewish centers wherever he set foot," Zelda wrote to him.[3]

My father's growing interest in Judaism was part of a broader movement that was reshaping American Jewish life and American culture in general. In addition to the attention to the Holocaust generated by the trial of Adolf Eichmann in 1961 and the Arendt and Hochhuth works that Zelda noted, interest in other aspects of Jewish experience was growing. By the time Zelda began work on *Herman Had Two Daughters*, many novelists, from Leon Uris to Isaac Bashevis Singer, had demonstrated that both Jews and non-Jews would indeed read books on Jewish themes. *Fiddler on the Roof* opened on Broadway in 1964 and was still running throughout the gestation of *Herman*. The Kennedy administration was friendlier to Israel than its predecessor; the Jewish state's "can-do" image fit with the optimism of the "New Frontier." The "Six Day War" between Israel and its neighbors in 1967, which took place while Zelda was writing her novel and which she followed through letters from her sister Helen, added to the American public's interest in Israel.

As she worked on her novel, Zelda turned her thoughts about the state of American Jewish life and her anxiety about the cultural atmosphere of the 1960s into a jeremiad she composed in 1966, lamenting the increasing alienation of Jewish youth from their tradition. "In the 1960s in the United States it is easy and agreeable to be a Jew. Yet, ironically, in this very period, our drop-out problem has become alarming," she proclaimed. American Jewish novelists—she named the familiar trinity of Bellow, Malamud, and Roth—had diagnosed the problem, but she was not optimistic about the solutions put forward by community leaders: "more Jewish day schools, for example, though where to find dynamic teachers who will capture the attention of the 'hip' generation no one seems to know; 'wall-to-wall Judaism' in the home, an artful phrase, meaning, I assume, return to the very formalism against which the parental generation had rebelled; organized 'study' tours to Israel where youth may inhale the spirit of the Land and be inspired." When she went on to lament that "there has been little *private* thinking-through, house by house, family by family, of how we got to the spot where indifference, intermarriage and assimilation threaten us with the loss of a generation," she may have been thinking about her own family, in which one son had married a Gentile.[4]

Rather than engaging in introspection, Zelda then summarized the main lines of the story of American Jewish life that she was in the process of integrating into her novel. "I grew up with the special richness of my generation: the enjoyment of two worlds, an American-born, Yiddish-speaking child, rooted in the warmth of Jewish family life, to whom the small shul up the street (a replica of those our elders knew in Lithuania and Poland) was as familiar as my parents' house," she began. Ten years earlier, in her autobiography, she had insisted that she was nothing but an American. Now, she wrote, "Our parents were the foreign-born, we the American generation, yet deep-down we were the same as they." The Holocaust, she claimed, had taught American Jews that they were responsible for their fellow Jews elsewhere in the world. The woman who had told the Jewish survivors she met in 1945 to clean up their camp themselves now said that "each survivor is precious, to be wrapped in cotton wool, cherished, healed. Each one is proof we Jews are indestructible." The establishment of Israel had also transformed American Jewish life. "No longer did we need to walk on eggs, looking over our shoulders, wondering will the Goy be tolerant of us. A brave, desperate handful, seven thousand miles away, had also liberated us."

And yet, despite these experiences, Zelda maintained that American Jews and even Israelis had failed to meet their responsibilities in keeping Jewish identity strong. "'For God's sake, don't give us the six million dead,' a women's luncheon chairman admonished me. 'We've had them up to here.' In Israel, a strange debate was starting: should one be encouraged to remember or forget?" she claimed. Alleging that young American Jews now regarded the Holocaust as "ancient history," she blamed "our omissions and commissions, through letting-go and *laissez-faire*, through naiveté and failure to communicate and by giving fund-raising top priority in the Jewish community." She denounced the 1950s, "that decade of shining slickness, of everything king-size and youth uncommitted," and its "belief that instant Judaism could be achieved by gadgets and gim-micks, by building large and lush, constructing architectural monstrosi-ties. . . . Most firmly, I believe that we have lost very many of our bright young people, our intellectual youth, estranged them, made them cynical and hostile, by the snobbery of large-scale fund-raising."

Drawing on her own intimate acquaintance with the culture of Jew-ish philanthropy, Zelda warned that there was "no cynicism more edged that that of the sensitive intellectual who sees the money-man exalted and himself deemed unworthy of a passing nod." Somewhat surprisingly, in view of her distaste for most manifestations of the rebellious spirit of the 1960s, she concluded by praising the aims of campus protesters. "It may be wise to ask the adult pundits to be quiet for a bit and to listen to the young, to learn where we failed and how we may retrieve our loss," she wrote. "By listening, we may discover that our lost generation isn't truly lost. It's merely temporarily out-of-town, in the Peace Corps or on the Civil Rights picket line, where it hews in explicit continuity to the oldest tenet of Hebrew morality, 'I am my brother's keeper.'" That there might be a contradiction between her call for a commitment to Jewish identity and her praise for young Jews who devoted themselves to uni-versalist causes does not seem to have occurred to her.

The new book on which Zelda was working as she composed her lament about the state of American Jewish life reflected both the more assertive version of identity that was gaining strength among American Jews in the 1960s and also the anxieties to which she gave voice. Her plot spanned a half century of American Jewish life, from the early decades of the twentieth century to the aftermath of the Holocaust and the creation of the state of Israel. In one respect, however, her project stood out from most other manifestations of the new interest in Jewish themes that characterized the mid-1960s. Unlike the more celebrated novels of authors such as Philip Roth and Saul Bellow, *Herman Had Two Daughters* highlighted the roles women had played in both the public and private spheres of American Jewish life.[5] None of the female characters in *Her-man Had Two Daughters* were conventional middle-class housewives and mothers; whether they were cast as heroines or villains, they were pow-erful and autonomous individuals, more than a match for the narrative's rather feckless males. *Herman Had Two Daughters* also anticipated, in its own way, some of the mixing of fiction and autobiography that character-izes many of Roth's novels. In her narrative, Zelda revisited many of the experiences she had already described in earlier books, putting them in new contexts; she also created, as her novel's main figure, a woman writer whose works were as self-consciously autobiographical as Zelda's own writings. *Herman Had Two Daughters* thus raises intriguing questions about the relations between fiction, autobiography, and "real life."

Discouraged as she was by the fiasco of her Molly Maguires project and by what she regarded as the lack of sociability at Yaddo—"after din-ner, the men sit around the magnificent parlor, looking at one another and asking 'Is there a movie to go to?'" she wrote to my parents—Zelda nevertheless made good use of her time there. "I started a new novel at Yaddo," she wrote shortly after she returned to her Manhattan apartment, "but don't know whether I care enough about it to put the next two years into it." For someone who thought of herself as a professional author and who had no other sources of income, the investment of so much time and effort in a project for which she had not even been able to obtain a publisher's advance was a risky gamble. The letters she wrote to my par-ents during the period when she was working on the book are rife with complaints about her poverty. "I don't believe you've really grasped what these last years have been for me. . . . I've been struggling on an income of less than fifty dollars a week," she wrote in the fall of 1967. Neverthe-less, as she worked her way through the project, she was clearly captured by her subject. "It came fast, completely, and interiorly," she told my parents. Midway through, her spirits and her bank account were buoyed when Lippincott, the publisher she had abandoned after the failure of *Quiet Street*, gave her a contract. "I am still floating in euphoria," she wrote. "Yesterday I had my first editorial conference with Tay Hohoff at Lippincott. As I came in, I ran into Maggie Carroll, Tay's secretary. She flung her arms around me, and said, 'You can't imagine all the excitement around here!' And when Tay told me how all of them felt about the book, those were words I hadn't heard in all my life."[6]

Summing up the story after she had completed it, Zelda wrote, "As any novel should be, this one is about people—the two daughters of

Herman and Ida Weiss and their loyal friend, Sam Rosenbaum. These three—Celia and Jessie Weiss and Sam grew up in the ghetto on the Hill in an American small town—and moved out of it into the mainstream of American life, particularly of American-Jewish life." Zelda made no secret of the fact that the book drew heavily on her own life story. "The background of this novel is out of a deep reservoir of personal knowledge and experience. . . . I needed no outside sources. . . . While the characters and incidents are fiction, the background is anything but," she told her publisher.[7] The town she called "Grady's Mills" in the book was Wilkes-Barre, Pennsylvania, where she had gone to high school. Focusing her comments on the two Weiss sisters and their male friend, Zelda failed to mention the fourth central figure in her story, the father whose name featured in the book's title. He and his wife, Ida, were modeled on her own Jewish immigrant parents, Harry and Annie Feinberg. In the file of documents she accumulated to help her write the book, Zelda included a collection of letters from her father, to help her accurately reproduce his Yiddish-inflected English.

Members of our family had no difficulty recognizing the novel's older daughter, Celia, as a vicious caricature of Zelda's older sister, Pauline, whom I remember as a kindly old lady always willing to indulge a grand-nephew; the publication of the book caused a permanent breach between the two of them. This was probably deliberate on Zelda's part: in one of the letters she wrote to my parents during the composition of the book, she rehearsed ancient grievances with her sister about the responsibility of caring for their parents that paralleled arguments between her two fictional characters. Once, when Zelda commented that several author friends of hers were using their writing to take revenge on their parents, my mother remarked in her diary, "Z. of course, does not recognize anything like this in her own work—*Herman*—but there she took it out on her sisters instead."[8]

Jessie, whose name recalled Zelda's "American" childhood name Jennie, was unquestionably to a large degree Zelda herself. Zelda endowed her protagonist with a more convoluted personal life and a more dazzling literary career than she herself had enjoyed, but the furnishings of the fictional Jessie's Gramercy Park apartment were those of the residence

Zelda had had there in her more prosperous days, and the details of Jessie's second husband's sudden death were those of Louis Popkin's heart attack. Zelda also put something of herself into the third main character in the book, the journalist and public relations man Sam Rosenbaum, who serves as the story's narrator. She drew on her own experience in small-town journalism and the public relations business for many of the incidents in his story, and, in the book, it was he rather than her female alter ego Jessie who undertook the trips to the postwar DP camps in Europe and to Israel during the 1948 war that had provided the basis for Zelda's novels on those topics. Throughout the novel, as Sam strives to "win an argument, just one, with the prize debater of Grady's Mills High School, class of 1918," his dialogues with Jessie provide opportunities for Zelda to question many of her own certainties.[9]

Lippincott's enthusiasm encouraged Zelda as she worked on the book, but the writing had certainly not proceeded as smoothly as her letters to my parents suggested. Throughout, she struggled to bring her central characters to life in convincing ways. Sam Vaughan, the first editor Zelda had approached about the book, had warned her that "there really is no major character. There's no one to identify strongly enough, to care about. Sammy . . . is too pale, too wishy-washy (even though I admire the strength he develops later). Neither of the daughters really captures center stage and holds it." Responding to such comments, Zelda told her agent that she was "strengthening [Sam's] backbone," admitted that Celia was "rather pale and flabby" and that the saintly Yuli, her representative Holocaust survivor, was "pretty much cardboard in this version," and promised that "I'm detailing Jessie, keeping closer focus on her, giving her additional pungent dialogue."[10] Sam remains, even in the published version, a Hamlet-like figure; it is difficult to understand his decades-long fixation on a woman who treats him as offhandedly as Jessie does. Jessie is certainly more vivid, but she disappears from Sam's life and from the narrative for long stretches. Celia and her unpleasant husband are stereotypes, presented in terms that sometimes evoke antisemitic representations of Jews, and Herman Weiss is equally one-dimensional. Zelda's writing style had not changed much since her first detective stories, written in the 1930s. Her somewhat dated diction and vocabulary may have been appreciated by older readers, but they certainly had less appeal to younger ones than Philip Roth's uninhibited prose.

The plot of *Herman* gave Zelda the chance to revisit almost every theme she had treated in her earlier novels and her autobiography, and often to write about them more freely than she had dared to do earlier. Attitudes to "sex and sensationalism" had changed in the years since Zelda had blamed low public taste for the failure of her books. I like to imagine that conversations at Yaddo with Philip Roth encouraged her to demonstrate her own liberation by slipping the word "cunt" into the first chapter of her novel and the word "fucking" into a passage near the end, but these constituted isolated instances of graphic language that she could not bring herself to employ on a regular basis.[11] Above all, however, she could now allow herself to create a panoply of Jewish characters who would demonstrate, as she had written in *Small Victory*, that a Jew could be "what all the world was. He was good; he was bad; he was weak; he was strong; he was brilliant or boorish; he was noble or cheap. . . . He was, in fact, everyman."[12]

From the start, editors realized that Zelda's novel contained two distinct and not always successfully integrated story lines. "Zelda really has two books here," an editor at Doubleday, the first publisher Zelda approached, wrote to her agent. "The first is the book she wants to write, 'the story of the American Jew from the ghetto to the country club.' . . . The second 'book' interested some as much as the first one. That is, roughly the story of fundraising, refugee resettlement, etc." Both these plots drew heavily from Zelda's own experience. In a letter to her literary agent, Zelda said she wanted to provide readers with "details of life in the ghetto on the Hill in Grady's Mills where an immigrant generation, early in this century, lived on terms not unlike Marc Chagall's Vitebsk. It will describe the self-imposed apartheid, the clinging to East European ways and Orthodox traditions, and the gradual emergence of a younger generation into the mainstream of American life."[13] In her autobiography, written twelve years earlier, she had depicted both her family, including her sister Pauline, and Wilkes-Barre warmly, and she had made no mention of prejudice. Now she drew a harsher portrait. Even the town's Jews were described in disparaging terms, with an emphasis on their crude pursuit of money and their lack of social graces.

Celia, the older of the two Weiss sisters in Zelda's novel, has good looks but no brains and is rigidly wedded to social convention; her younger sister, Jessie, is physically unattractive but bright and rebellious, a "strong, demanding, colorful bitch, attracting by her vitality, her redeeming humor," as Zelda described her in a memorandum to her agent.[14] Celia barely scrapes through high school, thanks to tutoring help from Sam, whereas Jessie makes such good grades that she is moved ahead, upstaging her sister by graduating as the valedictorian of their class. Unconventionally for the time—the novel starts in the years just prior to American entry into World War I—the father sends both daughters to college, Celia to study "domestic science" and Jessie to enroll in the "Emerson College of Oratory." Only toward the end of the novel do the characters—and the reader—learn of the sacrifice Herman Weiss made to pay for their education, by pawning his wife's diamond jewelry. In the meantime, the mystery of Ida Weiss's diamonds serves as a device for Zelda to dramatize the difference in character between the two women: the materialistic Celia obsesses about the fate of the jewels, and her suspicion that Jessie has somehow gotten her hands on them poisons their relationship. Ida Weiss, the girls' mother, who dies early in the book, had imagined Sam as a good match for Celia; Sam, for his part, had been attracted to Jessie, but he soon learns that she does not take him seriously. In an early scene in the novel, the two of them talk at a party, and he recognizes that she has deliberately made sure that he is seated in a chair, while she perches on its armrest. "Thus, by a casual arrangement, the design for our permanent relationship was set, Jessie higher than and looking down on me," Sam muses.[15]

After the Weiss girls finish college, they go very different ways. Jessie flees Grady's Mills for the bohemian cultural scene of New York City and, like Zelda, rushes into an impulsive marriage. Ida Weiss is scandalized when her new son-in-law explains that his parents are Reform Jews, "worse even than a Goy" in her eyes.[16] Jessie's sister is even more stricken when she realizes that her sister has stolen a march on her, and, horror of horrors, that she might now receive their mother's diamonds. Jessie's marriage, unlike Zelda's, turns out to be a disaster, but her sister does no better. Sam Rosenbaum finds himself a silent witness when Joe, the son of the wealthy junk dealer Max Slomowitz, is railroaded into matrimony with Celia in order to break up a relationship that has resulted in his impregnating an Irish coalminer's daughter. As for Sam himself, after serving in France during World War I, he settles down in Grady's Mills, writing for the local newspaper.

As the novel progresses chronologically through the 1920s and 1930s, the experiences of the three main characters reflect the changing nature of American Jewish life. Jessie quickly ditches her feckless husband and struggles to make a living as a playwright; on a visit to her Greenwich Village apartment before her first theatrical success, Sam finds her in such dire straits that he forces a ten-dollar bill on her, a humiliation for which she never forgives him. He describes her first play as "clearly auto-biographical," dealing with two sisters, "the younger a sensitive adolescent, shrinking from dogmatic parents . . . escaping through poetry into a fantasy world; the older complacent, conforming, preferred."[17] The play is sufficiently successful to allow Jessie to escape to Paris, giving Zelda the opportunity to imagine what her life might have been like if she had been able to join Ernest Hemingway and F. Scott Fitzgerald in Montparnasse cafés. Celia and her husband establish themselves in New York City. He changes his name from Slomowitz to Sloan and becomes a prosperous businessman dealing in scrap metal.

The two Weiss sisters disappear from the narrative for several chapters as Zelda turns her attention to depicting the rising tide of antisemitism in Grady's Mills in the 1930s. "Some anti-Semitism Grady's Mills has always had," Sam admits: "Ignorant kids yelling 'sheeny' and 'Christ-killer' at us," exclusion from the local country club. By the mid-1930s, however, "we'd begun to know fear."[18] The incidents Zelda recounted in her novel are easy to imagine for those who know the history of the period: vocal complaints about the arrival of German Jewish refugees from Germany, a local radio station broadcasting Father Coughlin's diatribes, a mysterious fire at a local synagogue, the desecration of the grave of a local Jewish boy who had died in World War I, a rock thrown through a synagogue window. When Sam is passed over for a promotion at the newspaper, he realizes that he is in danger of spending the rest of his life in a dead-end job because of unspoken prejudice. Before Sam can decide what to do about his own situation, he is drawn back into intimate contact with the Weiss sisters by the outbreak of another fire of mysterious origins: the widowed Herman Weiss's store burns down, nearly killing the old man. Zelda's description of the period's antisemitism evoked events that had actually taken place in Wilkes-Barre in the late 1930s and early 1940s, when a local lawyer named Robert Doran had launched a campaign of antisemitic agitation that included book burnings. "Liberals were threatened, their meetings boycotted, banned, while Elizabeth Dilling and Robert Edmundson came to preach their Swastika-tinged variety of patriotism," Zelda recalled in her autobiography. The circumstances of the fire in Herman Weiss's store resembled those that resulted in the death of Louis Weitzenkorn, the flamboyant journalist who had helped Zelda publish articles in the New York press when she first moved there. Weitzenkorn had later moved back to Wilkes-Barre, where he stood up to the local antisemites before being fatally burned in a fire in his home in 1943.[19]

The fire brings the two Weiss daughters back into the story. Celia rushes up from New York City, less out of concern for her father than out of determination to find her mother's diamonds, which she assumes must be buried in the ashes of the building. Jessie arrives belatedly and finds herself having to take charge of making arrangements for her father's care, including donating her skin to be grafted onto his wounds. As he does what he can to help his old friends, Sam concludes that it is high time for him to leave Grady's Mills as well. This leads him to New York City and to a dinner with Celia, her husband, and their daughter Ilene in their extravagant Park Avenue apartment. Celia has brought her father to live with the family, but keeps him confined to a back bedroom to avoid the embarrassment of being associated with his religiosity and his strange ways. Through his connection with Joe Sloan, Sam is hired to work for the "Jewish Aid Committee," a fictional version of the Jewish organizations Zelda knew so well, which is organizing a mass meeting at Madison Square Garden to protest against the Nazi persecution of the Jews.

Planting the fictional Sam Rosenbaum at the center of the American Jewish community's efforts to oppose Hitler allowed Zelda to introduce the second theme of *Herman Had Two Daughters*, her portrayal of the dynamics of Jewish fundraising and publicity work. She saw this as a major aspect of her project. "I have been interested in a phenomenon that began in the nineteen thirties, and grew into a colossus in the subsequent decades: the phenomenon of large-scale fundraising. It has hitherto been sacrosanct," she wrote in one of her memoranda about her manuscript. In the file of documents she put together to help her in writing her novel, Zelda included the article she had written in 1933 but apparently never published, describing the mass rally in Madison Square Garden organized by the American Jewish Congress in March 1933 to denounce Hitler.[20]

The full range of personalities in the American Jewish community and the full range of issues Zelda sought to deal with in her novel come together in the book's dramatic central episode, set at a Jewish community fundraising dinner in honor of Celia Weiss's husband in the fateful year of 1938. Jessie Weiss has just caused a sensation with her melodramatic play, *The Arsonists*, a lurid denunciation of small-town American. The imaginary play, perhaps inspired by the emotion-laden pageants produced by Ben Hecht during and after World War II, ends with the burning down of a synagogue. Unaware that he is about to bring about an explosive family reunion, Sam's new boss charges him to recruit Jessie as the keynote speaker at the fundraising dinner.

After six months on the job, Sam has become thoroughly disenchanted with his work, which consists, he concludes, in "speed[ing] appeals and resolutions, declarations and rebuttals, to wastepaper baskets in newsrooms from Florida to Oregon," as Zelda and Louis had done in the 1930s. Reading the plot summary of *The Arsonists*, Sam is privately appalled to recognize himself, travestied as a "confused newspaper reporter," but he cannot evade his orders to corral Jessie as the lead speaker at the upcoming event. Having done so, Sam feels obliged to see *The Arsonists* for himself. His verdict is unequivocal: "Claptrap! Junk! Phoney-baloney!" His old friend's depiction of the inhabitants of Grady's Mills was "black or white, no gray whatsoever. She'd entirely missed the crucial point, the fetid undercurrent of racial animosity that you could never reach and touch, drag to light and extirpate because it wasn't overt . . . the de facto second-class citizenship that custom imposed on Jews in all the little towns and cities that are the backbone of this republic." To his horror, the well-dressed audience loves the play, and he is particularly sickened by the realization that the imaginary hero in the drama, a blond "muscle-boy" who rescues the rabbi and the Torah scroll from the burning synagogue, must be what his old friend "wished I'd be so I might get the girl."[21]

Invited to speak at her brother-in-law's testimonial dinner, Jessie Weiss provides more melodrama of her own. The occasion is perfect for her sister, Celia, to show off her elegant clothing and jewelry, and, naturally, she has planned to leave her elderly Orthodox father at home. Halfway through the meal, the guests at the head table are informed that "a very strange old man" is trying to gain admission to the event. Sam immediately realizes who it is, rescues Herman from the policemen who have intercepted him, gets him seated at a table, and informs Jessie of his presence. When she rises to speak, Jessie sets aside her prepared speech and tells the guests, "There is, in this audience, a gentleman whom you should meet. A great gentleman who bears upon his fragile body the scars of the fires of hate. The gentleman whose personal ordeal inspired my play and whose noble character has been my lifelong source of inspiration." Celia is, of course, mortified to be publicly identified with her father, and Herman Weiss is overwhelmed by the storm of applause he receives. Meanwhile, Sam's fundraising colleagues are ecstatic: "That act, believe me, will be worth easy another hundred thousand bucks," one of them tells him.[22]

The banquet scene thus merges the intimate conflicts among the novel's four major characters with the book's public dimension. Celia, ostensibly the "good" daughter who is careful to keep a kosher kitchen and who has provided lodging for her father, in fact cares more about her social standing than about his welfare. Jessie, the rebellious daughter who, in addition to everything else, arrives at the banquet accompanied by her new lover, a married Gentile doctor, reveals herself as the one who truly respects him, even though her way of honoring him is acutely embarrassing for him. The "good shnook" Sam is the only one who knows the whole truth about the others.[23] Sam recognizes the cynicism of his organizational colleagues, but he also sees through the cynicism of his old friend Jessie, who has caricatured him, her father, and the people of Grady's Mills and, even more damningly, betrayed her own talents by writing a piece of melodramatic schlock. At the same time, however, he is also the only one who can sense the genuine love for Herman that underlies Jessie's sensationalistic transformation of him into a Jewish martyr.

The tone of *Herman Had Two Daughters* shifts as the story moves to the outbreak of the Second World War and the great tragedy of the Holocaust. In the wake of Pearl Harbor, Sam's boss dissuades him from trying to sign up to fight by telling him that he is needed in another conflict, the one against the Nazis' plan to exterminate the Jews. Sam understands the urgency of the situation, but also the awkward position of those like himself who are "earning bread and butter out of the Jewish catastrophe," as Zelda had during her time at the Joint Distribution Committee during the war. Even in this crisis, the paid staff like Sam find themselves humiliated by the wealthy donors who fund their activities: "We were 'paid professionals,' mercenaries, they, dedicated volunteers. Between us was a social chasm, never to be bridged." Unlike Zelda, Sam manages to escape from this bind when the Jewish Action Committee sends him to Europe to help arrange the rescue of Jews from the occupied countries. For the first time, Sam finds himself doing things he can truly regard as worthwhile. He also learns a harsh lesson about Jewish fate: "Christian nations, including ours, were indifferent to what was done to Jews, all except the Germans, who were dedicated to destroying them." Arthur Morse's pioneering exposé of American indifference to Jewish refugees, *While Six Million Died*, appeared almost simultaneously with her novel, but Zelda did not need Morse to teach her about the subject: the documents she gathered for the novel included the letter from the American consul in Berlin in 1939 denying her husband's request for visas for some of his Polish relatives because he had misspelled their family name, which she reproduced verbatim in *Herman*.[24]

After the war ends, Sam is still employed dealing with the survivors, and it is in the course of visiting a DP camp, as Zelda herself had done in the winter of 1945–1946, that he meets Yuli, a survivor of Auschwitz who has taken on the task of working with orphaned Jewish children. Zelda based the character of Yuli on "the Frau Doctor, a stunning Hungarian blonde," a Gentile woman married to a Jew who had narrowly survived the war. In her autobiography, Zelda described sharing a Christmas dinner with this woman in Vienna in 1945 and hearing of how, in spite of her hatred of the Germans, she had saved the life of a German soldier wounded in an air raid.[25] Zelda's decision to make a Gentile her representative Holocaust victim was a throwback to her habit, in her earlier novels, of making her main characters Gentiles rather than Jews. Sam is immediately attracted to Yuli, a woman who voluntarily chose to share the destiny of the Jews, but he does not know how to answer her question about his own motives. Her challenge starts a process analogous to what Zelda herself had experienced, when her encounters with camp survivors "shocked her into Zionism."[26]

Sam moves on, accompanying DPs to a British confinement camp in Cyprus and finally arriving in Palestine, where he "leaned against the rear wall of a room in a Tel Aviv museum while Ben-Gurion read the proclamation" of Israeli independence. Even in Israel, however, he still finds himself entangled with the Weiss family. Celia's daughter Ilene is there on her honeymoon, married to a man from another wealthy Jewish family as her mother had wished. To Sam, however, Ilene confides her deepest secret: she is hopelessly in love with another man, a liaison only her aunt Jessie knows about. Sam reluctantly agrees to smuggle a letter to her lover back in America for her, and then realizes with horror that it is addressed to the young man from Grady's Mills whom Ilene's father, Joe, had fathered so many years ago. Some readers of Zelda's draft manuscript objected to this incestuous subplot as contrived and even offensive, but Zelda argued that "I need Ilene's suicide . . . for its implications of sibling 'Schadenfreude,' as well as for its effect on Celia's character."[27]

Ready to return to the United States, Sam stops in Europe just long enough to propose marriage to Yuli, who accepts his ring but tells him she is not yet ready to start a new life. Sam's premonition of tragedy is confirmed soon after he returns to the United States: the lovesick Ilene has drowned herself off the beach in Tel Aviv. He rushes to Celia's home, and finds her with Jessie, grief-stricken but with her hair "immaculately coiffed." "It's easy to despise and hard to pity those whose lives are spent in vanity, acquiring show-off things," Sam thinks to himself. "What more was Ilene to her mother than another display piece?"[28] Jessie, to be sure, does not come off much better. After a long scene in which she tells Sam every detail of what she knew about Ilene's romance with her half-brother, she makes another of her periodic disappearances from the narrative.

Jessie's absence allows Zelda to return to her harsh depiction of the Jewish organizational milieu. Sam is dispatched on a nationwide lecture tour, raising money for Israel by recounting his stories about the DPs and the birth of the new state. He realizes that, with the disappearance of the European Jewish community from which his parents had come, "the child, the Jewish American, became head of the family. . . . The new man fed the children who were scattered over many lands or gathered into Israel. . . . However, since giving also is a greediness, he sought his status, built his stature here through misery and courage overseas. He functioned in a world whose yardstick for the measure of a man was, How much does he give?" With the passage of time, Sam also senses that American Jews are losing their interest in overseas events and turning inward. On a visit to Grady's Mills, his old Jewish friends explain to him that they have decided to use part of the funds he has helped them raise to build a local Jewish center. Sam decides that he doesn't want to discuss "the preservation of the Jewish heritage through a swimming pool in Grady's Mills." He also learns that appeals in the name of the victims of the Holocaust are losing their effectiveness. "'For God's sake, don't give us the six million dead,' one chairman told me. 'We've had them up to here,'" Zelda wrote, a line she claimed to have heard herself on one occasion in her own fundraising work. "And as for Israel, the flush of pride had ebbed, the annual drive had become routine."[29]

Zelda's denunciation of the pervasive materialism and obsessive self-absorption of postwar American Jewry reaches its climax in a final scene in which Sam, after marrying Yuli, brings his Holocaust-survivor wife back to Grady's Mills to meet his parents and his former friends. In a scene set at the swanky new Jewish country club, the locals compete to show off their complete incomprehension of her experiences. Zelda profited from the opportunity to take a swipe at her *bête noire*, Leon Uris, whose runaway best-seller *Exodus* had succeeded where her own novel about Israel had failed. When one of the Jewish women urges Yuli to read it, Sam thinks to himself, "I rated it with Jessie Weiss's *Arsonists*." The scene culminates when one woman catches sight of the tattooed number on Yuli's wrist and tells her, "You should remove that thing," offering to provide the name of a plastic surgeon. After she and Sam have escaped from this ordeal, Yuli tells him that she understands that there is an unbridgeable gulf between American Jews, with their sheltered lives, and those from Europe. But, she concludes, "We had them, too. . . . The comfortable people, the sophisticated people, the assimilated people, the self-satisfied people, who told themselves they could escape from Jewish history."[30]

Sam's departure for Europe and his marriage with Yuli suggest that he has embraced the notion that Jews cannot escape from history, but he is still not free of his entanglement with the Weiss sisters. Celia continues to insist that he visit her whenever he is in New York, but, as always, it is Jessie with whom Sam is really preoccupied. Baffled by the apparent indifference of the "dame who wrote *The Arsonists*" to the fate of the Jews in the post-Holocaust world, Sam finally provokes Jessie into a declaration of her real values and an explanation of her tortured personality. Her values, she insists, are universal ones: "The world—this is my absolute conviction—must offer bread and justice to all its people, brown and black, yellow, white, Christian, Moslem, Buddhist, Hebrew, Atheist." And, she goes on, this conviction is what drove her to leave her family and Grady's Mills. "I left the Hill to join the human race, not to be a willy-nilly, whining, pining member of a persecuted minority. . . . It was quite a thing to learn that I could walk alone and Jehovah's lightning didn't strike me dead when I ate steamed clams."[31]

Jessie's rebellion, like Zelda's own, was also a revolt against her family. "'Did you know, could you guess, what it was like to be the child of Herman Weiss?' she tells Sam. 'The daughter of a saintly man who part-time ran a grocery? . . . In that house Papa was a presence, not a human being. Remote, aloof. Wrapped up in his piety. Shul, morning, night, all day

Saturday. What time had he for me, for us?'" Ida Weiss fares no better: "The right-hand woman of the right-hand man of God! Why, she used him like a club! . . . Do you wonder why I hated everything and everybody in that house? Yes, even Papa, whom I didn't want to hate. Yet he *was* to blame. If he'd been a real father and a master in his house, not submissive to God and Ida Weiss. . . . So there you have it, why Jessie Weiss walked out on Judaism." Privately, Sam is unconvinced, perhaps reflecting Zelda's own divided thoughts on the subject: "Unhappy childhood is the alibi nowadays for every aberration from kleptomania to genocide. Why not for Jewish indifference?" But Jessie sticks to her position. In a subsequent encounter with Sam, she rehashes her grievances against her sister and insists again that her parents never loved her: "I've always been the misfit, the disappointment, from the hour I was born. I should have been a boy, you know, to perpetuate Papa's name, provide the kaddish so he'd rest easy in his grave. And don't think Mama didn't let me know it and Celia rub it in."[32]

Jessie's venting of her deepest feelings about her family and her Jewish origins still does not resolve the relationship between her and Sam. They have another emotional encounter when Jessie's doctor husband dies suddenly from a heart attack, a plot twist that allowed Zelda to draw once again on the details of her own husband's death. Sam has to step in to make the funeral arrangements and to comfort the widow when she pulls him into bed with her, using him, as he realizes, "instinctively . . . the always faithful friend, for reassurance that she had not also died." Immediately afterward, she turns on him, screaming "Pervert. . . . Lousy, filthy, fucking bastard!" and drives him out of the house. This experience makes Sam flee for Europe and Yuli, but Jessie will draw him back to her one last time, during his visit to America with his new bride a few years later. Before the pair can return to Europe, Sam learns that Jessie is dying of cancer. He finds her at the end of her strength, but able to make one last joke and give him a final wink. "'You loved her?' Yuli asks as they leave the sickroom. 'I'm not sure,' Sam replies, but in his heart, he knows he has just said farewell to his 'once and lifelong love.'"[33]

Listening to the rabbi engaged by Celia to preside over Jessie's funeral a few days later, Sam finds himself continuing his lifelong argument with her, both about Jewish identity and about family loyalty. When the rabbi calls her "'a distinguished and devoted and dedicated daughter of the Jewish people,' Sam thinks, 'What . . . was Jewish about Jessie? . . . Had she grieved for the Jewish tragedy? Had she rejoiced in the nationhood?'" When the rabbi goes on to call the deceased a "devoted daughter," Sam reminds himself that "she ran from her father's house." In the end, the only thing Sam can be sure of is his judgment of Celia. Talking to her after the funeral, he comments, "Never had I seen Celia look so well. . . . Celia had come out on top. All Jessie had achieved in school, career, and love would turn to ashes and yellowing newsprint. But Celia, ineffectual and unloved, was alive, and survival is what counts."[34]

The conclusion of *Herman Had Two Daughters* clearly reflects the grievances that Zelda had developed during the years in which her life had deviated so sharply from the image of herself as a successful woman that she had projected in her 1956 autobiography. A world in which a woman like Celia, a female character as monstrous as Alexander Portnoy's mother in Philip Roth's novel, has "come out on top" is obviously a world turned upside down, in which values Zelda regarded as false have triumphed. Are we to take it as Sam's final verdict on Jessie? This seems equally untenable: his disgust at Celia and everything she represents is unmistakable, as is his attachment to Jessie, despite the fact that she has kept him at a distance throughout their relationship. Was this last line then Zelda's own despairing verdict on the values of the American Jewish community whose evolution she had traced in her story? If so, she accomplished a remarkable feat, for it was that same Jewish public that made *Herman Had Two Daughters* her first commercially successful publication since *The Journey Home* in 1945, allowing her a feeling of vindication that had been denied to the fictional Jessie Weiss.

The reception of her book was a pleasant surprise for Zelda, who had predicted that "some Jews will like it, some [will] be furious." The reviews were generally positive, although the *New York Times*, which had printed unfavorable comments about her earlier books, ignored *Herman* completely. Another popular novelist of the period, Stephen Longstreet, volunteered a generous jacket blurb, calling it "the best novel of Jewish-American life that has come along in the last twenty years."

John Barkham, a reviewer who had admired Zelda's earlier novels, saw the novel's acerbic side, writing that "this rebarbative novel holds up a mirror to American Jewry, and what it reflects is not always pretty," but he praised the book's dialect passages: "Popkin's Jewish mamas, for example, are the funniest I have come across in years, and the dialogue she has written for them the richest since Hyman Kaplan."[35] The *Saturday Review*, a respected magazine that had tended to give Zelda's work positive evaluations, was more ambivalent. "As the story is stretched and strained to fill a documentary scale too large for it," its reviewer wrote, "the author begins to hedge her bets and pull her punches. . . . The coarse, the mean, the ruthless, the stingy, the obsessed—we are asked to make allowances for all of them, not because they are human, but because they are Jews, in the generic, self-placating sense that has served so well as a substitute for truthful insight in the best-selling sagas of [Herman] Wouk and Uris."[36]

Zelda could afford to ignore such criticism. Within a few weeks of the book's publication, she wrote triumphantly to my parents "to pass along the news that I've begun to have money problems, but of a sort quite different from any I have known before. Herman's causing them . . . that book went into its third big printing two weeks before publication. . . . I guess the Book of the Month Club recommendation gave it the third-edition push." *Herman Had Two Daughters* ended the money problems from which she had suffered for many years; after ten years, she was finally able to pay back the friends who had lent her money. Zelda's clip file filled with reviews from Jewish community publications around the country. The reviewer for one such paper wrote that "Many a Jewish nerve will be rubbed raw by this rich and biting novel by Mrs. Popkin. There is enough truth and history here to make material for hot discussion in Temple Youth, Brotherhood and Sisterhood groups in the synagogues of the United States for the next ten years." Zelda made a speaking tour, addressing Jewish audiences, including one in Detroit where, she claimed, "there were about 500 women for that speech—they had to open the back doors of the auditorium and set up extra seats. I guess they enjoyed what they heard, because they bought lots of books and drove me almost nuts, telling me I was the white hope of the

American Jewish Community." Her acid comments about the "oligarchy" that dominated that community and her demand to know "Where are today's giants to equal leaders such as Rabbi Stephen Wise, Judge Louis Brandeis, Louis Marshall, Nathan Straus, Jacob Schiff and others among whom I grew up?" did not seem to alienate her Jewish public.[37]

Although it lacks the satirical bite and the frenetic energy of Roth's *Portnoy's Complaint*, *Herman Had Two Daughters* provides some worthwhile insights into the development of American Jewish identity in the mid-twentieth century. The themes of the novel are those of the classics of modern American Jewish literature: the conflict between an older generation rooted in tradition and their children, the price of success in American life, the encounters with the Holocaust and with the alternative vision of Jewish identity constituted by Israel. There is sometimes a gritty realism to Zelda's novel that is missing in the work of her more gifted younger contemporaries. More than thirty years later, for example, Philip Roth would return to the issue of American antisemitism in the 1930s in his novel, *The Plot Against America*.[38] Roth's tale of a fascist takeover of the United States is pure fantasy, however, whereas Zelda had seen the Silver Shirts and the German American Bund marching through the streets and participated personally in the fight against Father Coughlin. Zelda was also willing to take a clear-eyed look at the growth of the American Jewish community's fundraising network, a feature of American Jewish life whose importance can hardly be denied but that rarely rates a mention in the major works of American Jewish literature. Zelda's critique of the American Jewish psyche certainly lacks the depth found in Roth's novels, but she had an insider's view of some issues that more prominent novelists ignored.

Zelda's novel is also significant because of her attempt to foreground the importance of women in American Jewish life, and not just of overbearing Jewish mothers such as Mrs. Portnoy. Zelda rejected the new feminism of the 1960s, but it was certainly not because she thought women's place was in the home. Unlike many other American Jewish women authors, Zelda did not give much attention to the relationship between immigrant-generation mothers and their daughters; the character based on her own mother dies early in the novel, whereas Annie Feinberg lived to be over eighty.[39] The negative role that the mother might have played is taken instead by Jessie's "bad" sister Celia, an unpleasant caricature, but unquestionably a force in her own right. Yuli surmounts the loss of her own family to devote herself to helping other Holocaust survivors, and she does not fall gratefully into Sam's arms when he proposes to her. And, of course, it is the character of Jessie Weiss, who never has children and who pursues an independent career as a playwright and public figure, that dominates the story. As she plotted out her novel, Zelda several times referred to Herman Wouk's 1955 book, *Marjorie Morningstar*, as a model for what she had in mind, but her heroine, unlike Wouk's, would not renounce her dreams of artistic success to become a typical suburban Jewish housewife. Jessie does, it is true, give up her career after her second marriage, but this is hardly presented as a happy outcome. Indeed, Zelda only inserted a few pages dealing with Jessie's life as a married woman in response to an editor's query, "how did Jessie keep busy after 'The Arsonists'? What happened to the spirit of the Jewish Joan of Arc?"[40]

One might have thought that writing her autobiography, *Open Every Door*, would have satisfied Zelda's urge to tell her own story. One obvious contrast between Zelda's autobiography and *Herman Had Two Daughters* is that the autobiography was told as an American story, whereas the novel was unmistakably a Jewish one. The message of *Herman Had Two Daughters* was not a simple affirmation of Jewishness, to be sure, but the story did suggest that Jews could never entirely escape their fate. When the cantor at Jessie Weiss's funeral chants "El Mole Rachamim," Sam thinks to himself, "Let her squirm inside that box; she's hooked, we've made her one of us again." And, he adds, "I'll bet she's pleased. Gathered up, gathered in, given the full treatment, reclaimed, redeemed."[41]

Although there is no doubt that the character of Jessie Weiss in *Herman Had Two Daughters* is modeled on Zelda herself, the book's status as fiction allowed her the freedom to imagine a life different from the one she actually lived. Jessie achieves a degree of literary celebrity that Zelda might have dreamed of but never achieved. Meanwhile, through her second stand-in, Sam, Zelda depicts the life she might have had if she had continued to work for the Wilkes-Barre *Times Leader*. Sam also allowed her to express her feelings about the profession she had practiced—public relations—and about the Jewish community organizations she had known so intimately in ways that she had not felt free to do in her autobiography. Zelda's creation of not just one but two fictional characters who were alter egos for their author created the opportunity for a dialogue in which Zelda could argue with herself about the questions that had dominated her life, rather than having to espouse one position over another.

When the fictional Jessie launches her literary career with a play whose plot closely resembles the story line of *Herman Had Two Daughters*, Sam is given the privilege of dismissing the play as "several steps down from Elmer Rice," suggesting that Zelda herself understood the psychological motives behind her treatment of her family members and some of the limitations of her own book. Toward the end of the novel, when Jessie voices her version of the secular and universalist worldview Zelda had espoused in her autobiography, Sam is there to remind her that "the Sermon on the Mount didn't save your crippled Vilna cousin," and to comment to himself that Jessie's tirade against her father is "as unreasoned, as subjective, as are most of the crucial decisions of most lives." By letting herself emerge, through the interaction of her two stand-ins, as a more complex and contradictory character than the Zelda Popkin of her earlier autobiography, Zelda showed that autobiographical fiction could sometimes achieve a truth that straightforward autobiography could not convey.[42]

The autobiographical elements in the novel also had their problematic aspects. Undoubtedly, thousands of readers enjoyed *Herman Had Two Daughters* without any idea that it drew so heavily not only on Zelda's experience of the period's public events but on her intimate family life. Among other things, the connection between the book's male narrator and its author that I have suggested could well be invisible, even to readers who might have deduced that Jessie Weiss was a stand-in for Zelda herself. For some family members, however, this inside knowledge made the novel literally unreadable: as I have mentioned, it led to a permanent rupture in relations between Zelda and her older sister. When I first read the novel, as a young man and the son of parents who had relentlessly inculcated in me a respect for "serious" literature, preferably foreign, I was embarrassed by the clunky prose, the melodramatic plot, and the lurid cover of the paperback edition, in which the character based on my grandmother is shown dressed only in her underwear.

Revisiting *Herman Had Two Daughters* now, after a career that has involved teaching courses in contemporary Jewish history, living through the feminist revolution that was just beginning as my grandmother was writing her book, and writing about issues involved in autobiographical literature, puts it in a different light. My grandmother's novel is certainly not great literature, but it has much to say about the tensions in twentieth-century American Jewish life, about the struggles of women authors to find a place for themselves in the Jewish literary world, and about the relationship between autobiography and fiction. Like *Portnoy's Complaint*, *Herman Had Two Daughters* rejects the sentimentality and triumphalism of mainstream narratives about twentieth-century American Jewish life, even those that Zelda had incorporated in her own earlier novels. At a time when both Roth and younger American Jewish women authors were emphasizing the politics of personal relations, Zelda defiantly projected her female protagonist into the great dramas of public life that had affected the Jewish community. Finally, through the dialogue between her two personas, Jessie and Sam, she exposed the tension between the universalist values she identified with America and her Jewish roots.

Herman Had Two Daughters had given Zelda the chance to make seemingly definitive statements about almost all the themes that had preoccupied her since the start of her writing career in the early 1920s. At first, she pretended to my parents that she no longer felt the urge to write another book, but before long she was back at her typewriter. The last two novels she completed, *A Death of Innocence* and *Dear Once*, were less personal than *Herman*, although, as always, episodes from her own life found their way into their pages.[43] Like *Herman*, both books reflected a more hard-boiled view of humanity than Zelda's earlier "serious" novels. *A Death of Innocence* was based on a murder case that had intrigued Zelda for years, in which a young woman from a good middle-class family helped her boyfriend rob and kill an older woman. The main character, Elizabeth Cameron, the mother of the murderess, has to come to terms with the fact that her beloved daughter is rotten to the core.

My mother, long familiar with Zelda's somewhat misanthropic view of human nature, categorized the book as her mother-in-law's attempt to show how children can ruin their innocent parents' lives. In fact, Zelda was harder on her main character than my mother realized. Reviving the polemic against permissive parenting from her magazine articles of the early 1930s, Zelda had the mother in the story admit to her daughter that she bore responsibility for what the young woman had done. "Apparently I never taught you what was right, what was wrong. I never put on the brakes, never said, 'Buffie, this and that you musn't do.'"[44]

To Zelda's surprise, her formidable editor, Tay Hohoff, liked the book "better than *Herman*. And truly, since it was such a hard book to do—such a monster—I find it a little incredible," Zelda told my parents. It appeared to favorable reviews in the spring of 1971, and even achieved the honor of a Spanish translation. "I never dreamed I could push the button twice in succession at this stage of my life," she wrote. With *A Death of Innocence*, Zelda achieved a long-held and previously unsatisfied ambition: she got to see one of her novels turned into a movie. Broadcast nationally on CBS in the fall of 1971, the production, which ironically starred the Jewish actress Shelley Winters playing the role of the good Christian mother, attracted the second-largest audience for a made-for-television movie that year. My younger sister, who watched the broadcast with her, remembered that "Zelda was furious that Shelley Winters had been cast as the mother, because she was a big weepy, emotional actress and Zelda had written the mother as a cold, thin woman."[45]

The movie of *A Death of Innocence* focused on the mother-and-bad-daughter story, largely omitting the parallel drama Zelda had constructed around the relationship between the Jewish lawyer who takes the young woman's case and his rebellious son. The book actually begins with Marvin Hirsch frantically searching among the hippies in Greenwich Village for his son Jonathan, who has walked out of the family Passover Seder and disappeared. Whereas the novel's mother-daughter conflict seems rather contrived—many girls are spoiled by their parents without growing up to commit murders—the drama in the Hirsch family captures something of the atmosphere of the 1960s, when even some of Zelda's grandchildren, like her fictional teenager, experimented with drugs and argued with their parents, telling them, as her character Jonathan does, "if you want to communicate, why don't you try listening to me for a change?" Later in the book, the boy expresses his resentment at having to enroll in college because of "the draft. That war. My generation's in a bind, the whole Establishment."[46]

The story of the Hirsch family also gave Zelda an opportunity to write about the tensions involved in intermarriage; as she was working on the novel, her son Roy, having divorced his first Gentile wife, married another Catholic woman, "going into another inter-marriage, repeating the pattern of the added tension," as Zelda lamented to my parents.[47] The fictional Marvin Hirsch is married to a Christian woman. When he finds himself obligated to host a Passover seder for his extended family, after the death of an older brother who had performed that function, his son attacks him for his hypocrisy: "To pretend you are Jews. Put on a show for a pack of relations we don't see from one year to the next." Hirsch wonders if his son has inherited antisemitic attitudes from his mother. Hirsch himself "was aware that, like most Jews, his skin was thin, his arrogance defensive, and in the pit of his stomach was a tight knot of dread. For he knew that no matter how decently you conducted your personal life . . . no matter how much success and professional prestige you achieved, you weren't safe from the slur and the slap, the scourge of ancient canards." But his own family drama ends on a positive note, even though he fails to persuade the jury of his client's innocence. When he returns home after the end of the trial, having stayed out late drinking with his law partners to assuage his sense of defeat, he finds his son on the phone, calling area hospitals in fear that something bad had happened to his father. Despite his frustration with the outcome of the trial, the father finds himself "experiencing the small victory of his family's solicitude" and realizes that, unlike the murderous daughter he had defended in court, his son understands that his father's strictures are a way of showing his love for his child.[48]

Having written a novel dealing with contemporary issues, Zelda then turned back to the past again, but with an up-to-date twist. *Dear Once*, the final publication in a fiction-writing career that spanned nearly four decades, was, like *Herman Had Two Daughters*, the saga of an East

European Jewish immigrant family. The title came from the misspelled salutation Zelda's father, Harry Feinberg, had used in his letters to relatives, but the novel's plot had little in common with the actual Feinberg family. By this time, I was old enough for Zelda to discuss her writing plans with me, and I remember her telling me that her story was inspired by a newspaper story about a famous Broadway actor, one of the Barrymores, who had died in his mistress's bed. "What did they tell the children?" Zelda had asked herself.

With that ending in mind, she constructed a story about a young Jewish woman, Mildred (Millie) Samuelson, roughly her own age, who is swept off her feet into marriage with a charming actor, Jay Bernstein, a character with some traits in common with Noel Airman, the male protagonist of Herman Wouk's *Marjorie Morningstar*. Jay, who eventually makes a Hollywood career under the name of James Burns, proves to be chronically unfaithful, but Millie, out of motives that Zelda never convincingly conveys, remains loyal to him and raises their two children in ignorance not only of their father's affairs but of their parents' Jewish origins. This is possible because the couple make their home in Los Angeles, where they are visited only on rare occasions by relatives. Despite Millie's distance from her *mishpoche*, the reader is kept informed on the lives of numerous members of the clan whom her Uncle Reuben, the self-appointed head of the family, refers to as his "dear once," the phrase used by Zelda's father, Harry Feinberg. Millie cannot separate herself from them because she feels responsible for the sad fate of one of them, her Aunt Daisy. As a ten-year-old child, Millie had blurted out the secret of Aunt Daisy's affection for Reuben Samuelson's young brother-in-law Ben. Unwilling to approve the match, Reuben and his wife force Daisy into an arranged marriage with an Orthodox Jewish man from a wealthy family and fix Ben up with a cold and snobbish bride from another rich family.

Dear Once appeared in 1975, the same year that saw the publication of Susan Brownmiller's *Against Our Will*, a classic feminist denunciation of "rape culture." Despite her generally disparaging attitude toward 1970s feminism—"she doesn't approve of the women's movement's attacks on men and the dropping of family responsibilities," an Associated Press interview reported—Zelda's novel reflected the period's new outspokenness about the sexual abuse of women.[49] The depiction of Jay Bernstein's infidelities was not particularly daring, but other episodes in Millie's life went far beyond anything Zelda would have ventured to put in her novels in the 1940s and 1950s. The full extent of the tragedy of her Aunt Daisy's marriage is made clear when Daisy's loathsome husband corners the young Millie in a darkened hallway. "He raised my skirt. I wriggled, squirmed, and tried to pull away. One hand held my shoulder tightly; the other, with a swift and sudden motion, opened up his pants. And he pushed a swollen penis hard against my body." Such episodes were certainly not unknown in earlier periods—my mother recalled one of her cousins telling her how her dentist uncle had exposed himself while treating her teeth—but they were not discussed in public. In Zelda's novel, Millie and the reader are spared any further encounters with the perpetrator when he is caught molesting young girls at Coney Island and chased out into the water, where he drowns. The episode jolted several reviewers, and should have made it clear to others that the book was anything but a sentimental re-creation of early twentieth-century Jewish life.[50]

Zelda went on to depict the effect of this traumatic experience on her main character's married life. She begins to sleep with Jay before their marriage, but "my body found no pleasure, though at his bidding, I spread my thighs and pretended to welcome him." Her frigidity is one of the things that drives him to pursue other women; in their Hollywood mansion, they sleep in separate beds. But, in an illustration of one of the themes that feminist writers such as Brownmiller were exploring at the time, Jay is depicted as using his masculine privilege as a weapon against his wife. After she interrupts him in bed in her own home with another woman during a drunken party, he takes out his anger on her. "One thing led to another. Now to this, my drunken husband raped me in my bed." Rather than apologizing the next morning, he tells her, "You had it coming, pet. Long time overdue. . . . I'm not in the priesthood, Mrs. B. No vow of celibacy."[51]

Even though *Dear Once* thus depicted a marriage at the antipodes from the egalitarian partnership Zelda had described in her autobiography, the novel was not intended as a feminist tract. Even after Jay has beaten and raped her, Millie insists to herself that "it was plausible—I didn't discount it—that, in his own way, my husband loved me." In addition to her sense of guilt about her inability to respond to his sexual desires, she acquires a new sense of guilt after one of her East Coast relatives arrives in Los Angeles and persuades her husband to host a fundraiser for the Spanish Loyalists in their home. Jay and Millie even provide overnight lodging for the Comintern agent who supervises the affair, an echo of an episode in Zelda's own life during the years when she and Louis were doing publicity work for the Spanish cause. At the time, many other Hollywood actors and writers shared these sentiments, but, as Zelda herself had feared once the political atmosphere changed, "being an anti-Fascist in 1936 would make you anti-American in 1947."[52] The husband of Millie's best Hollywood friend denounces Jay as a Communist sympathizer and his career is ruined. When Jay is summoned to testify before a congressional committee, Millie stands by him and takes her son with her to attend the hearing. When Jay states his original name, Bernstein, rather than the name under which his son has always known him, the son is suddenly confronted both with the realization that he is Jewish and with the existence of antisemitism, which Millie has to hurriedly try to explain to him.

Published a few months before Lillian Hellman's celebrated memoir of the McCarthy period, *Scoundrel Time*, this episode in *Dear Once* was Zelda's most extended treatment of the politics of that era. She had never been harassed herself, despite the involvement with the Spanish Loyalist cause that she mentioned in her autobiography, but memories of the McCarthy period still angered her. The main target of *Dear Once*, however, was neither abusive husbands nor rabid anti-Communists, but rather the extended Jewish families evoked by the book's title. In sharp contrast to Irving Howe's *World of Our Fathers*, a best-seller about the East European Jewish immigration that came out around the same time and captivated readers with its sentimental portrayal of a lost world, Zelda's novel emphasized the stifling atmosphere of Jewish family life. In her narrative, not only parents but uncles, aunts, and cousins interfere freely in each other's affairs, imposing their prejudices about money and status and ignoring individual desires. Aided by his wife, Millie's Uncle

Reuben, who dreams of binding the family together in a "Family League" like the one Harry Feinberg had had Zelda propose to their relatives in 1920, leaves a trail of emotional wreckage throughout the story, ruining the lives of his sister, Daisy, his wife's brother, Ben, and Ben's son. Millie's stuffed-shirt cousin Karl never forgives her for ignoring his warning about Jay Bernstein's character and cuts off relations with several of his own brothers because of political differences. Jay's own wealthy family shuns Millie and their children. At the end of the book, as she fights off Karl's bid to dictate Jay's funeral arrangements, Millie thinks bitterly of all the ways in which "those loving people Uncle Reuben called dear once" have soured her life. The unimpressed reviewer for the Kirkus service, who called it "one of those sincerely sentimental books that other landswomen will enjoy," certainly misled readers who were looking for anything that could be called "heartwarming."[53]

Like Zelda's earlier novels, her trio of late-life publications were avowedly middlebrow literature. She may have crossed paths with the likes of Roth and Kazin at Yaddo, but she had no ambition to compete with them for literary glory. In contrast to the four "serious" novels she had published between 1945 and 1951, her last three novels did not have overtly positive messages for their readers. Hardened by her own difficult experiences during the "golden age" of American Jewish life in the 1950s and early 1960s, Zelda now created female characters—Jessie Weiss, Elizabeth Cameron, and Millie Burns—forced to confront incomprehension and hostility, even within their own families.

A book talk about *Dear Once* gave Zelda a final chance to deliver her thoughts about her own life and the state of the world to a live audience. Much of what she said repeated things she had said many times before, such as her lament that the Jewish community no longer had leaders of the stature of Jacob Schiff, Louis Marshall, or Stephen Wise, but she was still observing the world around her and making new connections with her own experiences. "I marched in suffrage parades in my teens and was sure the millennium had come when women got the vote," she said. "A fortnight ago, I voted again for women's rights and the cause was lost," referring to the defeat of an equal rights amendment on the New York ballot. "I shared the triumph of Israel at the U.N. in New York, the day

Figure 7.1. Zelda Popkin on her final book tour (1976): In 1976, when Zelda gave a lecture to promote her last novel, *Dear Once,* in Saint Louis, a photographer captured her vivid personality.

partition was voted," she recalled, but "last July I shared the fear that swept Jerusalem when a booby-trapped refrigerator blew up in Zion Square." She feared that American Jews had become too comfortable and secure. She may even have been thinking of me when she mentioned "a young man, brilliant, a fellowship student at a leading university," who had asked her, "Why are you so emotional about Hitler and that period? It's ancient history, isn't it?" (If I did express this sentiment to my grandmother during my student days, I hope I have made up for it by teaching courses on the Holocaust at the University of Kentucky for nearly 40 years.) Even as she denied that her novels were autobiographical, she admitted, "I am completely fascinated by all this—by steps by which we came from there to here, the twistings and turnings of our passage from the Jewish family that knew its purposes and served its brothers' needs, to a groping and bewildered upward mobile mass of Jewish Americans." Declining to give her audience any prognostication about the future, she concluded by telling them that, in spite of the frustrations she had identified, "we have no choice except to go back, start fresh and open new doors."[54]

As her 1975 speech shows, Zelda was convinced that her late-life novels had managed to highlight some of the period's big questions: the inability of American Jews to define a positive project for themselves once they had achieved material prosperity; the conflict of generations that was particularly evident in the 1960s but that, as her stories showed, had existed in own youth as well; and the difficulties facing women who aspired to have careers, happy marriages, or simply to succeed as mothers. Despite the streak of pessimism that runs through Zelda's last three novels, they also convey one positive message: rather than sinking into depression or unrelieved bitterness after her long years of misery in the 1950s and 1960s, my grandmother did indeed create a second chance for herself. Even in her seventies, she could still connect with readers and draw them into the stories she wove.

Epilogue

In 1974, a telephone-service outage in Manhattan cut off communication between Zelda and my parents for several days. Once she was assured that her mother-in-law was safe, my mother wrote a short character sketch:

> *She is a 76 year old woman with lots of nerve, not to say chutzpah. When she visits us in La Jolla, she gives the Pacific Ocean a very cool nod and complains because the New York Times is not around to accompany her morning coffee. She scoffs at the news and radio and t.v. because it is not relevant, to New York, that is, and she persists in resubscribing to New York Magazine for us because she thinks that even renegades like us need its special salt and wisdom. She is also a professional writer and extremely verbal in her rationales for staying snugly in Stuyvesant Town in New York where crime and filth surround her but where she is near everything she needs and besides she doesn't get around that much anymore. Mostly, with advanced years, a minor heart condition and whatever toll 60 years of smoking four packs a day can do to one, she sticks pretty close to her 1-bedroom apartment which is furnished with books, magazines, radio, t.v., ash trays and perhaps, most important, two telephones which the phone company has equipped with amplifiers for a lady whose hearing is rapidly disappearing.*[1]

My mother's description captures the grandmother I remember from her last years. She did not exactly mellow with age—one of her regular remarks to me was, "one good thing about getting older is that you don't have to be nice to people you don't like"—and she was still capable of provoking a family crisis, as when she threatened to boycott an awards ceremony at which my father was honored by Columbia University in 1977 because she had gotten it into her head that my mother had arranged for her own sister to be given a better seat than Zelda herself. She made a trip to Israel in 1975 to visit her sister Helen and renew her acquaintance with the country, her first visit there since the publication of *Quiet Street*, but it was not a success. She fought with Helen about old issues from their childhood; found the Western Wall, which had been in Jordanian hands during her earlier trips, less impressive than she had expected; and judged the Israelis "provincial and trivial and unaware of what democracy is."[2] In her letters to my parents, complaints about the indignities of old age replaced her laments about financial problems: in addition to her hearing, she had problems with her vision and numerous other aches and pains.

Even after the publication of *Dear Once*, when Zelda was seventy-seven, however, she still had ambitions to continue writing. Her routine, she explained to me, was simple: "I get up, I sit down at my typewriter at 9 a.m., and I stay there until 1 p.m. Then, whether I've written ten pages or one line, I stop, pour myself a double scotch, and take the rest of the day off." In the last years before her death, she was still working away on another novel with a Jewish theme, a story "about the parallel lives of two adopted war orphans, one raised in Israel one in the U.S., the Israeli one having first been rejected by the prospective well-to-do American family because he cried the whole night that they first took him," as my mother summarized the plot. Unfortunately, several publishers rejected the book, which she never finished. Had she been able to complete it, this project would have brought together all of her major concerns: the impact of the Holocaust, the shortcomings of American Jewish life, and the challenge represented by Israel. Zelda still adamantly defended the identity as an author that she had constructed for herself over so many years. When someone sent her a copy of *Weightwatchers Magazine*, which had committed the faux pas of publishing a story about an overweight woman with Zelda's name in 1981, she wrote the editor an angry letter, protesting that the piece "hold[s] me up to ridicule, which we professionals who write fiction are careful to avoid," and demanding an apology.[3]

Zelda always livened up when she was around other people. The younger novelist Gail Godwin, who overlapped with Zelda at Yaddo on one of the several later stays she was able to make there, remembered "exchang[ing] a bit of shoptalk over our sandwiches and oatmeal cookies," as Zelda "confided cheerfully that she could never live long enough to translate all of her rich fund of memories and experience of people into fiction."[4] She thoroughly enjoyed the eightieth birthday party my mother and other relatives organized for her in 1978. When I took advantage of Zelda's couch in her last years, she would wait up for me to come home, eager to trounce me at Scrabble, cackling happily that "it's the little ones that make the big ones" as she piled up extra points by making multiple words on a single play. I would watch the cigarette in her mouth, planning to announce that I needed to go to bed when she finished it, but she was always too quick for me: before I had noticed, she would have a new "coffin nail" started. "They're my life insurance," she said: she did not want to end up in a retirement home, as her parents had. As her health problems mounted, she finally agreed to try going to live with my uncle Roy and his second wife in Maryland, but she kept the lease on her New York apartment in case she didn't like the arrangement. She died peacefully in her sleep two weeks after the start of the experiment.

Zelda had dreamed of maintaining a posthumous presence in her beloved New York City by leaving her literary papers to the New York Public Library. Unfortunately, the library declined her gift, informing her heirs that they did not consider her important enough to merit inclusion in their collection. My mother discovered the Howard Gotlieb Twentieth-Century American Authors Collection in the Boston University Library, which was happy to accept the donation and where I have done much of the research for this account of her life. Zelda left few other tangible traces of her life behind. Burglars had stolen most of her jewelry some years before her death, and she had given away most of her small collection of art. Material possessions had never much concerned her, and the small apartments she occupied for the last forty years of her life did not give her space for many acquisitions. What she treasured were stories: the stories of her own life that she loved to tell and retell, and the stories she had turned into books.

Zelda Popkin died just as academic scholars were beginning to develop their own stories about the epoch of American Jewish history through which she had lived and to which she had contributed. Deborah Dash Moore's foundational monograph, *At Home in America*, which described the Bronx neighborhoods in which Zelda had spent the first half of her adulthood, was published in 1982, just a few months before the end of my grandmother's life. Since then, excellent scholarship has illuminated many of the other multiple contexts in which Zelda moved: the world of small-town Jewry in which she grew up, the atmosphere of political and sexual experimentation in the New York City to which she moved as a young woman, the public relations business in which she worked, the controversies about child-rearing to which she contributed, the growth of the American Jewish fundraising world with which she was connected for much of her life, the struggle against antisemitism in which she took part, the impact of the Second World War on women, the role of American Jews in the popularization of psychology for the masses, American Jews' reactions to the Holocaust and the birth of Israel, and the revival of interest in the American Jewish past that made her last novels successful.

My grandmother experienced all these developments as part of a unique generation: the first cohort of American-born children of the "Great Migration" of Jews from eastern Europe, and the first cohort of American women to have the right to vote. She and her contemporaries, the first generation of American Jews not to be continually faced with new arrivals bringing older traditions with them from the Old World, created the distinctive culture of modern American Jewry. She and other women her age were "emancipated" but discovered that achieving equality between the sexes was an ongoing challenge. Zelda's story shows how all these different currents flowed together over the decades from the First World War to the Reagan era, and how one articulate American Jewish woman saw them affecting her own life. She had her own understanding of what her life had been, and she told it in many forms: in private letters, in her stories and novels, and in her autobiography. If I have chosen to retell her story in my own way, it is because situating her experiences and writing in the broader perspective provided by historical scholarship gives them new meaning. Through her experiences and the way she depicted them, we gain a better understanding of what challenges American Jews and American women of her generation faced and why they reacted to them as they did.

Zelda's life and her writings reflect the ways in which her generation of American Jews were both "at home in America," as the title of Deborah Dash Moore's book put it, and yet never entirely at ease, either with their country or their Jewish inheritance. To the end of her life, Zelda was never entirely confident that she had seen the last of antisemitism or that the liberal political values she espoused were firmly entrenched. The election of Donald Trump, who was launching his career in New York City just as she was reaching the end of her life in the 1970s, would have appalled her but not surprised her. As her final novels demonstrated, she was also less than confident in the future of Jews and Judaism. As the debates between the two main characters in her late-life novel *Herman Had Two Daughters* showed, she saw the issues facing American Jews clearly, but she could never really make up her mind about where she herself stood on them. Her late-life novels also showed her keen awareness of the problems that still beset even the most determined and energetic American women.

The fate of Judaism in her own family reflected Zelda's own ambivalences. As she herself said in her autobiography, she made no effort to transmit any kind of meaningful Jewish heritage to her own children. Having assumed that the universalist values she espoused were fully compatible with Jewish identity, she could hardly complain when one of her sons married a Gentile, and none of her five grandchildren married a Jew. Her own way of being Jewish had little to do with the idiosyncratic way in which her younger son, my father, found his own way of identifying with Judaism, through the study of the interactions of descendants of Spanish and Portuguese exiles of the sixteenth and seventeenth centuries with their Christian milieu. He made a number of trips to Israel and developed a lively interest in the country's politics, but he kept his distance from American Jewish life. My father's interest in Judaism in turn has little in common with my own, more conventional, status as a member of a Conservative Jewish congregation and a teacher of university courses on the Holocaust and on modern Jewish history.

Zelda was more successful in inspiring her descendants with her ambition to write. I grew up staring at the shelf in our home that contained her publications. Zelda lived long enough for me to present her with a copy of my first academic monograph, published in 1980 and full of the footnotes she disdained. I had ignored her often-repeated advice to "never publish anything that isn't going to make you some money," and I imagine she was a little disappointed: during my college years, when I wrote for campus newspapers, she had hoped that I would wind up on the *New York Times*. Nevertheless, she was proud to have formed a dynasty of writers. She displayed copies of my father's books in her living room, and in the mid-1960s, when my uncle Roy joined my father by writing several books, Zelda commented happily, "It is a bit extraordinary, I think, that all of us have the writing skill. Almost as if it was a genetic trait."[5] Eventually, my two sisters also became published authors, and although I have never made it into the *New York Times*, my oldest son, whom Zelda met when he was one year old, has had several articles in her favorite daily newspaper.[6]

In 2021, as I was finishing the writing of this book, two excellent biographies of American women who were roughly my grandmother's contemporaries were published. Dvora Hacohen's *To Repair a Broken World: The Life of Henrietta Szold* recounts the life of a Jewish saint, the founder of Hadassah; Debby Applegate's *Madam: The Biography of Polly Adler, Icon of the Jazz Age* tells the story of flamboyant Jewish sinner, the most notorious brothelkeeper of her day. Henrietta Szold set her sights on making the world, especially the Jewish world, a better place; Adler accepted the world, including some of its most disagreeable aspects, as she found it. Like most human beings, Zelda Popkin fell somewhere between these two extremes. She cared deeply about certain causes and hoped to have an impact on public issues, but she was not prepared to sacrifice her personal life for the sake of others, as Szold did. She was too much of an individualist and too attracted to the world of men to be at home in the world of synagogue sisterhoods and women's clubs through which, as recent scholarship has shown, middle-class American Jewish women collectively exercised a real influence on public life. An acute critic of the excesses of Jewish charitable fundraising, she rarely acknowledged the positive accomplishments it made possible.

No prude about sexual matters—she described the public relations business she practiced for many years as "another trade in which your bedfellows are whoever picks up the tab"—and unembarrassed about occasionally flouting laws like Prohibition, Zelda nevertheless believed in family life and social order. As her detective novels show, she had no illusions about the incorruptibility of politicians or policemen, but she also recognized the necessity of governments and courts. In the years when, as Applegate describes, other women contributors to the *New Yorker* sometimes accompanied their male colleagues to Polly Adler's establishment, Zelda was home with her children. She had no illusions about the effects of prostitution on the ordinary women caught up in the sex trade. If she was present on the occasion in the mid-1930s when Adler was hauled up before her friend Anna Kross, Zelda would certainly not have had much sympathy for her.[7] Over the course of her life, Zelda met a number of the men who were clients of Adler's establishment, but she encountered them in the course of their public occupations, not during their nocturnal diversions.

How, then, should one describe the impact Zelda Popkin had on the world in which she lived? She did not create new institutions and save lives, as Szold did through Hadassah and her work with children escaping Hitler's Europe, and her life story does not pull back the curtain on behind-the-scenes aspects of her times, as Adler's story does. She was an observer of and a commentator on the world around her, but she aspired to be something more than that. She wanted to show that women could do whatever men could do, and that Jews could be full members of American society. She hoped to make a difference in the combat against antisemitism and she wanted to help consolidate American support for Israel. At the same time, she wanted to be an independent voice. In her later years, when American Jews seemed to be becoming too comfortable with their own past, Zelda reminded them of the family quarrels and the mistreatment of women that had characterized "the world of our fathers."

Zelda may not have had the impact on history of Henrietta Szold or Polly Adler, but she certainly had an impact on those who knew her. This book is one testimony to that impact; another is the life of my mother, Juliet Popkin. She never published a book, but when the time came for me to clean out the apartment where she lived in her later years, I discovered that she had been as dedicated to the written word as Zelda or any other member of our family. In the "Popkin Family Archive," from which I have drawn much of the documentation in this volume, the thirty notebooks of her diaries and the dozens of essays she wrote occupy twice as much space as my files on Zelda. Like Zelda, my mother was inspired by the events of her own life. She wrote about her childhood, her family, and the trips abroad that she made with my father. For many years, she documented in excruciating detail the agony of living with a husband who suffered from bipolar disorder. And she wrote about Zelda. It was she, rather than my father and my uncle, who put together the obituary that the family sent out when my grandmother died, and I have had a number of occasions to quote from a piece she titled "Yiches and Naches," an essay on Zelda that she probably composed shortly afterward. My mother saved many of Zelda's documents, and it was she who found a depository that would conserve Zelda's literary papers.

As a young woman, my mother explained in one of her autobiographical essays, she had dreamed of working in publishing, and Zelda's achievements fascinated her. "She let me read her manuscripts and offer suggestions and in general helped me to draw closer to the publishing world which seemed so glamorous and inviting," my mother recalled.[8] Unlike Zelda, she subordinated her own ambitions to the demands of my father's academic career and the obligations of raising her three children. By the early 1980s, once her youngest daughter had left home, she did start to publish short articles and book reviews in local newspapers. When my father retired and my parents settled in the Los Angeles suburb of Pacific Palisades, my mother finally got the chance to enter the publishing world that she had dreamed of participating in decades earlier. She created her own literary agency, and her first successful transaction was an arrangement to have Zelda's six murder mysteries from the early 1940s translated into German, where they have now been in print for nearly three decades. Over a period of twenty years, she shepherded more than forty other books to publication.

If my mother had written a more extensive memoir of her mother-in-law, she would not have needed to do all the reading in the scholarship about American Jewish history that I found necessary. Like Zelda, she was the daughter of a Jewish immigrant father, although her mother was born in the United States around the same time as Zelda. My mother knew about Jewish life in the Bronx in the interwar years because she grew up in an apartment just off the Grand Concourse. She had been a young woman during the Second World War, and her marriage to my father in 1944, when she was just nineteen, made her part of the cohort who opted for domesticity in the years that followed. The earliest of her unpublished essays in my files, written in the mid-1950s, shows her wrestling with the question of whether she had the right to pursue a career outside the home, as Zelda had. My mother would have had the advantage over me of having known Zelda over a much longer period of her life, from the late 1930s to her death. She knew much more about the relationship between Zelda and my father than I could understand from my child's perspective, and she saw the connections between the plots of Zelda's novels and Zelda's own life, even without the benefit of reading the correspondence between my grandmother and her editors that I have perused.

I regret that my mother left her essay "Yiches and Naches" unfinished. She never forgot my grandmother; she continued to entertain friends with her store of "Zelda stories" throughout her life. She chose, however, to put her energy into helping other authors get their books published, work that gave her great satisfaction. She often jokingly asked me when I was going to write something that she would be able to market, and I can imagine how delighted she would have been to try to find a publisher for this book about Zelda. We did collaborate in getting *Quiet Street*, Zelda's novel about Israel, reissued in 2002. Ironically, however, I could not have written this book as I have before my mother's gradual descent into dementia allowed me to begin going through her files, where I found documents such as the letters Zelda wrote from Europe and from Israel that my mother had forgotten decades earlier, as well as my mother's voluminous diaries and the unpublished essays from which I have drawn. No doubt a book about Zelda written by my mother would have been very different from what I have written. (Certainly it would have had fewer footnotes!) Nevertheless, I think of this biography as a continuation of the effort my mother began many years before I was even born: the effort to capture the essence of a complicated American Jewish woman who those who knew her could never forget.

ACKNOWLEDGMENTS

THIS BIOGRAPHY OF MY GRANDMOTHER IS THE OUTGROWTH OF A LIFE-time of curiosity about her life. In its present form, it owes a great deal to numerous scholars who have encouraged me to think of this project not just as an exercise in family history but as a contribution to knowledge and thinking about history and life-writing. Andrew Furman gave me my first opportunity to present an academic paper about Zelda Popkin at a conference on Jewish American Literary Studies at Florida Atlantic University in 1999, and my thoughts on the subject developed as a result of discussions at meetings of the Association for Jewish Studies; the International Auto/Biography Association; the Association pour l'auto-biographie; a conference on "Women and the Holocaust" at the University of South Carolina in 2013; the Groupe Sociétés, Religions, Laïcités; and presentations to my colleagues in the History Department and the Jewish Studies Program at the University of Kentucky.

When the conditions created by the COVID-19 pandemic in 2020 forced me to put aside other research projects, I took the opportunity to devote myself seriously to this project, and I quickly realized how much I needed to learn about American Jewish history, scholarship on women in American history and literature, and numerous other topics. I reached out to many colleagues, some of whom I already knew but others whom I have not had the opportunity to meet in person, and all were generous in providing encouragement and advice, via email, Zoom, and other media. I would like to thank Joyce Antler, Samantha Baskind, Jack Censer, Deborah Daley, Sebastiaan Faber, Leah Garrett, Emily Alice Katz, Carole Kessner, Rachel Kranson, Josh Lambert, Meg Lamme, Nadia Malinovich, Deborah Dash Moore, Pamela Nadell, Riv-Ellen

Prell, Karen Russell, Shelley Spector, Eric Smith, Ellen Umansky, Beth Wenger, and Stephen Whitfield for their willingness to answer questions and offer guidance. Melissa Klapper took the time to read the full manuscript and provide valuable suggestions. My old friends from graduate school, David and Rachel Biale and Fred Rosenbaum, have provided much-appreciated moral support, as have my University of Kentucky Jewish studies and history colleagues, particularly Dan Frank in the early phases of my work and Jan Fernheimer, Sheila Jelen, Karen Petrone, and Francie Chassen-López in recent years. My daughter-in-law, Ruth Popkin, found several crucial documents online.

Particularly under COVID-19 conditions, the support of librarians and archivists has been indispensable for my work. For more than twenty years, the staff of Boston University's Mugar Library's Special Collections Department have obliged me whenever I have asked them to "take my grandmother out of the vault" for me. At the Hebrew Union College Library, Abigail Bacon helped me track down Zelda Popkin's many contributions to the *American Hebrew* magazine, and Dana Herman of the American Jewish Archives found a folder of papers about Zelda's husband Louis Popkin of which I was completely unaware. Laura Harding from the Osterhout Free Library in Wilkes-Barre, Pennsylvania, forwarded me a number of articles from the city where Zelda attended high school. The University of Kentucky Library and especially its Interlibrary Loan department have also been indispensable.

Peter Bernstein, my agent, worked with dogged determination to find a publisher willing to take a chance on a "grandmother story." Research for this book was supported by the University of Kentucky's William T. Bryan Chair fund. Jon Sisk at Rowman & Littlefield has been willing to take a chance on a book that doesn't fit in any comfortable pigeonhole. Katherine Berlatsky, Sally Rinehart, Sarah Sichina, and Hannah Fisher have helped make the production process go smoothly.

I am also indebted to many relatives who provided documents and, sometimes, memories of Zelda Popkin. Thanks to my cousins Gail Ohnsman and Raymond Popkin for sharing papers and photographs inherited by their father, my uncle the late Roy Popkin; to my sister Sue Popkin, who read and commented on the whole manuscript; and to

Irma Megiddo, one of Zelda's favorite cousins. My father's cousin Henry Pinsker allowed me to quote from his own father William Pinsker's diary. My parents, Richard and Juliet Popkin, enjoyed discussing the first stages of my research twenty years ago. Neither of them lived to see the final product, but I cannot help considering my mother especially as a collaborator. Without her efforts to find a suitable home for Zelda's literary papers, this book could never have been written. In addition to the documents now preserved in the Mugar Library's Howard Gotlieb Twentieth-Century American Authors Collection, she kept a number of other files of Zelda's papers and publications. The unpublished sketches and essays she wrote about her mother-in-law have been another valuable source of information and inspiration.

Finally, I have to thank my grandmother herself, even though she never dreamed that her academic grandson, set on making a career by studying the French Revolution, would someday take on the task of writing about her life. She probably thought she had done enough in that regard by publishing her autobiography, *Open Every Door*, in 1956. Nevertheless, by preserving so many of her papers, as well as correspondence from other family members, she made it possible for me to take a fresh look at her life. Equally importantly, by inspiring me to become a writer, she encouraged me to develop the skills that have allowed me to carry out this project.

NOTES

INTRODUCTION

1 Zelda Popkin, speech to Detroit Book Fair, 13 November 1975, in Zelda Popkin Papers, Howard Gotlieb Twentieth-Century American Authors Collection, Boston University Library (hereafter ZP Papers, BU Library), box 11.

2 Joyce Antler, *The Journey Home: Jewish Women and the American Century* (New York: Free, 1997). For my first publication about Zelda Popkin's novels on the Holocaust and Israel, see Jeremy D. Popkin, "A Forgotten Forerunner: Zelda Popkin's Novels of the Holocaust and the 1948 War," *Shofar* 20 (2001): 36–60.

3 Zelda Popkin (hereafter ZP) to Richard and Juliet Popkin, 19 October 1953, in Popkin Family Archive (hereafter PFA).

4 Suzanne Selengut, "Quietly Ahead of Her Time," *Jerusalem Post*, 3 February 2006.

5 On Zelda Popkin's evolving attitudes toward the Holocaust, see Jeremy D. Popkin, "From Displaced Persons to Secular Saints: Holocaust Survivors, Jewish Identity, and Gender in the Writings of Zelda Popkin," *Studies in American Jewish Literature* 37, no. 1 (2018): 1–20.

6 Pierre Nora, "Entre mémoire et histoire," in *Les Lieux de mémoire*, t. 1 (Paris: Seuil, 1984), 1:xxxiii (my translation). For Nora's own venture into personal memoir, see Pierre Nora, *Jeunesse* (Paris: Gallimard, 2021). For my exploration of historians' memoirs, see Jeremy D. Popkin, *History, Historians and Autobiography* (Chicago: University of Chicago Press, 2005).

7 Bliss Broyard, *One Drop: My Father's Hidden Life—A Story of Race and Family Secrets* (New York: Back Bay, 2007); Daniel Mendelsohn, *The Lost: A Search for Six of Six Million* (New York: Harper, 2006); Mark Mazower, *What You Did Not Tell: A Father's Past and a Journey Home* (New York: Other, 2018); Modris Eksteins, *Walking Since Daybreak: A Story of Eastern Europe, World War II, and the Heart of Our Century* (Boston and New York: Houghton Mifflin, 1999). For an analysis of the genre of "family memoir," see Jeremy D. Popkin, "Family Memoir and Self-Discovery," *Life Writing* 12, no. 2 (2015): 127–38, reprinted in Paul Arthur, ed., *Border Crossings: Essays in Identity and Belonging* (Routledge, 2018).

8 This is acknowledged in the autobiographical essays by American Jewish historians collected in Jeffrey S. Gurock, ed., *Conversations with Colleagues: On Becoming a Jewish Historian* (Boston: Academic Studies, 2018).

9 Paul Murray Kendall, *The Art of Biography*, cited in Sara Alpern, Joyce Antler, Elisabeth Israels Perry, and Ingrid Winther Scobie, eds., *The Challenge of Feminist Biography* (Urbana: University of Illinois Press, 1992), 10.

10 The final edition of Richard H. Popkin's most influential book was *The History of Scepticism: From Savonarola to Bayle* (New York: Oxford University Press, 2003). He wrote and edited over forty other books and several hundred scholarly articles. For my own venture into autobiography, see Jeremy D. Popkin, "History, a Historian, and an Autobiography," *Rethinking History* 14 (2010): 387–300, reprinted in Alun Munslow, ed., *Authoring the Past: Writing and Rethinking History* (London: Routledge, 2013), 183–95.

11 "Introduction," in *Challenge of Feminist Biography*, 5, 2–3.

12 Significant biographies devoted to American Jewish women include Dianne Ashton, *Rebecca Gratz: Women and Judaism in Antebellum America* (Detroit: Wayne State University Press, 1997); Elisabeth Israels Perry, *Belle Moskowitz: Feminine Politics and the Exercise of Power in the Age of Alfred E. Smith* (New York: Oxford University Press, 1987); Julie G. Gilbert, *Ferber: A Biography of Edna Ferber and Her Circle* (New York: Doubleday, 1978); Brooke Kroeger, *Fannie: The Talent for Success of Writer Fannie Hurst* (New York: Random House, 1999); Dvora Hacohen, *To Repair a Broken World: The Life of Henrietta Szold* (Cambridge, MA: Harvard University Press, 2021); Carole S. Kessner, *Marie Syrkin: Values Beyond the Self* (Hanover, NH: Brandeis University Press, 2008); and Debby Applegate, *Madam: The Biography of Polly Adler, Icon of the Jazz Age* (New York: Doubleday, 2021).

CHAPTER 1

1 Birth certificate, marriage license, notarized affidavit from Harry Feinberg, dated Wilkes-Barre, Pennsylvania, 31 May 1945, in PFA.

2 ZP to Richard and Juliet Popkin, 11 January 1955, in PFA; Hasia R. Diner, *Roads Taken: The Great Jewish Migrations to the New World and the Peddlers Who Forged the Way* (New Haven, CT: Yale University Press, 2018); Zelda F. Popkin, "The Jewish Covered Wagon," *B'nai B'rith Magazine* XLI, no. 11 (August 1927): 453–55.

3 Zelda Popkin, *Open Every Door* (New York: E. P. Dutton, 1956), 31.

4 Harry Feinberg, "The Story of My Life. Uri Ben Aharen Yitzchock Feinberg Harry Feinberg March 15, 1954," and "My Life's History Beginning from 1871 to 1955 Adar 17, 5631," in PFA.

5 Harry Feinberg, "History of Harry Feinberg and Annie S. Feinberg," in PFA; Popkin, *Open Every Door*, 38.

6 Harry Feinberg, "My Life's History"; Lee Shai Weissbach, *Jewish Life in Small-Town America: A History* (New Haven, CT: Yale University Press, 2005); Popkin, *Open Every Door*, 24.

7 ZP, Detroit Book Fair lecture, ZP Papers, BU Library, box 11; letter signed Noel Bullock to Feinberg family, 7 January 1907, in PFA; Popkin, *Open Every Door*, 26–27.

8 Juliet Popkin, "Yiches and Naches," unpublished manuscript, and interview with Helen Rossi Koussewitsky, 1981, in PFA.

9 Popkin, *Open Every Door*, 35, 40, 39. On Jewish immigrants' commitment to educating their daughters, see Melissa Klapper, *Jewish Girls Coming of Age in America, 1860–1920* (New York: New York University Press, 2005), 47.

10 Popkin, *Open Every Door*, 41, 44.

11 Online biography of physicist David Joseph Bohm, by F. David Peat, at http://www.fdavidpeat.com/interviews/bohm.htm; "The Hero of Tel Aviv," *Wilkes-Barre Times Leader*, 15 August 2010, interview with Lou Lenart.

12 Popkin, *Open Every Door*, 44–45; *Wilkes-Barre Times Leader*, 2 November 1915.

13 Her magazine articles about Wilkes-Barre include "That's A Strike," *Nation* 115 (23 August 1922): 185–86; "A Barn for School," *Survey* 49 (15 November 1922): 253–55; "An Experiment in Education," *American Hebrew* 113 (28 December 1923); "Abdication of King Coal," *Nation* 126 (4 January 1928): 11–12; "Gone With the Flood," *New Yorker* (24 October 1936): 32, 34, 36–39; "Not to Reason Why," *New Yorker* (6 March 1937); "Annals of Crime: Sing a Song of Homicide," *New Yorker* (30 October 1937): 46–56; and a novella, "Bitter Bondage," *American Magazine* 149 (May 1950): 52–58. Her detective novel, *Dead Man's Gift* (Philadelphia: J. B. Lippincott, 1941) and the first half of *Herman Had Two Daughters* are set in Pennsylvania towns that are modeled on Wilkes-Barre, although they are given different names.

14 Popkin, *Open Every Door*, 53, 52.

15 Edna Ferber, *A Peculiar Treasure* (New York: Doubleday, Doran, 1938), 6, 103; Julien Gorbach, *The Notorious Ben Hecht: Iconoclastic Writer and Militant Zionist* (West Lafayette, IN: Purdue University Press, 2019), 9; Popkin, *Open Every Door*, 17. In 1999, the *Times Leader* commemorated Zelda's breaking of "Wilkes-Barre's gender barrier in journalism." Tara Baxter, "A Woman of Substance," *Times Leader,* 27 June 1999.

16 Popkin, *Open Every Door*, 17; Joy Stilley, "Zelda Popkin Lives Life to the Fullest," *Bridgeport [Connecticut] Sunday Post*, 9 November 1975; "Former Local Woman is Editor of Jerusalem Post," *Wilkes-Barre Times Leader*, 3 April 1971. The *Times Leader* did not put bylines on its reporters' stories, so Zelda's contributions cannot be identified, with the exception of a story, "Quarantined Leper Plays Card Game at a Neighbor's House" (3 October 1916), whose genesis she described in *Open Every Door*, 86–90.

17 Popkin, *Open Every Door*, 20, 70.

18 Popkin, *Open Every Door*, 95. On Louis Weitzenkorn, see Abraham Schachner, "Editor and Playwright: Concerning Louis Weitzenkorn, Latest Addition to Editors of New York City Newspapers and Author of a Broadway Play," *Jewish Tribune*, 11 October 1929, 3. Sam Hoffenstein (1890–1947) became a successful Hollywood screenwriter in the 1930s.

19 Popkin, *Open Every Door*, 100, 104. On Hillquit's mayoral campaign, see Zosa Szajkowksi, "The Jews and New York City's Mayoralty Election of 1917," *Jewish Social Studies* 32, no. 4 (1970): 286–306; and Ross J. Wilson, *New York and the First World War* (Farnham: Ashgate, 2014), 177–78.

20 Popkin, *Open Every Door*, 102–3, 107–8; *Microcosm* 53 (1913): 174–75. Louis Popkin's name also appears in the list of "Students of the Evening Session," 173.

21 Paul A. Peters, undated clipping, probably from *Jewish Ledger*, "Between You and Me." The Cowens celebrated their golden wedding anniversary in 1937, so the

silver-wedding dinner described would have taken place in 1912. Jacob Schiff was a banker and prominent Jewish community leader; Cyrus Adler, a scholar of Middle Eastern antiquity, became chancellor of the Jewish Theological Seminary; the banker Felix Warburg was another prominent philanthropist and community leader. Solomon Schechter was the first president of the Jewish Theological Seminary. Cyrus Sulzberger was a leading philanthropist and the father of Arthur Hays Sulzberger, longtime publisher of the *New York Times*. On Cowen, see the obituary in the *New York Times*, 21 April 1943.

22 Israel Zangwill, letter of 29 December 1915, in ZP Papers, BU Library, box 9.

23 Louis Popkin himself described the origins of the Jewish Welfare Board in an article in the *American Hebrew:* "The Problem of the Jewish Youth in America: An Interview with Justice Irving Lehman," *American Hebrew* 109 (8 July 1921): 196ff. On the formation and character of the Joint Distribution Committee, see Jaclyn Granick, *International Jewish Humanitarianism in the Age of the Great War* (Cambridge: Cambridge University Press, 2021), 29–36.

24 Applegate, *Madam*, 89–92.

25 Popkin, *Open Every Door*, 106; *Wilkes-Barre Times Leader*, 30 June 1917.

26 Zelda Feinberg, "Hope Springs Eternal—Seeing 'Papa' Joffre," *Wilkes-Barre Times Leader*, 12 May 1917; *Scranton Republican*, 31 December 1917; William Pinsker diary, 2 January 1918, cited with permission of Henry Pinsker.

27 Popkin, *Open Every Door*, 106; Jewish Welfare Board archives, n.d. Louis Popkin's salary was $200 a month.

28 Popkin, *Open Every Door*, 110; Pinsker diary, n.d. but late 1919, cited with permission of Henry Pinsker.

29 *Wilkes-Barre Times Leader*, 31 October 1919; Popkin, *Open Every Door*, 118; letter to Feinberg family relatives, 15 January 1920, in ZP Papers, BU Library, box 7.

CHAPTER 2

1 Zelda Popkin, *Open Every Door*, 110.

2 Zelda Feinberg, "Home Comforts for the Soldiers," *American Hebrew* 104 (8 November 1918): 15–16; "The East Side Emerges," *American Hebrew* 104 (15 November 1918): 27.

3 Popkin, *Open Every Door*, 117–18; *New Yorker* (19 December 1925): 32. On "Heterodoxy," see Sandra Adickes, *To Be Young Was Very Heaven: Women in New York Before the First World War* (New York: St. Martin's, 1997).

4 "Leah Morton," [Elizabeth G. Stern], *I am a Woman—and a Jew*, ed. Ellen M. Umansky (New York: Markus Wiener, 1986 [orig. 1926]), 200, 202. When it was published, the novel was widely assumed to be a memoir, but in real life its author was married to a Jew, not to a Gentile. After the republication of the book in 1986, evidence emerged indicating that the author was probably a Christian child adopted by an Orthodox Jewish family, adding an additional layer of complications to its interpretation. See Ellen M. Umansky, "Representations of Jewish Women in the Works and Life of Elizabeth Stern," *Modern Judaism* 13, no. 2 (1993): 165–76.

5 Popkin, *Open Every Door*, 110, 114–15. On the early history of the American public relations business, see Larry Tye, *The Father of Spin: Edward L. Bernays and the Birth of Public Relations* (New York: Crown, 1998).

6 Popkin, *Open Every Door*, 114, 115. Schiff went to Versailles as the representative of the American Jewish Committee. See Naomi W. Cohen, *Jacob H. Schiff: A Study in American Jewish Leadership* (Hanover, NH: Brandeis University Press, 1999), 240. I have been unable to confirm Zelda's story in the Jacob Schiff papers in the American Jewish Archives.

7 Popkin, *Open Every Door*, 114, 116; Jeffrey S. Gurock, *Jews in Gotham: New York Jews in a Changing City, 1920–2010* (New York: New York University Press, 73–74. On Abraham Fromenson, see the obituary published by the Jewish Telegraphic Agency, 14 April 1935, which mentioned his collaboration with the Popkins on "many fund-raising campaigns." Unlike the Popkins, Fromenson was active in the Zionist movement. See A. H. Fromenson, "The Real Causes of the Zionist Controversy," *Jewish Tribune* (6 June 1928): 2, 11. Doris Fleischman Bernays, *A Wife Is Many Women* (New York: Crown, 1956), 171. On Fleischman's role in the Bernays publicity firm, see Susan Henry, "Anonymous in Her Own Name: Public Relations Pioneer Doris E. Fleischman," *Journalism History* 23, no. 2 (1997): 50–62.

8 Bernhard Lichtenberg, cited in Heywood Broun, *Christians Only: A Study in Prejudice* (New York: Vanguard, 1931), 240; "An Advertising Man," "Personal Experience With Prejudice," *Jewish Tribune* 97 (15 August 1930): 2.

9 Press release, 1929, in Popkin Family Archive; ZP, lecture to Detroit Book Fair, 13 November 1975, in ZP Papers, BU Library, box 1. Louis Popkin's published articles with Jewish leaders include "Who's Who in Philanthropy—1920," *American Hebrew* 108 (3 December 1920): 65; "The Problem of the Jewish Youth in America. An Interview with Justice Irving Lehman," *American Hebrew* 109 (8 July 1921): 196; and "The Future of the Jew in America, interview with Nathan J. Miller," *American Hebrew* 115 (31 October 1924): 779, which also appeared in the *American Israelite*, 30 October 1924. On the Popkins' work for Temple Emanu-El, see documents in American Jewish Archives, Mss. Col. 11, "Louis Popkin."

10 Arthur Garfield Hays, *City Lawyer: The Autobiography of a Law Practice* (New York: Simon and Schuster, 1942), 177–78 (Hays refers to "Lionel Popkin," but it is hardly likely that there were two Popkins engaged in political publicity work in 1924); Kenneth Campbell MacKay, *The Progressive Movement of 1924* (New York: Columbia University Press, 1947), 70–71; Popkin, *Open Every Door*, 209–10.

11 Popkin, *Open Every Door*, 166–68; Louis Popkin to Earl Browder, 29 October 1935, in ZP Papers, BU Library, box 9.

12 Popkin, *Open Every Door*, 124; citation in Riv-Ellen Prell, *Fighting to Become Americans: Assimilation and the Trouble between Jewish Women and Jewish Men* (Boston: Beacon, 1999), 97; Pamela S. Nadell, *America's Jewish Women: A History from Colonial Times to Today* (New York: Norton, 2019), 162, 177. On Jewish women's involvement in social causes during this period, see Melissa R. Klapper, *Ballots, Babies, and Banners of Peace: American Jewish Women's Activism, 1890–1940* (New York: New York University Press, 2013).

13 Doris E. Fleischman, *An Outline of Careers for Women* (Garden City, NJ: Doubleday, Doran, 1928), 394.

14 Zelda Popkin, "The Jew and Aviation," *B'nai B'rith Magazine* XLI, no. 10 (July 1927), 417–18. An editorial in the same issue of the magazine insinuated that antisemitism was behind the accusations against Levine, an accusation echoed in an editorial in the *Jewish Tribune* (10 June 1927): 8. In later life, Levine was repeatedly accused of various forms of financial fraud. Nevertheless, he was remembered at his death in 1991 as "the first trans-Atlantic air passenger" (*New York Times*, 18 December 1991).

15 "Art: Three Aisles Over," *Outlook and Independent* 156 (26 November 1930): 502–3, 515–16; "Russia Goes to the Movies," *Outlook and Independent* 155 (28 May 1930): 129–31, 154–55; "Camera Explorers of the New Russia." *Travel* 58 (December 1931): p. 37–40, 52–54. On the vogue for Soviet cinema in these years, see Jon Wilkman, *Screening Reality: How Documentary Filmmakers Reimagined America* (New York: Bloomsbury, 2020), 81–82; and William Alexander, *Film on the Left: American Documentary Film from 1931 to 1942* (Princeton, NJ: Princeton University Press, 1981), 7–8, 21–22. It seems unlikely that Zelda, who was never attracted by communism, had actually seen many of the films she wrote about. She may have derived her information from her younger sister Helen, who had just returned from a stay in Russia at the beginning of 1930. Juliet Popkin, interview with Helen Rossi Koussewitsky, in PFA.

16 Rion Bercovici, *For Immediate Release* (New York: Sheridan House, 1937), 249, 252; Popkin, *Open Every Door*, 124; Louis Popkin, "Interesting People: Henry J. Gaisman, the Edison of the Safety Razor Field," *Jewish Tribune* 97 (29 August 1930): 4–5, 16.

17 "Shifters," *New York Times*, 25 March 1922; "Shifters No Longer Appeal to Flapper," *New York Times*, 26 March 1922; Ben Schott, "A Ponzi Scheme for Flappers," *New York Times*, 30 November 2012. For Popkin's account of the concoction of the Shifters, see *Open Every Door*, 130–33. The Popkins were not the only publicists who invented imaginary organizations for the benefit of their clients: on behalf of the tobacco industry, Edward Bernays created a phony group to promote the claim that smoking was good for the throat. Tye, *Father of Spin*, 35.

18 Zelda Feinberg, "Jewish Women with the A.E.F.," *American Hebrew* 104 (11 April 1919): 524, 544, 597; Zelda Popkin, "Women to 'Sell' Philanthropy," *American Hebrew* 107 (1920): 440; "Mother Love in Mean Streets," *American Hebrew* 110 (5 May 1922): 700; "Spotting 'Star-Dust,'" *American Hebrew* 108 (29 April 1921): 712; "Jewish Dolly Madisons," *American Hebrew* 109 (30 September 1921): 488, 514–15. For a critical reading of Zelda's article on Jewish women's role in philanthropy, see Beth S. Wenger, "Federation Men: The Masculine World of New York Jewish Philanthropy, 1880–1945," *American Jewish History* 101, no. 3 (2017): 392–94.

19 On the *American Hebrew*, see Yehezkel Wyszkowski, "'The American Hebrew': An Exercise in Ambivalence," *American Jewish History* 76, no. 3 (1987): 340–53, and Peter Levine, "The *American Hebrew* Looks at 'Our Crowd': The Jewish Country Club in the 1920s," *American Jewish History* 83, no. 1 (1995): 27–49. On Isaac Landman, see Michael Berenbaum, "Isaac Landman," *Encyclopedia Judaica*, 2nd ed., 12:472–3.

20 "The Week in Review," *American Hebrew* 117 (6 November 1925): 811; Rabbi Lee J. Levinger, "Shall Women Be Rabbis?," *American Hebrew* 111 (14 July 1922): 222.

21 *American Hebrew* 109 (July 1921): 249; and 114 (4 January 1924): 249. Myra May was probably the same person as Myra May Haas, an author of cookbooks published in the 1930s.

22 Letter in PFA. Wise made a regular habit of writing such letters to his friends' newborn babies. Melvin I. Urofsky, *A Voice That Spoke for Justice: The Life and Times of Stephen S. Wise* (Albany: State University of New York Press (SUNY), 1982), 81.

23 Zelda Popkin, "National Jewish Hospital for Consumptives," *American Israelite*, 22 August 1923, 1; "New York State Sisterhoods Outside of the Metropolis," *American Hebrew* 114 (4 January 1924): 236, 246; "The Caravan of Hope in Europe: A Regenerated People Sing Praises of Providence and O.R.T." *American Israelite*, 4 December 1924, 1; "Nearly Seventy Thousand Volumes in College Library," *American Israelite*, 22 October 1925, 5; "The Hebrew Union College Library is Leader of Jewish Learning," *American Israelite*, 19 August 1926, 1, 5.

24 "The Changeable Petticoat," *American Hebrew* 111 (14 July 1922): 221, 224, 228; "Curb Lizards," *American Hebrew* 112 (24 November 1922): 30, 32, 33, 34.

25 Review of Luigi Pirandello, *Three Plays, American Hebrew* 117 (3 July 1925): 281; "Romain Rolland and the Jews," *American Hebrew* 110 (7 April 1922): 542; review of Theodore Dreiser, *The Color of a Great City, American Hebrew* 114 (18 April 1924): 724; review of *My Musical Life*, by Walter Damrosch, *American Hebrew* 114 (29 February 1924): 473; review of *Lummox*, by Fannie Hurst, *American Hebrew* 113 (2 February 1923): 672–73. Zelda Popkin's reviews in the *American Hebrew* were usually signed with her initials, Z.F.P.

26 "Rachel as Viewed by a Writer of Her Day," *American Jewish World* (Minneapolis), 8 July 1921; "'The Jew and Civilization': A Review of Ada Sterling's Remarkable Book Just From The Press," *American Israelite*, 24 February 1924,1; review of William Henry Warner, *Sacrilegious Hands, American Hebrew* 117 (14 August 1925): 425; "A New Adventurer in the Promised Land," review of Yezierska, *Hungry Hearts, American Hebrew* 108 (3 December 1920): 112–13.

27 "The Jew on Stage and Screen," part 1, *B'nai B'rith Magazine* XLII, no. 1 (October 1927): 548–49; "The Jew on Stage and Screen," part 2, *B'nai B'rith Magazine* XLII, no. 2 (November 1927): 18–19.

28 "A South African Writes About the Jews," *B'nai B'rith Magazine* 43 (November 1928): 66–67. Virtually unknown in the United States, Millin has become a controversial figure in South Africa since the end of the apartheid regime, which she supported in her later years. See J. M. Coetzee, "Blood, Flaw, Taint, Degeneration: The Case of Sarah Gertrude Millin," *English Studies in Africa* 23, no. 1 (1980): 41–58; Lavinia Braun, "Not Gobineau but Heine—Not Racial Theory but Biblical Theme: The Case of Sarah Gertrude Millin," *English Studies in Africa* 34, no. 1 (1991): 27–38; and Margaret Lenta, "Choosing Difference: South African Jewish Writers," *Judaism: A Quarterly Journal of Jewish Life and Thought* 50, no. 1 (2001): 92–103.

29 Popkin, *Open Every Door*, 142.

30 "East Side Night Life," *New Yorker* (5 June 1926): 68–69 (a longer version of this article appeared as "Changing East Side," *American Mercury* 10 (February 1927): 168–75); "Z.F.P," [Zelda F. Popkin], "Reflections of Silent New Yorkers," *New Yorker*

(30 October 1926): 38–39; "Reflections of More-or-Less Silent Citizens," *New Yorker* (11 December 1926): 103–4; "Reflections of Silent Citizens," *New Yorker* (12 February 1927): 82; "Reflections of Silent Citizens: The Bus Conductor," *New Yorker* (26 February 1927): 69; Ben Yagoda, *About Town: The New Yorker and the World It Made* (New York: Scribner, 2000), 70–71.

31 Charles Nessler [sic], *The Story of Hair: Its Purpose and Its Preservation* (New York: Boni and Liveright, 1928), 270. For Popkin's authorship, see *Open Every Door*, 151. In a 1940 interview, Zelda boasted that "she has 'ghost-written' books and articles on a wide range of subjects for many well-known personalities." *Wilkes-Barre Times Leader*, 2 February 1940.

32 ZP to Katherine White, 14 July 1936; White to ZP, 10 September 1936; ZP to White, 11 September 1936, in New York Public Library, *New Yorker* archives, Ms. Coll. 2236, box 261, folder 7; Zelda Popkin, "Plot Isn't a Dirty Word," *Writer* 82 (July 1969): 11–12.

33 Popkin, *Open Every Door*, 119, 123, 124; Zelda Popkin, "Curb Lizards," *American Hebrew* (24 November 1922): 30, 32–34; Richard H. Popkin, "Intellectual Autobiography: Warts and All," in Richard A. Watson and James E. Force, eds., *The Sceptical Mode in Modern Philosophy: Essays in Honor of Richard H. Popkin* (Dordrecht: Nijhoff, 1988), 104. There is a fleeting glimpse of "curb lizards" with their children in Jay Leyda's experimental film, *A Bronx Morning* (1931).

34 On the Jewish migration to the Bronx, see Deborah Dash Moore, *At Home in America: Second Generation New York Jews* (New York: Columbia University Press, 1981); and Beth Wenger, *New York Jews and the Great Depression: Uncertain Promise* (Syracuse, NY: Syracuse University Press, 1999).

35 Property deed, dated 1 July 1924, in PFA; *Open Every Door*, 143–45; "Manhattan Vista," in PFA; Theresa Bernstein, "Spuyten Duyvil," 1925, private collection.

36 "A Jewish Palette: Theresa Bernstein Wins Laurels as Painter," *American Hebrew* 111 (16 June 1922): 133, 135; Popkin, *Open Every Door*, 127–30; portraits in author's collection and collection of Gail Ohnsman.

37 Popkin, *Open Every Door*, 139, 141; Zelda Popkin, "Mistress and Maid in Autumn Line-Up," *Daily News* (Los Angeles), 8 November 1925.

38 Popkin, *Open Every Door*, 155–57. On the Jewish contribution to American psychology, see Andrew Heinze, *Jews and the American Soul: Human Nature in the Twentieth Century* (Princeton, NJ: Princeton University Press, 2004).

39 Citation in Zelda F. Popkin, "An Experiment in Education," *American Hebrew* (28 December 1923); see also Zelda F. Popkin, "A Barn for School," *Survey* 49 (15 November 1922): 253–55. On Lillian Rifkin Blumenfeld (1897–1982), see Paul Avrich, *Anarchist Voices: An Oral History* (AK Press, 2005), 243–45. Rifkin was listed as a guest at a luncheon Zelda hosted in Wilkes-Barre in June 1917.

40 Zelda Popkin, "A Good School for the Children," *New Yorker* (10 September 1927): 55; *Open Every Door*, 158.

41 Zelda Popkin, "Wonderful Institution, Our Schools," *New Yorker* (14 November 1931): 52–54; "Panic of the Parents," *Outlook and Independent*, 158 (1 July 1931): 267–69, 286.

42 Popkin, *Open Every Door*, 160–61; Roy (Sandy) Popkin, "Respect for Teachers, a Contrast," in PFA. My uncle's article includes details on the "stink bomb raid" that Popkin mentioned in her autobiography. Richard H. Popkin, "Intellectual Autobiography," 104–5.

43 Zelda Popkin, "The Finer Things of Life," *Harper's Magazine* 164 (April 1932): 602–11. She expressed similar sentiments in a 1935 interview cited in Sidonie Matsner Gruenberg, *Radio and Children* (New York: Radio Institute for the Audible Arts, 1935). Zelda Popkin, "Children of the Racketeer Age," *Harper's Magazine* 166 (February 1933): 164–75.

44 Popkin, *Open Every Door*, 153–54.

45 Richard H. Popkin, "Intellectual Autobiography," 103.

46 Popkin, *Open Every Door*, 199.

47 Israel Goldstein, *Jewish Justice and Conciliation: History of the Jewish Conciliation Board of America, 1930–1968* (New York: Ktav, 1981), 249; letter to Louis Popkin, 9 November 1931, in PFA; Louis Popkin, letter to Joseph C. Hyman, 2 December 1935, in Joint Distribution Committee archives; Richard Breitman, Barbara McDonald Stewart, and Severin Hochberg, eds., *Refugees and Rescue: The Diaries and Papers of James G. McDonald* (Bloomington: Indiana University Press, 2009),103.

48 Zelda Popkin, "Conciliation Court," *New Yorker* (10 September 1932).

49 ZP to St. Clair McKelway, 2 June 1937, in New York Public Library, Ms. Coll. 2236, box 283, folder 12; Harry Feinberg to Zelda Popkin, 7 February 1939, in PFA.

50 Jewish Telegraphic Agency, 17 June 1935. On Helen's early experiences in Palestine, see Juliet Popkin, interview with Helen Rossi Koussewitsky, in PFA. Popkin, *Open Every Door*, 200.

51 "The American Jewish Tragedy," *Jewish Criterion* (Pittsburgh), 30 September 1932.

52 "The American Jewish Tragedy," *Jewish Criterion* (Pittsburgh), 30 September 1932.

53 Popkin, *Open Every Door*, 168. Ford's apology was widely reprinted in the Jewish press; see *B'nai B'rith Magazine* XLI, no. 10 (July 1927): 412. For American Jewish leaders' reluctance to oppose Ford openly, see Gulie Ne'eman Arad, *America, Its Jews, and the Rise of Nazism* (Bloomington: Indiana University Press, 2000), 66. On Marshall's role in obtaining Ford's signature, see M. M. Silver, *Louis Marshall and the Rise of Jewish Ethnicity in America: A Biography* (Syracuse, NY: Syracuse University Press, 2013), 397–400, and Charles Reznikoff, *Louis Marshall: Champion of Liberty*, 2 vols. (Philadelphia: Jewish Publication Society of America, 1957), 1:374–81. Neither of these sources mentions Louis Popkin or Fromenson, nor do the documents on this episode in the Louis Marshall papers at the American Jewish Archives (box 155).

54 Theodore Dreiser, letter to C. Halliwell Duell, 8 May 1933, copy in PFA. On Dreiser's antisemitism, see Donald Pizer, *American Naturalism and the Jews* (Pittsburgh: University of Pittsburgh Press, 2008). The book in question was Edgar Ansel Mowrer, *Germany Puts the Clock Back* (New York: William Morrow, 1933). Zelda's copy is autographed by the author.

55 Press release for American Jewish Congress, 26 March 1933, in ZP Papers, BU Library, box 4; "Snowball Rolling Downhill," ZP Papers, BU Library, box 7. On the 27 March 1933 anti-Nazi rally, see Robert G. Waite, "'Raise My Voice Against

Intolerance.' The Anti-Nazi Rally in Madison Square Garden, March 27, 1933, and the American Public's Outrage over the Nazi Persecution of the Jews," *New York History Review* (online), 20 October 2013; and Frederick A. Lazin, "The Response of the American Jewish Committee to the Crisis of German Jewry, 1933–1939," *American Jewish History* 68, no. 3 (1979): 283–304.

56 Elisabeth Israels Perry, *After the Vote: Feminist Politics in La Guardia's New York* (New York: Oxford University Press, 2019), 146–48. Perry's account draws heavily from Popkin's articles. The report Kross and Popkin compiled is in the Anna Kross Papers, American Jewish Archives, Ms. Coll. 176, box 37.

57 Zelda Popkin, "Vignettes from a Women's Court," *Independent Woman* 14 (December 1935): 398–400, 414–16; *Open Every Door*, 188–96. See also Zelda Popkin, "Sociological Court is Urged for Women," *New York Times*, 25 November 1934, and "Magistrates' Courts Bureau is Designed to Deal With Problems Presented by Arraigned Persons," *New York Times,* 5 January 1936.

58 Zelda Popkin, "Abdication of King Coal," *Nation* 126 (4 January 1928): 11–12; "Gloucester Honors its Sailors," *Nation* 128 (17 April 1929): 448–49; "Folk Festivals Lure: Annual Trips Begin in May to Centres of Primitive American Arts and Music," *New York Times*, 21 April 1935; "Tent Show Turns to Sex," *Outlook and Independent* 156 (24 September 1930): 128–30, 157.

59 Zelda Popkin, "Heaven Bound: Authentic Negro Folk Drama Out of Old Savannah," *Theatre Guild* 11 (6 August 1931): 14–17. On Jewish blackface performers, see Michael Alexander, *Jazz Age Jews* (Princeton, NJ: Princeton University Press, 2001).

60 Zelda Popkin, "Changing East Side," *American Mercury* 10 (February 1927): 168–75. The "Chasidim" she referred to in her articles were probably not actually members of any of the organized Hasidic sects that established themselves in New York after the Holocaust.

61 Popkin, "Conciliation Court," *New Yorker* (10 September 1932): 40–47.

62 Zelda Popkin, "Gone With the Flood," *New Yorker* (24 October 1936): 32, 34, 36, 37–39; "Not To Reason Why," *New Yorker* (6 March 1937); "Annals of Crime: Sing a Song of Homicide," *New Yorker* (30 October 1937): 46–56.

63 On American Jews' wrestlings with their identity in the interwar years, see Eric L. Goldstein, *The Price of Whiteness: Jews, Race, and American Identity* (Princeton, NJ: Princeton University Press, 2006).

64 Ferber, *Peculiar Treasure*, 10.

CHAPTER 3

1 Popkin, *Open Every Door*, 182, 180, 179; press releases in ZP Papers, BU Library, box 4.

2 Popkin, *Open Every Door*, 180, 182; "Roy Parker" [Roy Popkin], "The Band Will Now Play 'Hearts and Flowers,'" *Daily Worker*, n.d. but August or September 1938, in PFA; Richard H. Popkin, "Intellectual Autobiography," 104.

3 Popkin, *Open Every Door*, 182.

4 Louis Popkin, File #136 (JDC Personnel), Joint Distribution Committee archives.

5 Zelda Popkin, *Open Every Door*, 206–7. On Zerwick, see Phoebe Zerwick, "Memory: Father's War Tales Masked a Dark Truth," *Winston-Salem Journal*, 27 May 2001. Zerwick's campaign against Schmeling at the time of his first fight with Louis was featured in the *New York Times* on 12 January 1937: "Schmeling Tour Opposed."

6 Popkin, *Open Every Door*, 204–6; "Democracy Pledge Circulated Throughout Country," press release, 23 June 1939, in ZP Papers, BU Library, box 4. Leon Birkhead has not yet received the study he obviously deserves. The most extensive treatment of his activities is a three-part series of articles, "Democracy's Friend," by E. J. Kahn Jr., that appeared in the *New Yorker* (26 July, 2 August, 9 August 1947).

7 "Memorandum to the Federal Bureau of Investigation," 29 August 1940; press release about Joseph McWilliams, 13 September 1940, in ZP Papers, BU Library, box 4; Popkin, *Open Every Door*, 204–6. Derounian's book *Under Cover: My Four Years in the Nazi Underworld of America*, published in 1943 under the pseudonym "John Roy Carlson," remains a classic source on the subject of the period's pro-fascist movements.

8 Letter from Louis Popkin to American consulate, 3 June 1939, and reply from Raymond H. Geist, in ZP Papers, BU Library, box 7.

9 Popkin, *Open Every Door*, 220.

10 Louis Popkin to Zelda, 19 October 1940, in PFA; Popkin, *Open Every Door*, 226, 231; Moses Zerwick to ZP, 6 January 1944, in ZP Papers, BU Library, box 12.

11 Kathleen Gregory Klein, *The Woman Detective: Gender and Genre* (Urbana: University of Illinois Press, 1988), 143.

12 Popkin, *Open Every Door*, 183–86.

13 Popkin, *Open Every Door*, 187.

14 Willy Cuppy, *New York Herald-Tribune*, in ZP Papers, BU Library, box 8; *Murder in the Mist*, 35, 195; letter to J. A. McKaughan, n.d. [1944], in PFA.

15 Popkin, *Time Off for Murder*, 8–9.

16 Zelda Popkin, "Highest Standard of Living on Earth," *Independent Woman* 19 (April 1940), 101; Popkin, *Time Off*, 16.

17 *Wilkes-Barre Times Leader*, 1 February 1940; *Wilkes-Barre Record* 2 February 1940; Juliet Popkin, "Yiches and Naches," in PFA.

18 Popkin, *White Gardenia*, 239.

19 Charles Wagner, *Daily Mirror*, in ZP Papers, BU Library, box 8; Popkin, *Time Off*, 273.

20 Popkin, *White Gardenia*, 139.

21 Supplement to *Philadelphia Inquirer*, 24 July 1938; also in *San Francisco Examiner*; A. S. Burdack, ed., *Writing Detective and Mystery Fiction* (Boston: Writer, 1945). The other women authors represented were Dorothy Sayers and Dorothy B. Hughes. Zelda's article was first published in 1942.

22 Zelda Popkin, *Mary Carner et ses voisins*, trans. Simone Périer (Ghent: Editions Lumière, [1946]); Zelda Popkin, *La Lune de miel de Mary Carner*, trans. Simone Périer (Ghent: Editions Lumière, [1946]); Zelda Popkin, *Una Gardenia per il boia* (Milan: Mondadori, 1952). I would like to thank Denis Reynaud for sending me copies of these translations. The German and French translations published in the 1990s were

arranged by my mother, Juliet Popkin, who had established a small literary agency in the late 1980s.

23 ZP to "Minnie," n.d. but 1943, in PFA.

24 On widowhood memoirs, see Jeffrey Berman, *Writing Widowhood: The Landscapes of Bereavement* (Albany: SUNY Press, 2015).

25 Popkin, *Open Every Door*, 241–57.

26 Zelda Popkin to Richard Popkin, 20 February 1964; Juliet Popkin diaries, July 1976, both in PFA.

27 Moses Zerwick to ZP, 25 July 1943, in ZP Papers, BU Library, box 12; Popkin, *Open Every Door*, 244, 245, 247.

28 Popkin, *Open Every Door*, 246; Popkin, memorandum to J. C. Hyman, 1 September 1943, in American Jewish Joint Distribution Committee archives (accessed online, 30 September 2015).

29 ZP to Richard Popkin, "Thursday," [July or August 1943], in PFA. "Short-arm inspection" was military slang for examinations for venereal disease.

30 Popkin, *Open Every Door*, 253.

31 Juliet Popkin, "Another Era, Another Train Wreck," *Los Angeles Times*, 16 January 1987; Wesley S. Griswold, *Train Wreck!* (Brattleboro, VT: Stephen Greene, 1969), 116–19; *New York Daily News*, 10 September 1943.

32 Zelda Popkin, letter to J. A. McKaughan, n.d. [1944], in PFA.

33 Roy Popkin to ZP, no date, in PFA.

34 Popkin, *So Much Blood*, 219.

35 Popkin, *Open Every Door*, 255.

36 Popkin, *Open Every Door*, 257.

37 Popkin, *Open Every Door*, 259–63.

38 Popkin, *Open Every Door*, 257.

39 "Survivors of Wreck Tell How Servicemen Helped," *New York Times*, 7 September 1943; Juliet Popkin, "Another Era"; ZP to "Dear Barbara," 13 May [1945?], in ZP Papers, BU Library, box 11, file 1.

40 On the role of Jewish writers in creating the canon of American war literature, see Leah Garrett, *The Young Lions: How Jewish Authors Reinvented the American War Novel* (Evanston, IL: Northwestern University Press, 2015).

41 Zerwick to ZP, 15 March 1945, ZP Papers, BU Library, box 12, quoted in ZP, letter to unnamed correspondent beginning "Last March," n.d. but 1945, in ZP Papers, BU Library, box 11.

42 E. J. Kahn Jr., "No Place Like Home," *New Yorker*, 20 May 1944, 49–57; Josiah Macy Jr. Foundation to Zelda Popkin, 23 May 1944, in ZP Papers, BU Library, box 11, file 1. A review of the published report in 1945 commended its case studies of "free-floating anxiety states, both severe and mild, somatic regressions, psychosomatic visceral disturbances," and other syndromes. Wendell Muncie, review of *War Neuroses in North Africa*, *Quarterly Review of Biology* 20 (1945): 191–92.

43 Popkin to "Dear Barbara," 13 May [1945?]; "Outline for a novel tentatively entitled *The Journey Home*," n.d., both in ZP Papers, BU Library, box 11.

44 "Outline for a novel," in ZP Papers, BU Library, box 11.

45 "Outline for a novel," and ZP to Henry Klinger, 18 May 1944, both in ZP Papers, BU Library, box 11. The American Women's Voluntary Service (AWVS) was set up to organize women to support the war effort. ZP, letter to unnamed correspondent beginning "Last March," n.d. but 1944, in ZP Papers, BU Library, box 11.

46 ZP, letter to "Dear Barbara," and "Outline for a Novel," both in ZP Papers, BU Library, box 11.

47 Zelda Popkin, *The Journey Home* (Philadelphia: J. B. Lippincott, 1945), 5, 9, 36, 41.

48 Melissa A. McEuen, *Making War, Making Women: Femininity and Duty on the American Home Front, 1941–1945* (Athens: University of Georgia Press, 2011), xiii; Popkin, *Journey Home*, 41, 99.

49 Popkin, *Journey Home*, 35, 108–9, 114–16.

50 Popkin, *Journey Home*, 93; memo, "The Journey Home, by Zelda Popkin," 23 February 1945, in ZP Papers, BU Library, box 11.

51 Popkin, *Journey Home*, 113, 115, 117, 118.

52 Popkin, *Journey Home*, 118, 119.

53 Popkin, *Journey Home*, 50, 51, 52.

54 Popkin, *Journey Home*, 81–83, 137–38; ZP interview with Chip Bontell, *New York Post*, 30 August 1945, in ZP Papers, BU Library, box 11.

55 Popkin, *Journey Home*, 22, 125.

56 ZP to Blumenthal, 2 August 1944, in Jewish Welfare Board Archives, Center for Jewish History.

57 Studs Terkel, *"The Good War": An Oral History of World War Two* (New York: Ballantine, 1984), 114–16.

58 Popkin, *Journey Home*, 128.

59 Popkin, *Journey Home*, 159–60.

60 Laura Z. Hobson, *Gentleman's Agreement* (New York: Simon and Schuster, 1947). On Hobson's book and the challenges facing Jewish authors who wanted to expose American antisemitism in this period, see Rachel Gordan, "Laura Z. Hobson and the Making of *Gentleman's Agreement*," *Studies in American Jewish Literature* 34, no. 2 (2015): 231–56.

61 Popkin, *Journey Home*, 172–73.

62 Popkin, *Journey Home*, 175.

63 Popkin, *Open Every Door*, 254.

64 Popkin, *Journey Home*, 185.

65 Popkin, *Journey Home*, 206, 222.

66 Popkin, interview in *Palestine Post*, n.d. but December 1948, clipping in PFA; receipt for advance, 13 July 1945, and George Stevens to ZP, 15 November 1946, in ZP Papers, BU Library, box 12.

67 *Omnibook Magazine* (October 1945): 121–60. The male version of war literature was Robert J. Casey, *This Is Where I Came In* (New York: Bobbs-Merrill, 1945), a journalistic account of the American army's advance into Germany.

68 Harry Feinberg to ZP, 29 July 1945, and 25 August 1945, PFA.

69 Nathan L. Rothman, *Saturday Review*, 28 July 1945; E. Beatrice Fox, *Chicago Daily Bulletin*, 10 July 1945.

70 Eleanor Roosevelt, newspaper column, clipping in ZP Papers, BU Library, box 11.

71 Saul Bellow, *Commentary*, December 1945, 95–96.

72 Emily Yellin, *Our Mothers' War: American Women at Home and at the Front During World War II* (New York: Free, 2004); Popkin, *Journey Home*, 173.

73 Paul Griffith, "Train Ride North," *New York Times*, 27 July 1945; ZP, letter to Ernest Cody, n.d., in ZP Papers, BU Library, box 11.

CHAPTER 4

1 Mary Egan Winter, "Writing Fiction Is 'Messy' But Easy," *Brooklyn Daily Eagle*, 22 July 1945; Chip Bontell, "Authors Are Like People," *New York Post*, 30 August 1945; Juliet Popkin, "Yiches and Naches," in PFA.

2 "War Brides and Europe," *Gramercy Graphic* (n.d.), clipping in PFA.

3 Richard Popkin to ZP, 10 April 1947, in PFA.

4 Zelda Popkin, "A Widow's Way," *McCall's Magazine* (October 1945): 17, 60, 66, 68.

5 Popkin, *Open Every Door*, 261.

6 Joanne Meyerowitz, "Beyond the Feminine Mystique: A Reassessment of Postwar Mass Culture, 1946–1958," in Joanne Meyerowitz, ed., *Not June Cleaver: Women and Gender in Postwar America, 1945–1960* (Philadelphia: Temple University Press, 1994), 232–37.

7 Marynia Farnham, "Women and Wives," *McCall's* (October 1945): 16, 56, 59, 60. For Farnham's review of *The Second Sex*, see *Annals of the American Academy of Political and Social Science* 291 (January 1954): 178.

8 ZP to Richard and Juliet Popkin, 24 October 1945, in PFA. The "Bob" mentioned in the letter was her nephew Robert Pinsker, then stationed in Europe.

9 ZP to Richard and Juliet Popkin, 3 November 1945, in PFA.

10 ZP to Richard and Juliet Popkin, 3 November 1945, in PFA. On postwar Jewish "DPs" in 1945–1946, see Atina Grossmann, *Jews, Germans, and Allies: Close Encounters in Occupied Germany* (Princeton, NJ: Princeton University Press, 2007), 131–82; and David Nasaw, *The Last Million: Europe's Displaced Persons from World War to Cold War* (New York: Penguin, 2020), 65–126, 169–82.

11 *Open Every Door*, 266, 280–81. Max Lowenthal (1888–1971) was a prominent Washington lawyer and political insider and a longtime family friend of the Popkins. Lowenthal's book, *The Federal Bureau of Investigation* (New York: Harcourt Brace Javonich, 1950) was one of the first critical treatments of the agency. The story about Zelda confirming the death of his relatives was verified by his son, David Lowenthal (email of 21 February 2015). Sandy and Dick were the nicknames of Zelda's two sons, Roy and Richard Popkin.

12 ZP to Richard and Juliet Popkin, 23 December 1945, in PFA.

13 Moses Zerwick to ZP, Berlin, 24 August 1945, in PFA; ZP to Richard and Juliet Popkin, Salzburg, 23 December 1945, in PFA.

14 Interview with Sophie Reagan Herr, 4 August 2000; ZP to Richard and Juliet Popkin, Paris, 10 January 1946, in PFA. In *Open Every Door*, Zelda claimed that her intervention had resulted in an immediate change of policy (304).

15 ZP to Richard and Juliet Popkin, Frankfurt, 23 October 1945 and Berlin, 11 November 1945, in PFA.

16 Among the relief workers she mentions by name were Ruth Kluger, not the famous Holocaust memoirist but a representative of the Jewish Agency who worked with survivor children; Miriam Warburg, whose report on "Conditions of Jewish Children in a Bavarian Rehabilitation Camp" has become an essential source for scholars working on the treatment of postwar DPs; and Simon Rifkind, the official Jewish liaison to the American Military Government, appointed at the behest of the Joint Distribution Committee.

17 Zelda Popkin, "Shoes for the Children of Drancy," *Red Cross Courier* 25 (February 1946): 6; reprinted in *Reader's Digest* 48 (March 1946): 38; Zelda Popkin, "Europe's Children," *Ladies' Home Journal* 63 (August 1946): 168, 170–71.

18 Popkin, "Europe's Children."

19 ZP to Richard and Juliet Popkin, 10 January 1946, in PFA.

20 Saul Bellow, letter to Cynthia Ozick, cited in Garrett, *Young Lions*, 12; Christopher Hobson, cited in Rachel Gordan, "Laura Z. Hobson and the Making of *Gentleman's Agreement*," *Studies in American Jewish Literature* 34, no. 2 (2015): 236.

21 Ruth Gruber, letter of 1 October 1947, in ZP Papers, BU Library, box 1; *Small Victory*, 164.

22 The US Army's treatment of camp survivors had already become an issue before Popkin arrived in Germany, with the issuance of the Harrison report, circulated in August 1945. See Leonard Dinnerstein, *America and the Survivors of the Holocaust* (New York: Columbia University Press, 1982), 43; and Nasaw, *Last Million*, 106–9.

23 Zelda Popkin, *Small Victory* (Philadelphia: J. B. Lippincott, 1947), 279, 225.

24 Richard Plant, review in *New York Times*, 7 December 1947, in ZP Papers, BU Library, box 1.

25 *Small Victory*, 228, 142–44, 47. On early American descriptions of camp survivors, see the citations collected by Peter Novick in *The Holocaust in American Life* (Boston: Houghton Mifflin, 1999), 68.

26 Popkin, *Small Victory*, 174, 211.

27 Popkin, *Small Victory*, 135.

28 Popkin, *Small Victory*, 135, 136, 139, 144.

29 Popkin, *Small Victory*, 174–75.

30 Popkin, *Small Victory*, 218, 228; *Open Every Door*, 291. On Rifkind's role, see Leonard Dinnerstein, "The U.S. Army and the Jews: Policies Toward the Displaced Persons After World War II," *American Jewish History* 68, no. 3 (1979), 359.

31 Popkin, *Small Victory*, 251–52.

32 James Kelly, letter of 8 August 1947, in ZP Papers, BU Library, box 1; Fletcher Isbell, *Washington Star*, 30 November 1947; Richard Plant, *New York Times*, 7 December 1947.

33 For an extended discussion of *Small Victory*, see Werner Sollors, *The Temptation of Despair* (Cambridge, MA: Harvard University Press, 2014), 144–50.

34 Suzanne Rhoads, letter of 24 September 1947, Stephen Wise, letter of 13 January 1948; Ira Rosenthal, letter of 11 November 1947; Philip Slomovitz, *Detroit Jewish News*, n.d., in ZP Papers, BU Library, box 1.

35 Abraham Duker, *The Day*, 11 July 1948; Louis Kraft, *In Jewish Bookland* 4, no. 3 (January–February 1948); "L. H.," in *Palestine Post*, 2 January 1948; Joseph Hamburger, *The Answer*, 30 January 1948, documents in ZP Papers, BU Library, box 1.

36 On the changing nature of American policy toward the DPs, see Leonard Dinnerstein, *Antisemitism in America* (New York: Oxford University Press, 1994), 161.

37 Barbara Frost to Popkin, 6 January 1948, citing comments of Harold Schiff, in ZP Papers, BU Library, box 1.

38 Charles [illeg.] to Popkin, 25 October 1947, letter in ZP Papers, BU Library, box 1.

39 Richard Plant, *New York Times*, 7 December 1947.

40 Popkin, *Small Victory*, 35, 276.

41 Popkin, *Small Victory*, 202–3.

42 Helen Koussewitsky to ZP, letter of 22 June 1947, in PFA.

43 Zelda Popkin to "Jim," 5 June 1948; George Stevens to ZP, 25 June 1948, in ZP Papers, BU Library, box 14.

44 Zelda Popkin, *Walk Through the Valley* (Philadelphia: J. B. Lippincott, 1949), 21, 128, 54–55.

45 Janice A. Radway, *A Feeling for Books: The Book-of-the-Month Club, Literary Taste, and Middle-Class Desire* (Chapel Hill: University of North Carolina Press, 1997), 284–85.

46 J. F. Wilsey to Popkin, 30 October [1949], in ZP Papers, BU Library, box 14.

47 Eleanor Schorer, "When a Woman Is Alone," *Everybody's Weekly* (Sunday supplement), *Philadelphia Inquirer*, 1 May 1949.

48 Popkin, *Walk Through the Valley*, 139.

49 Popkin, *Walk Through the Valley*, 205.

50 ZP to Richard and Juliet Popkin, "Wednesday evening," [early 1949], in Popkin Family Archive. Betty MacDonald's *The Plague and I*, the story of its author's nine-month stay in a tuberculosis sanitorium, was one of the more widely read books by a woman author on the market at the time.

51 Katherine Gauss Jackson, in *Harper's Magazine* (July 1949): 109–10, in ZP Papers, BU Library, box 14.

52 Frances M. Allen, letter of 29 September 1949; Irma Pharylles Torem, 18 May 1949, H. Webster, n.d., ZP Papers, in BU Library, box 14.

53 Florence Haxton Bullock, *New York Herald Tribune*, 20 February 1949; Marjory Stoneman Douglas, *Saturday Review*, 5 March 1949; Karen Horney to Stanley Chambers, 19 February 1949, all in ZP Papers, BU Library, box 14.

54 Popkin, *Walk Through the Valley*, 270.

55 Juliet Popkin, letter of 18 April 1949; ZP to Juliet Popkin, April 1949, in PFA.

56 ZP to Richard and Juliet Popkin, 1 July 1949; "8-Year Widowhood Average Prospect," *New York Times*, 20 April 1949; Zelda Popkin, "Widows and the Perilous Years," *Harper's Magazine* (September 1949): 69–74; Norman Thomas, *Mirror News* (Los Angeles), 15 September 1949.

57 Berman, *Writing Widowhood*.

CHAPTER 5

1 ZP to Richard and Juliet and Roy and Dot Popkin, 15 November 1948 and 30 November 1948, in PFA; Popkin, *Open Every Door*, 316.

2 RHP to Judah Goldin, 31 December 1960, in PFA.

3 Tay Hohoff, memorandum, 12 June 1950, in ZP Papers, BU Library, box 14; I. F. Stone, *This is Israel* (New York: Boni and Gaer, 1948); Ruth Gruber, *Israel Without Tears* (New York: A. A. Wyn, 1950).

4 Cited in Ira B. Nadel, *Leon Uris: Life of a Best Seller* (Austin: University of Texas Press, 2010), 116.

5 Juliet Popkin, "Interview with Helen Rossi," PFA; Popkin, *Open Every Door*, 31–32; Helga Dudman, "The Fighter Who Built the Funds," *Jerusalem Post*, 6–12 December 1981; Greer Fay Cashman, "Remembering Helen Rossi," *Jerusalem Post*, 26 May 1990. "Rossi" was the last name of Helen's first husband and the name by which she was known in Israeli public life; within the family, she used the last name of her second husband, Alexander "Sasha" Koussewitsky.

6 Roy Popkin to Zelda and Louis Popkin, "Saturday night" [fall 1938]; Harry Feinberg to Zelda and Louis Popkin, 30 June 1940, in PFA.

7 Popkin, interview, *Palestine Post*, n.d., in PFA; *Small Victory*, 211.

8 I. F. Stone, *Underground to Palestine* (New York: Boni and Gaer, 1946); Ruth Gruber, *Destination Palestine* (New York: A. A. Wyn, 1948).

9 Helen Rossi to ZP, 9 October 1947, in PFA; Helen Rossi, "Army Goes in for Art: Posters for Psychological Warfare," *Palestine Post*, 27 August 1948; Molly Abramowitz, "The Mysterious Case of the Haganah Posters," *Na'Amat Woman* 24 (summer 2009), 12–15. Zelda was rewarded with a set of the posters, three of which now hang in my home. Letters from Robert L. Leslie, a typographer who met David in New York, confirm the role that Helen and Zelda played in making the production of the posters possible. Robert L. Leslie to Ismar David, 22 April 1948 and 1 February 1949, in Ismar David archives, Rochester Institute of Technology.

10 Helen Koussewitsky to ZP, 19 November 1947, 9 January [1948?], and telegram, 5 February 1948; letter of T. G. Thackrey, editor, *New York Post*, to ZP, 2 March 1948, with undated clipping; Juliet Popkin, "Interview," all in PFA.

11 Helen Rossi to ZP, 15 May 1948, 15 August 1948, in PFA. I. F. Stone later became a severe critic of Israeli policy toward the Palestinians, but in 1948 he wrote enthusiastic articles about the creation of Israel and President Truman's unexpectedly swift recognition of the Jewish state. I. F. Stone, "Born Under Fire," *New Republic*, 31 May 1948; "Against All Rules," *New Republic*, 14 June 1948; "Palestine, Britain and the UN," *New Republic*, 2 August 1948. On Stone's support for Israel in 1948, see D. D. Guttenplan, *American Radical: The Life and Times of I. F. Stone* (New York: Farrar, Straus and Giroux, 2009), 228–31. On Ruth Gruber's 1948 trip, see Ruth Gruber, *Witness* (New York: Schocken, 2007), 161.

12 Memorandum, two pages, n.d., addressed to "Dear George [Stevens] and Tay [Hohoff]," in ZP Papers, BU Library, box 12. Zelda may have known Agronsky, who spent the early 1920s as a journalist in New York.

13 ZP, letter to Roy and Dot, Richard and Juliet Popkin, Jerusalem, 16 October 1948, in PFA.

14 Norman Grieser, articles editor, *New Republic*, letter of 15 September 1948; ZP to Roy and Dot, Richard and Juliet Popkin, 15 and 30 November 1948, in PFA.

15 Notebooks and script of interview with Arthur Holzman, WMCA radio, in ZP Papers, BU Library, box 14; *Palestine Post* interview, n. d. (Dec. 1948), clipping in PFA.

16 "Sunday night," n.d. but early 1949; Ruth H. Kaufman, "Jewish Briefs," *Temple Israel Journal*, 26 January 1949 [Wilkes-Barre], both in PFA; *Montreal Star*, 19 October 1949.

17 Some elements of this project, but not the antisemitism theme, were incorporated into a short novella she published in 1950: "Bitter Bondage," *American Magazine* 149 (May 1950), 52–58.

18 Contract, 4 May 1949, in ZP Papers, BU Library, box 12; "Outline for a novel tentatively called The Silver Salver," n.d. but spring 1949, in ZP Papers, BU Library, box 14.

19 For an overview of American literature on Israel in the first years after its creation, see Emily Alice Katz, *Bringing Zion Home: Israel in American Jewish Culture, 1948–1967* (Albany: SUNY Press, 2015), 19–39.

20 "Novelist Tells of Scenes Witnessed on Palestine Trip," *Wilkes-Barre Times Leader*, 26 January 1949; ZP to Helen Dean Fish, 1 December 1949, in ZP Papers, BU Library, box 12.

21 See the comments of Stephen Longstreet and James Yaffe in the symposium, "Why I Wrote a Jewish Novel," in Harold U. Ribalow, ed., *Mid-Century* (New York: Beechhurst, 1955), 327, 331.

22 "Outline for a novel tentatively called The Silver Salver," in ZP Papers, BU Library, box 14. Alterman's poem is better known in English today under the title "The Silver Platter." On the significance of the poem in Israeli literature, see Yael Seliger, "After 'Postmemory': Coping with Holocaust Remembrance in Postmodern Hebrew Literature," PhD dissertation, York University, 2015, 252–59.

23 Draft of prospectus for novel, one page, in ZP Papers, BU Library, box 14; Helen Koussewitsky to ZP, letter of 15 May 1949, in PFA.

24 Tay Hohoff, memo of 12 June 1950; George Stevens to ZP, 19 June 1950, both in ZP Papers, BU Library, box 14; ZP to Richard and Juliet Popkin, 4 May and 29 June 1950, in PFA.

25 Popkin, *Quiet Street*, 332. On American volunteers who fought for Israel in 1948, see Amy Weiss, "1948's Forgotten Soldiers? The Shifting Reception of American Volunteers in Israel's War of Independence," *Israel Studies* 25, no. 1 (2020): 149–73.

26 "Widow of Israel Dreyfus Fought to Shield Son," *New York Post*, 11 July 1949. For an account of the affair by an Israeli historian, see Shabtai Teveth, *Ben-Gurion's Spy: The Story of the Political Scandal that Shaped Modern Israel* (New York: Columbia University Press, 1996), 3–58. Teveth sees the Tubiansky scandal as a foreshadowing of the far more explosive Lavon Affair that dominated Israeli political life in the early 1960s.

27 ZP to George Stevens, Managing Editor, Lippincott, letter of 23 September 1950, in ZP Papers, BU Library, box 14. Avraham Harman later became president of Hebrew University.

28 Popkin, *Open Every Door*, 346, 349; ZP to Richard and Juliet Popkin, February 1951, in PFA; Kloetzel to ZP, letter of 23 March 1951, in ZP Papers, BU Library, box 14. Popkin may been thinking of a prominent German-American Jewish figure, Rabbi Joachim Prinz, when she chose her character's name, but the real-life Prinz never lived in Jerusalem.

29 Richard Dana, Lippincott promotion manager, to ZP, letter of 17 April 1951, in ZP Papers, BU Library, box 14. Other documents in the same box refer to appearances before a variety of groups, mostly Jewish. Office of the Prime Minister of Israel, letter from Chicago, 18 May 1951, in ZP Papers, BU Library, box 14.

30 *San Francisco Chronicle*, 15 July 1951; Mendel Kochanski, *Middle Eastern Affairs* (August–September 1951): 289–90; C. Z. Kloetzel, *Jerusalem Post*, 6 July 1951.

31 Bill Corum, "When Popkin Pitched for Brooklyn," *New York Journal-American*, n.d. [1951], PFA.

32 Red Barber to ZP, letter of 2 July 1951; interview transcript; Newman review, all in ZP Papers, BU Library, box 14.

33 Gertrude Samuels, "Jerusalem Delivered," *New York Times Book Review*, 20 May 1951. Samuels was a long-time staffer for the *Times* and later wrote a book about Israel herself.

34 Lynne Weiner to ZP, letter of 21 May 1951, in ZP Papers, BU Library; ZP to Richard and Juliet Popkin, 25 May 1951, in PFA; Marie Syrkin to ZP, letter of 21 September 1951, in ZP Papers, BU Library, box 14. On Syrkin, an important figure in the New York Jewish journalistic world and author of one of the first books about Jewish resistance during the Holocaust, see Carole S. Kessner, *Marie Syrkin: Values Beyond the Self* (Hanover, NH: Brandeis University Press, 2008). Like Syrkin, Popkin's character Edith Hirsch was described as the American-raised daughter of an important early collaborator of Herzl.

35 Letter from Lippincott to ZP, 6 February 1952, in ZP Papers, BU Library, box 14. There are hints in letters from Lippincott that concerns about libel suits may have inhibited a Hebrew translation.

36 Interview in *The Jewish News*, 28 December 1951; contribution to "'Why I Wrote a Jewish Novel,' by Nine Contemporary Novelists," *Congress Weekly*, n.d., clipping in ZP Papers, BU Library, box 14, reprinted in Harold U. Ribalow, ed., *Mid-Century*, 316–32.

37 On Uris and *Exodus*, see M. M. Silver, *Our Exodus: Leon Uris and the Americanization of Israel's Founding Story* (Detroit: Wayne State University Press, 2010); and Ira B. Nadel, *Leon Uris: Life of a Best Seller* (Austin: University of Texas Press, 2010).

38 Transcript of interview, in ZP Papers, BU Library, box 14.

39 Radway, *A Feeling for Books*, 285.

40 Popkin, *Quiet Street*, 346.

41 Goldie Joseph to ZP, letter of 24 November 1948, in PFA; notebook and "Outline for a novel," in ZP Papers, BU Library, box 14.

42 Popkin, *Quiet Street*, 18–20, 171–72.

43 Popkin, *Quiet Street*, 220.

44 Katz, *Bringing Zion Home*, 33–39. Bar-David's columns were collected in a book, *My Promised Land*, published a year after *Quiet Street*, but she had already reached a wide audience through the Hadassah magazine, which had a circulation of 250,000.

45 Popkin, *Quiet Street*, 121, 378. Helen had told Zelda, "Goldie Joseph's daughter died as she definitely taunted her comrades with the word 'cowards' as she firmly stuck to the center of the road—as if with her frail body she would fend off the Egyptian bombers." Helen Koussewitsky, letter to ZP, 15 May 1949, in PFA.

46 Popkin, *Quiet Street*, 315.

47 Suzanne Selengut, "Quietly Ahead of Her Time," *Jerusalem Post*, 3 February 2006.

48 In his overview of "Zionist Contemporary Fiction" in 1952, the well-informed Jewish journalist and author Harold Ribalow compared *Quiet Street* favorably to Alex Comfort's *On This Side of Nothing* and Ernst Pawel's *The Island in Time*, two stories set in years of the Mandate and critical of Zionism. Ribalow's essay, originally published in *Reconstructionist* magazine, is in Ribalow, ed., *Mid-Century*, 570–91.

49 Andrew Furman, *Israel Through the American-Jewish Imagination* (Albany: SUNY Press, 1997); Zelda Popkin, *Quiet Street* (Lincoln, NE: Bison, 2002).

CHAPTER 6

1 "Quiet Street," *Eternal Light*, chapter 385 (3 May 1953), script in PFA. On "The Eternal Light," see Jeffrey Shandler, "Religion, Democracy, and Radio Waves: *The Eternal Light*," in J. Hoberman and Jeffrey Shandler, eds., *Entertaining America: Jews, Movies, and Broadcasting* (Princeton, NJ: Princeton University Press, 2003), 130–32.

2 *Wilkes-Barre Times Leader*, 17 March 1952; *Scranton Tribune*, 17 March 1952.

3 On the anxieties of postwar American Jewish life, see Rachel Kranson, *Ambivalent Embrace: Jewish Upward Mobility in Postwar America* (Chapel Hill: University of North Carolina Press, 2017).

4 Zelda Popkin, "A Warsaw Fighter in Israel," *Commentary* (January 1952): 34–37.

5 On Liebman, see Heinze, *Jews and the American Soul*, 195–97.

6 ZP to Richard and Juliet Popkin, 18 February 1953, in PFA.

7 Heinze, *Jews and the American Soul*, 296.

8 Juliet Popkin, "Yiches and Naches," in PFA; Zelda Popkin, "Anyone Can Be Brave," *Coronet* 33 (November 1952): 100–3; "What Are We Afraid Of?," *Coronet* 33 (February 1953): 36–38; "What Do You Know About Love?," *Coronet* 33 (April 1953): 138–40; "Some New Ways of Making Friends," *Coronet* 34 (August 1953): 98–100; "Middle Age: The Time to Live," *Coronet* 35 (December 1953): 162–65; ZP to Richard and Juliet Popkin, 1 October 1953, in PFA.

9 Zelda Popkin, "On Sources," n.d. but probably 1953, and "Memorandum on: 'The Inheritance," in PFA.

10 Saxe Commins, editor at Random House, letter of 4 June 1953, in PFA.

11 ZP to Richard and Juliet Popkin, 6 November 1952; 9 May 1953; 26 June 1953; 7 July 1953, in PFA.

12 ZP to Richard and Juliet Popkin, "Thursday," n.d. but 1954, in PFA.

13 ZP to Richard and Juliet Popkin, 2 December 1953; 20 March 1954, "Thursday," n.d. but 1954; 8 September 1954, in PFA.

14 Walter O'Hearn, "Zelda's Revenge," *Montreal Star*, undated clipping in ZP Papers, BU Library, box 14. This box also contains a letter from O'Hearn to Zelda, dated 19 March 1956. He told her, "While I didn't agree with all your opinions, I admired your spirit."

15 Pauline Pinsker to Richard and Juliet Popkin, 19 September 1954, in PFA; ZP to Richard and Juliet Popkin, "Monday," n.d. but early 1956, in PFA.

16 ZP to Richard and Juliet Popkin, 19 October 1953, in PFA.

17 Fannie Hurst, *Anatomy of Me: A Wonderer in Search of Herself* (Garden City, NY: Doubleday, 1958), foreword. For an overview of the American autobiographical tradition, see Diane Bjorkland, *Interpreting the Self: Two Hundred Years of American Autobiography* (Chicago: University of Chicago Press, 1998).

18 Zelda Popkin, "If Tragedy Comes," *Coronet* 33 (March 1953): 61–64.

19 Jeremy D. Popkin, *History, Historians and Autobiography* (Chicago: University of Chicago Press, 2005).

20 ZP to Richard Popkin, 4 July 1961, in PFA.

21 Paul John Eakin, *Fictions in Autobiography: Studies in the Art of Self-Invention* (Princeton, NJ: Princeton University Press, 1985), 3; Patricia Meyer Spacks, *Imagining a Self: Autobiography and Novel in Eighteenth-Century England* (Cambridge, MA: Harvard University Press, 1976), 310–11.

22 ZP to Richard and Juliet Popkin, April 1954; fall 1954; 11 January 1955, in PFA.

23 Zelda Popkin, "Memorandum Re: Open Every Door," n.d. but 1954, in ZP Papers, BU Library, box 14.

24 ZP, "Memorandum Re: Open Every Door," ZP Papers, BU Library, box 14.

25 Zelda Popkin, *Open Every Door*, 22–23.

26 Hurst, *Anatomy of Me*; Alfred Kazin, *Starting Out in the Thirties* (Boston: Little, Brown, 1965); Irving Howe, *A Margin of Hope: An Intellectual Autobiography* (New York: Harcourt Brace Jovanovich, 1982).

27 Zelda Popkin, *Open Every Door*, 257, 312, 331.

28 Interview notes, in ZP Papers, BU Library, box 14.

29 On Wouk's novel's message for women, see Barbara Sicherman, "Reading *Marjorie Morningstar* in the Age of the Feminine Mystique and After," in Hasia Diner, Shira Kohn, and Rachel Kranson, eds., *A Jewish Feminine Mystique? Jewish Women in Postwar America* (New Brunswick, NJ: Rutgers University Press, 2010), 194–204.

30 Doris Fleischman Bernays, *A Wife Is Many Women* (New York: Crown, 1956).

31 Popkin, *Open Every Door*, 29.

32 Popkin, *Open Every Door*, 281, 310.

33 Antler, *The Journey Home*, xv.

34 Popkin, *Open Every Door*, 281, 345, 379.

35 Popkin, *Open Every Door*, 367, 373.

36 Popkin, *Open Every Door*, 375, 376, 379.

37 Alfred Kazin, *A Walker in the City* (New York: Harcourt Brace, 1951), 172; Kazin, *Starting Out in the Thirties*.

38 Harry Feinberg to ZP, 25 April 1956, in PFA; Helen Rossi to ZP, 10 February 1956, in ZP Papers, BU Library, box 14; Richard Popkin to ZP, 6 February 1956, in PFA.

39 W. G. Rogers, Associated Press, February 1956; Sterling North, *World-Telegram and Sun*, 13 March 1956; review by "Burstein," source unknown; Harold Ribalow, *Hadassah Newsletter*, June 1956; Harold Ribalow, *Jewish Affairs*, April 1956, in ZP Papers, BU Library, box 14.

40 Ribalow, *Hadassah Newsletter*, June 1956; North, *World-Telegraph and Sun*, 13 March 1956; Ishbel Ross, *Herald Tribune*, 26 February 1956.

41 Kate Simon, *A Wider World: Portraits in an Adolescence* (New York: Harper and Row, 1986).

42 ZP to Richard and Juliet Popkin, 17 March 1956, in PFA; "Open Every Door: A Self-Help Program for Women," in ZP Papers, BU Library, box 14; ZP to Richard and Juliet Popkin, 11 August 1956, in PFA.

43 ZP to Richard and Juliet Popkin, 6 April 1956, in PFA.

44 ZP to Richard and Juliet Popkin, 25 October 1956. Ellen Glasgow's *The Woman Within* (New York: Harcourt Brace, 1954), "written in great suffering of mind and body," according to its author, reflected a very different attitude toward life than what Zelda had tried to communicate in her autobiography.

45 ZP to Richard and Juliet Popkin, n.d. but spring 1957; 15 February 1957, in PFA; letter of reference from Mrs. D. P. Gotlieb, national chair of Women's Division, State of Israel Bonds (Canada), 29 August 1957; letter from Belle Eichler, administrative assistant, America-Israel Cultural Foundation, 13 June 1958, stating that ZP was Director of Publicity and Public Relations from 16 September 1957 to 13 June 1958, with a salary of $8,000 a year; letters from the American Friends of the Hebrew University about her resignation, all in PFA.

46 Richard Popkin to Juliet Popkin, 18 June 1961, in PFA.

47 Roy Popkin to ZP, n.d. but 1963?, in PFA.

48 ZP to Richard and Juliet Popkin, November 1964 and 20 February 1964, in PFA.

49 ZP to Richard and Juliet Popkin, 23 February 1963, in PFA.

50 ZP to Richard and Juliet Popkin, 31 August 1963, in PFA.

51 ZP to Richard and Juliet Popkin, 27 November 1963, 3 August 1966. The 1966 mass killings she was referring to were the massacre committed on the University of Texas campus by Charles Whitman and the murder of eight student nurses in Chicago by Richard Speck.

52 ZP to Richard and Juliet Popkin, 29 April 1965, in PFA. Andrea Dworkin later became famous for her writings against pornography.

53 ZP to Richard and Juliet Popkin, 17 December 1963, in PFA. ZP to Richard Popkin, 19 January 1965; 9 September 1965; and "Saturday," early 1966, in PFA.

54 Richard H. Popkin, *The Second Oswald* (New York: Avon, 1966).

CHAPTER 7

1 Zelda Popkin file, Yaddo Archives, New York Public Library; marketing questionnaire for *Herman Had Two Daughters*, 12 October 1967, in ZP Papers, BU Library, box 7; Zelda Popkin, *A Death of Innocence* (Philadelphia: J. B. Lippincott, 1971), 73.

2 ZP to Richard Popkin, 18 April 1963 and 16 March 1964, in PFA.

3 ZP to RP, 16 March 1964, in PFA.

4 Zelda's papers contain two copies of this composition, both with handwritten corrections. It seems to have been intended as a public lecture, and I have dated it to 1966 because it refers to the eighteenth anniversary of the Israeli Declaration of Independence. There is mention in one of her letters to my parents of an invitation to address a Hadassah group in late 1965 or early 1966; it is possible that this is the talk she gave. ZP to Richard and Juliet Popkin, 9 September 1965, in PFA.

5 The only critical discussion to date of *Herman Had Two Daughters* places it in the context of American Jewish women's writing: Ellen Serlen Uffen, *Strands in the Cable: The Place of the Past in Jewish American Women's Writing* (New York: Peter Lang, 1995), 95–109.

6 ZP to Richard Popkin, 13 July 1965 and 9 September 1965; 28 September 1967; 10 September 1966; and ZP to Richard and Juliet Popkin, "Tuesday," n.d. but spring 1967, in PFA.

7 ZP, marketing questionnaire, 12 October 1967, in ZP Papers, BU Library, box 7.

8 Juliet Popkin diary, 23 October 1976, in PFA.

9 Zelda Popkin, *Herman*, 329.

10 Samuel Vaughan to ZP, letter of 21 February 1967; memorandum to Cyrilly Abels, n.d., both in ZP Papers, BU Library, box 7.

11 Popkin, *Herman*, 16, 332.

12 Popkin, *Small Victory*, 174.

13 Samuel Vaughan to Zelda Popkin and Cyrilly Abels, 21 February 1967; "Memorandum from Zelda Popkin," n.d., both in ZP Papers, BU Library, box 7.

14 Memorandum to Cyrilly Abels, n.d., in ZP Papers, BU Library, box 7.

15 Zelda Popkin, *Herman*, 29.

16 Zelda Popkin, *Herman*, 43.

17 Zelda Popkin, *Herman*, 61.

18 Zelda Popkin, *Herman*, 105.

19 Popkin, *Open Every Door*, 232–35. Dilling and Edmundson were antisemitic agitators; Dilling had connections with Paul Winter, leader of the Ku Klux Klan chapter in Wilkes-Barre. Philip Jenkins, *Hoods and Shirts: The Extreme Right in Pennsylvania, 1925–1950* (Chapel Hill: University of North Carolina Press, 1997), 87. Weitzenkorn's death was reported in the *New York Times*, 6 February 1943. Some aspects of his career as a playwright in the 1930s may have inspired elements of the story of Jessie Weiss.

20 "Memo" and "Snowball Rolling Downhill," in ZP Papers, BU Library, box 7.

21 Zelda Popkin, *Herman*, 164, 168, 181–82.

22 Zelda Popkin, *Herman*, 188–89.

23 Popkin, memorandum to Cyrilly Abels, in ZP Papers, BU Library, box 7.

24 Arthur D. Morse, *While Six Million Died: A Chronicle of American Apathy* (New York: Random House, 1968); Popkin, *Herman*, 213, 225, 234. The original letter from American consul Raymond Geist is in ZP Papers, BU Library, box 7.

25 Popkin, *Open Every Door*, 298–301.

26 Zelda Popkin, interview in *Palestine Post*, n.d., clipping in PFA.

27 Popkin, *Herman*, 255–56, 276; "Memorandum to Cyrilly Abels," n.d., ZP Papers, BU Library, box 7.

28 Zelda Popkin, *Herman*, 289, 311.

29 Zelda Popkin, *Herman*, 313, 325, 339.

30 Zelda Popkin, *Herman*, 365, 369, 372.

31 Zelda Popkin, *Herman*, 329, 330.

32 Zelda Popkin, *Herman*, 331–33, 339.

33 Zelda Popkin, *Herman*, 346, 377.

34 Zelda Popkin, *Herman*, 379, 380, 381–82.

35 ZP to Richard and Juliet Popkin, 6 October 1966, in PFA; John Barkham, review in *New York Knickerbocker*, 28 April 1968. Hyman Kaplan was the protagonist of two humor books by Leo Rosten, originally published in the 1930s. One of the Kaplan character's distinguishing characteristics was his fractured English.

36 Paul Kersh, review in *Saturday Review*, 18 May 1968.

37 Popkin to Richard and Juliet Popkin, "Monday," in PFA; Calhoun Ancrum, review in *Charleston News and Courier*, 19 May 1968; Popkin, letter to Alice [Allen], 14 November 1968; Popkin, interview with Ruth Maizlish, *California Jewish Voice*, 19 July 1968 in ZP Papers, BU Library, box 7.

38 Philip Roth, *The Plot Against America* (Boston: Houghton Mifflin, 2004).

39 On the role of mothers in American Jewish fiction by women, see Janet Handler Burstein, *Writing Mothers, Writing Daughters: Tracing the Maternal in Stories by American Jewish Women* (Urbana: University of Illinois Press, 1996).

40 Memorandum to Sam Vaughan, in ZP Papers, BU Library, box 7.

41 Zelda Popkin, *Herman*, 381.

42 Zelda Popkin, *Herman*, 55, 329, 333. Zelda had known the playwright Elmer Rice (1892–1967) during the 1920s, when his career was at its peak. He died as she was completing *Herman*.

43 Zelda Popkin, *A Death of Innocence* (Philadelphia: J. B. Lippincott, 1971); paperback edition (New York: Dell, 1972); Spanish translation: *Inocencia Violada* (Barcelona: Editoriale Pomaire, 1972). Zelda Popkin, *Dear Once* (Philadelphia: J. B. Lippincott: 1975); paperback edition (New York: Signet, 1977).

44 Zelda Popkin, *Innocence*, 307.

45 ZP to Richard and Juliet Popkin, n.d. but spring 1970 and n.d. but spring 1971, in PFA; Susan Popkin, email, 20 September 2021.

46 Zelda Popkin, *Innocence*, 28, 272.

47 ZP to Richard and Juliet Popkin, 25 June 1970, in PFA.

48 Zelda Popkin, *A Death of Innocence*, 27, 7, 314.

49 Joy Stilley, "Zelda Popkin Lives Life to the Fullest," *Bridgeport [Connecticut] Sunday Post*, 9 November 1975; Susan Brownmiller, *Against Our Will: Men, Women and Rape* (New York: Simon and Schuster, 1975).

50 Zelda Popkin, *Dear Once*, 95–96, 117–18; Juliet Popkin, diary, 13 February 1978, in PFA. For reactions to this scene in the novel, see notes on reviews by Edith Dunham Webber and Eileen C. Spraker in ZP Papers, BU Library, box. 11.

51 Zelda Popkin, *Dear Once*, 239, 242.

52 Zelda Popkin, *Dear Once*, 258, 319.

53 Zelda Popkin, *Dear Once*, 91, 370; Kirkus Reviews, 1 October 1975.

54 Detroit Book Fair talk, ZP Papers, BU Library, box 11.

EPILOGUE

1 Juliet Popkin, "Improbabilities," unpublished essay (1974), in PFA.

2 ZP to Irma Megiddo, 22 June 1975, in PFA. For her fights with her sister, see Richard Popkin to Juliet Popkin, 15 January 1977, in PFA.

3 Juliet Popkin to Grace Goldin, 8 June 1977, in PFA; Leslie Lewinter-Suskind, "The Story of Zelda Popkin," *Weight Watchers Magazine* (November 1981); Zelda Popkin to Judith Nolte, 5 November 1981, in PFA.

4 Gail Godwin, "House Parties and Box Lunches: One Writer's Summer at Yaddo," *New York Times*, 10 August 1986.

5 ZP to Richard and Juliet Popkin, 7 November 1965. Roy Popkin published *The Environmental Science Services Administration* (New York: Praeger, 1967); *Desalination: Water for the World's Future* (New York: Praeger, 1968); and *Technology of Necessity: Scientific and Engineering Development in Israel* (New York: Praeger, 1971).

6 Margaret Popkin, *Peace Without Justice: Obstacles to Building the Rule of Law in El Salvador* (University Park, PA: Penn State University Press, 2000); Susan J. Popkin, *No Simple Solutions: Transforming Public Housing in Chicago* (Lanham, MD: Rowman & Littlefield, 2016).

7 Popkin, *Open Every Door*, 209–10; Applegate, *Madam*, 386–88.

8 Juliet Popkin, letter, 21 November 1980, in PFA.

Sources and Bibliography

Manuscript Sources

Zelda Popkin papers, Mugar Library (Boston University), Howard Gottlieb Archival Research Center, Twentieth-Century American Authors Collection. Contains manuscripts of Zelda Popkin's novels, including unpublished works, correspondence with editors and publishers, published reviews, correspondence from readers, research materials connected to Popkin's books, and miscellaneous items including some personal correspondence.

Popkin Family Archive, author's collection. Contains Zelda Popkin personal documents; correspondence with Zelda Popkin's son Richard Popkin and his wife Juliet Popkin; letters to Zelda Popkin from other relatives including her father Harry Feinberg, sister Helen Rossi Koussewitsky, son Roy Popkin; miscellaneous publications by and about Zelda Popkin; souvenirs from Zelda Popkin's 1948 trip to Israel; Juliet Popkin diaries and essays; family photographs; and inscribed books from Zelda Popkin's library.

New York Public Library. Documents related to Zelda Popkin in archives of the *New Yorker* magazine and the Yaddo Writers Colony.

Center for Jewish History. Documents related to Zelda and Louis Popkin in archives of Joint Distribution Committee and Jewish Welfare Board.

American Jewish Archives. File on Louis Popkin.

Printed Sources
Books by Zelda Popkin

Death Wears a White Gardenia (Philadelphia: J. B. Lippincott, 1938). Paperback edition (New York: Dell, 1943). German translation: *Rendezvous nach Ladenschluß* (Munich: Deutscher Taschenbuch Verlag, 1992). Italian translation: *Una Gardenia per il boia* (Milan: Mondadori, 1952).

Time Off for Murder (Philadelphia: J. B. Lippincott, 1940). Paperback edition (New York: Dell, 1944). French translation: *Congés pour meurtre* (Paris: Métailié, 1993). German translation: *Karrierefrauen leben schneller* (Munich: Deutscher Taschenbuch Verlag, 1993).

Murder in the Mist (Philadelphia: J. B. Lippincott, 1940). Paperback edition (New York: Dell, 1944). French translation: *La lune de miel de Mary Carner* (Brussels: Les Éditions de Lumière, 1946); French translation: *Meurtre dans la brume* (Paris: Métailié, 1994). German translation: *Die Tote nebenan* (Munich: Deutscher Taschenbuch Verlag, 1994).

Dead Man's Gift (Philadelphia: J. B. Lippincott, 1941). Paperback edition (New York: Dell, 1944). French translation: *Le Cadeau du mort* (Paris: Métailié, 1999). German translation: *Ein teuflisches Testament* (Munich: Deutscher Taschenbuch Verlag, 1995).

No Crime for a Lady (Philadelphia: J. B. Lippincott, 1942). Paperback edition (New York: Dell, 1944). French translation: *Mary Carner et ses voisins* (Brussels: Les Éditions de Lumière, 1946). German translation: *Die Dame mordet nicht* (Munich: Deutscher Taschenbuch Verlag, 1996).

So Much Blood (Philadelphia: J. B. Lippincott, 1944). German translation: *So viel Blut* (Munich: Deutscher Taschenbuch Verlag, 1996).

The Journey Home (Philadelphia: J. B. Lippincott, 1945). Paperback edition (New York: Pocket, 1946).

Small Victory (Philadelphia: J. B. Lippincott, 1947).

Walk Through the Valley (Philadelphia: J. B. Lippincott, 1949).

Quiet Street (Philadelphia: J. B. Lippincott, 1951). Paperback edition (Lincoln, NE: Bison, 2002).

Open Every Door (New York: E. P. Dutton, 1956).

Herman Had Two Daughters (Philadelphia: J. B. Lippincott, 1968). Paperback edition (New York: Dell, 1970).

A Death of Innocence (Philadelphia: J. B. Lippincott, 1971). Paperback edition (New York: Dell, 1972). Spanish translation: *Inocencia Violada* (Barcelona: Pomaire, 1972).

Dear Once (Philadelphia: J. B. Lippincott, 1975). Paperback edition (New York: Signet, 1977).

Book Ghost-Written by Zelda Popkin

Nessler, Charles [sic], *The Story of Hair: Its Purpose and Its Preservation* (New York: Boni and Liveright, 1928).

Articles

By Zelda Feinberg

"Quarantined Leper Plays Card Game at a Neighbor's House," *Wilkes-Barre Times Leader*, 3 October 1916.

"Hope Springs Eternal—Seeing 'Papa' Joffre," *Wilkes-Barre Times Leader*, 12 May 1917; *Scranton Republican*, 31 December 1917.

"Home Comforts for the Soldiers," *American Hebrew* 104 (8 November 1918): 15–16.

"The East Side Emerges," *American Hebrew* 104 (15 November 1918): 27.

"An Oasis in the East Side," *American Hebrew* 104 (15 November 1918): 41–42.

"Jewish Women with the A.E.F.," *American Hebrew* 104 (11 April 1919): 524, 544, 597.

By Zelda Popkin

"The Council's Work on Blackwell's Island," *Womankind* (16 April 1920): 5.

"Women to 'Sell' Philanthropy," *American Hebrew* 107 (10 September 1920): 440.

"A New Adventurer in the Promised Land," review of *Hungry Hearts* by Anzia Yezierska, *American Hebrew* 108 (3 December 1920): 112–13.

"Spotting 'Star-Dust,'" review of *Star-Dust* by Fannie Hurst, *American Hebrew* 108 (29 April 1921): 712.

"Rachel as Viewed by a Writer of Her Day," *American Jewish World* (Minneapolis), 8 July 1921.

"Jewish Dolly Madisons," *American Hebrew* 109 (30 September 1921): 488, 514–15.

"Who's Who in the Short Story—1921," *American Hebrew* 110 (1921): 86, 126.

"Romain Rolland and the Jews," *American Hebrew* 110 (7 April 1922): 542.

"Mother Love in Mean Streets," *American Hebrew* 110 (5 May 1922): 700.

"A Jewish Palette: Theresa Bernstein Wins Laurels as Painter," *American Hebrew* 111 (16 June 1922): 133, 135.

"The Changeable Petticoat," *American Hebrew* 111 (14 July 1922): 221, 224, 228.

"That's A Strike," *Nation* 115 (23 August 1922): 185–86.

"A Barn for School," *Survey* 49 (15 November 1922): 253–55.

"Curb Lizards," *American Hebrew* 112 (24 November 1922): 30, 32, 33, 34.

"National Jewish Hospital for Consumptives," *American Israelite*, 22 August 1923, 1.

Review of *Lummox* by Fannie Hurst, *American Hebrew* 113 (2 November 1923): 672–73.

"An Experiment in Education," *American Hebrew* 113 (28 December 1923).

"New York State Sisterhoods Outside of the Metropolis," *American Hebrew* 114 (4 January 1924): 236, 246.

"'The Jew and Civilization': A Review of Ada Sterling's Remarkable Book Just From The Press," *American Israelite*, 24 February 1924, 1.

Review of *My Musical Life* by Walter Damrosch, *American Hebrew* 114 (29 February 1924): 473.

Review of *The Color of a Great City* by Theodore Dreiser, *American Hebrew* 114 (18 April 1924): 724.

Review of *Birth* by Zona Gale, *American Hebrew* 115 (6 June 1924): 144.

"The Caravan of Hope in Europe: A Regenerated People Sing Praises of Providence and O.R.T.," *American Israelite*, 4 December 1924, 1.

"The Paradox of John Singer Sargent," *American Hebrew* 117 (26 June 1925): 229.

Review of *Three Plays* by Luigi Pirandello and *The Swan* by Ferenc Molnár, *American Hebrew* 117 (3 July 1925): 281.

Review of *Unveiled* by Beatrice Kean Seymour, *American Hebrew* 117 (31 July 1925): 363.

Review of *Sacrilegious Hands* by William Henry Warner, *American Hebrew* 117 (14 August 1925): 425.

"Gloucester Hangs Art on Its Trees," *New York Times Magazine* (6 September 1925): 17, 21.

"Nearly Seventy Thousand Volumes in College Library," *American Israelite*, 22 October 1925.

"Mistress and Maid in Autumn Line-Up," *Daily News* (Los Angeles), 8 November 1925, 11.

Review of *The Happy Failure* by Solita Solano, *American Hebrew* 118 (4 December 1925): 167.

Review of *I Meet My Contemporaries* by Maximilian Harden, *American Hebrew* 118 (16 April 1926).

"East Side Night Life," *New Yorker* (5 June 1926): 68–69.

"The Hebrew Union College Library is Leader of Jewish Learning," *American Israelite*, 19 August 1926, 1, 5.

"The Synagogue in the Wilderness: First Place of Worship in Pennsylvania Founded by Early Colony Near Lancaster," *American Hebrew* 119 (10 September 1926): 522, 577.

"Reflections of Silent New Yorkers," *New Yorker* (30 October 1926): 38–39.

"Reflections of More-or-Less Silent Citizens," *New Yorker* (11 December 1926): 103–4.

"Reflections of Silent Citizens," *New Yorker* (12 February 1927): 82.

"Changing East Side," *American Mercury* 10 (February 1927): 168–75.

"Reflections of Silent Citizens: The Bus Conductor," *New Yorker* (26 February 1927): 69.

"The Jew and Aviation," *B'nai B'rith Magazine* XLI, no. 10 (July 1927): 417–18.

"The Jewish Covered Wagon," *B'nai B'rith Magazine* XLI, no. 11 (August 1927): 453–54, 476.

"A Good School for the Children," *New Yorker* (10 September 1927): 55.

"The Jew on Stage and Screen," *B'nai B'rith Magazine* XLII, no. 1 (October 1927): 548–49.

"The Rivals of Bridge that Come and Go," *New York Times*, 30 October 1927.

"The Jew on Stage and Screen," *B'nai B'rith Magazine* XLII, no. 2 (November 1927): 18–19.

"Abdication of King Coal," *Nation* 126 (4 January 1928): 11–12.

"Class of '28 Gets Down to Business," *New Yorker* (19 October 1928): 92–94.

"A South African Writes About the Jews," *B'nai B'rith Magazine* 43 (November 1928): 66–67.

"Gloucester Honors its Sailors," *Nation* 128 (17 April 1929): 448–49.

"Russia Goes to the Movies," *Outlook and Independent* 155 (28 May 1930): 129–31, 154–55.

"Tent Show Turns to Sex," *Outlook and Independent* 156 (24 September 1930): 128–30, 157.

"Art: Three Aisles Over," *Outlook and Independent* 156 (26 November 1930): 502–3, 515–16.

"Panic of the Parents," *Outlook and Independent* 158 (1 July 1931): 267–69, 286.

"Heaven Bound: Authentic Negro Folk Drama Out of Old Savannah," *Theatre Guild* 11 (6 August 1931): 14–17.

"Wonderful Institution, Our Schools," *New Yorker* (14 November 1931): 52–56.

"Camera Explorers of the New Russia," *Travel* 58 (December 1931): 37–40, 52–54.

"Saturday Morning at Carnegie," *New Yorker* (6 February 1932).

"Finer Things of Life," *Harper's Magazine* 164 (April 1932): 602–11.

"Conciliation Court," *New Yorker* (10 September 1932): 40–47.

[Anonymous] "The American Jewish Tragedy," *Jewish Criterion* (Pittsburgh), 30 September 1932.

"Children of the Racketeer Age," *Harper's Magazine* 166 (February 1933): 364–75.

"Boy Wonder," *New Yorker* (4 August 1933): 40–42.

"Sociological Court is Urged for Women," *New York Times*, 25 November 1934.

"Folk Festivals Lure: Annual Trips Begin in May to Centers of Primitive American Arts and Music," *New York Times*, 21 April 1935, X13.

"Vignettes from a Women's Court," *Independent Woman* 14 (December 1935): 398–400, 414–16.

"Magistrates' Courts Bureau is Designed to Deal With Problems Presented by Arraigned Persons," *New York Times*, 5 January 1936, 166.

"Gone With the Flood," *New Yorker* (24 October 1936): 32, 34, 36–39.

"Not to Reason Why," *New Yorker* (6 March 1937).

"Annals of Crime: Sing a Song of Homicide," *New Yorker* (30 October 1937): 46–56.

"The Trousseau," *New York Daily News*, 23 September 1938.

"Madame Jumel: Vice-Queen," *American Mercury* 48 (November 1939): 327–33.

"Highest Standard of Living on Earth," *Independent Woman* 19 (April 1940): 101.

"A Corpse Can't Leer," *Writer* 55 (October 1942): 291–94.

"A Widow's Way," *McCall's Magazine* (October 1945): 59–60, 66, 68.

"Shoes for the Children of Drancy," *Reader's Digest* 48 (March 1946): 36–38.

"Europe's Children," *Ladies' Home Journal* 63 (August 1946): 168, 170–71.

"Glory at Twilight," *American Magazine* 144 (October 1947): 48–49.

"New Youth for a New Land," *Parents' Magazine* 24 (1949): 36–37, 84.

"Widows and the Perilous Years," *Harper's Magazine* 199 (September 1949): 69–75.

"Bitter Bondage," *American Magazine* 149 (May 1950), 52–58.

"Tolerance: For Snobs Only," *Negro Digest* 10 (November 1951): 38–39. (Originally in *Compact* magazine, September 1951.)

"A Warsaw Fighter in Israel," *Commentary* (January 1952): 34–37.

"Anyone Can Be Brave!," *Coronet* 33 (November 1952): 100–103.

"What Are We Afraid Of?," *Coronet* 33 (February 1953): 36–38.
"If Tragedy Comes," *Coronet* 33 (March 1953): 61–64.
"What Do You Know About Love?," *Coronet* 33 (April 1953): 138–40.
"Some New Ways of Making Friends," *Coronet* 34 (August 1953): 98–100.
"What's Right with Our Schools," *Coronet* 34 (October 1953): 23–28.
"Middle Age: The Time to Live," *Coronet* 35 (December 1953): 162–65.
"Something for Nothing," *Coronet* 35 (January 1954): 124–26.
"Budget Your Emotions," *Coronet* 35 (February 1954): 154–56.
"Technical Charge of Homicide," *New Yorker* 30 (13 March 1954): 100, 102–10.
"Plot Isn't a Dirty Word," *Writer* 82 (July 1969): 11–12.

OTHER PRINTED SOURCES

Abramowitz, Molly. "The Mysterious Case of the Haganah Posters," *Na'Amat Woman* 24 (summer 2009): 12–15.

Adickes, Sandra. *To Be Young Was Very Heaven: Women in New York Before the First World War* (New York: St. Martin's, 1997).

Adler, Polly. *A House Is Not a Home* (New York: Rinehart, 1953).

Alexander, Michael. *Jazz Age Jews* (Princeton, NJ: Princeton University Press, 2001).

Alexander, William. *Film on the Left: American Documentary Film from 1931 to 1942* (Princeton, NJ: Princeton University Press, 1981).

Alpern, Sara, Joyce Antler, Elisabeth Israels Perry, and Ingrid Winther Scobie, eds. *The Challenge of Feminist Biography: Writing the Lives of Modern American Women* (Urbana: University of Illinois Press, 1992).

Anonymous. "An Advertising Man," "Personal Experience With Prejudice," *Jewish Tribune* 97 (15 August 1930): 2.

Antler, Joyce. *The Journey Home: Jewish Women and the American Century* (New York: Free, 1997).

———. *Talking Back: Images of Jewish Women in American Popular Culture* (Hanover, NH: Brandeis University Press, 1998).

Applegate, Debby. *Madam: The Biography of Polly Adler, Icon of the Jazz Age* (New York: Doubleday, 2021).

Arad, Gulie Ne'eman. *America, Its Jews, and the Rise of Nazism* (Bloomington: Indiana University Press, 2000).

Ashton, Dianne. *Rebecca Gratz: Women and Judaism in Antebellum America* (Detroit: Wayne State University Press, 1997).

Baxter, Tara. "A Woman of Substance: From Age 16, Zelda Feinberg Popkin Was A Role Model For Women," *Wilkes-Barre Times Leader*, 27 June 1999.

Bellow, Saul. "Review of *The Journey Home*," *Commentary*, December 1945, 95–96.

Bercovici, Rion. *For Immediate Release* (New York: Sheridan House, 1937).

Berenbaum, Michael. "Isaac Landman," *Encyclopedia Judaica*, 2nd ed., 12:472–3.

Berman, Jeffrey. *Writing Widowhood: The Landscapes of Bereavement* (Albany: SUNY Press, 2015).

Berman, Lila Corwin. *The American Jewish Philanthropic Complex: The History of a Multibillion-Dollar Institution* (Princeton, NJ: Princeton University Press, 2020).

Bernays, Doris Fleischman. *A Wife Is Many Women* (New York: Crown, 1956).

Bjorklund, Diane. *Interpreting the Self: Two Hundred Years of American Autobiography* (Chicago: University of Chicago Press, 1998).

Breitman, Richard, Barbara McDonald Stewart, and Severin Hochberg, eds. *Refugees and Rescue: The Diaries and Papers of James G. McDonald, 1935–1945* (Bloomington: Indiana University Press, 2009).

Brodkin, Karen. *How Jews Became White Folks and What That Says About Race in America* (New Brunswick, NJ: Rutgers University Press, 1998).

Broun, Heywood. *Christians Only: A Study in Prejudice* (New York: Vanguard, 1931).

Brownmiller, Susan. *Against Our Will: Men, Women and Rape* (New York: Simon and Schuster, 1975).

Broyard, Bliss. *One Drop: My Father's Hidden Life—A Story of Race and Family Secrets* (New York: Back Bay, 2007).

Burnham, Patricia M. "Theresa Bernstein," *Woman's Art Journal* 9, no. 2 (1988), 22–27.

Burstein, Janet Handler. *Writing Mothers, Writing Daughters: Tracing the Maternal in Stories by American Jewish Women* (Urbana: University of Illinois Press, 1996).

Carlson, John Roy [Arthur Derounian]. *Under Cover: My Four Years in the Nazi Underworld of America* (New York: E. P. Dutton, 1943).

Cohen, Naomi W. *Jacob H. Schiff: A Study in American Jewish Leadership* (Hanover, NH: Brandeis University Press, 1999).

DeMarr, Mary Jean. "The Mysteries of Zelda Popkin," *Clues: A Journal of Detection* 3 (1982): 1–8.

Diner, Hasia R. *Roads Taken: The Great Jewish Migrations to the New World and the Peddlers Who Forged the Way* (New Haven, CT: Yale University Press, 2018).

Diner, Hasia R., Shira Kohn, and Rachel Kranson, eds. *A Jewish Feminine Mystique? Jewish Women in Postwar America* (New Brunswick, NJ: Rutgers University Press, 2010).

Dinnerstein, Leonard. "The U.S. Army and the Jews: Policies Toward the Displaced Persons After World War II," *American Jewish History* 68, no. 3 (1979): 353–66.

———. *America and the Survivors of the Holocaust* (New York: Columbia University Press, 1982).

———. *Antisemitism in America* (New York: Oxford University Press, 1994).

Douglas, Ann. *Terrible Honesty: Mongrel Manhattan in the 1920s* (New York: Farrar, Straus and Giroux, 1995).

Eakin, Paul John. *Fictions in Autobiography: Studies in the Art of Self-Invention* (Princeton, NJ: Princeton University Press, 1995).

Eksteins, Modris. *Walking Since Daybreak: A Story of Eastern Europe, World War II, and the Heart of Our Century* (Boston and New York: Houghton Mifflin, 1999).

Faber, Sebastiaan. "Image Politics: U.S. Aid to the Spanish Republic and its Refugees," *Revista Forma* 14 (2016): 21–34.

Ferber, Edna. *A Peculiar Treasure* (New York: Doubleday, Doran, 1938).

Fermaglich, Kirsten. *A Rosenberg by Any Other Name: A History of Jewish Name Changing in America* (New York: New York University Press, 2018).

Fleischman, Doris E. *An Outline of Careers for Women: A Practical Guide to Achievement* (Garden City, NJ: Doubleday, Doran, 1928).

Furman, Andrew. *Israel Through the American-Jewish Imagination: A Survey of Jewish-American Literature on Israel, 1928–1995* (Albany: SUNY Press, 1997).

Gabler, Neal. *An Empire of Their Own: How the Jews Invented Hollywood* (New York: Crown, 1988).

Garrett, Leah. *Young Lions: How Jewish Authors Reinvented the American War Novel* (Evanston, IL: Northwestern University Press, 2015).

Gilbert, Julie G. *Ferber: A Biography of Edna Ferber and Her Circle* (New York: Doubleday, 1978).

Godwin, Gail. "House Parties and Box Lunches: One Writer's Summer at Yaddo," *New York Times*, 10 August 1986.

Goldstein, Eric L. *The Price of Whiteness: Jews, Race, and American Identity* (Princeton, NJ: Princeton University Press, 2006).

Goldstein, Israel. *Jewish Justice and Conciliation: History of the Jewish Conciliation Board of America, 1930–1968* (New York: Ktav, 1981).

Gorbach, Julien. *The Notorious Ben Hecht: Iconoclastic Writer and Militant Zionist* (West Lafayette, IN: Purdue University Press, 2019).

Gordan, Rachel. "Laura Z. Hobson and the Making of *Gentleman's Agreement*," *Studies in American Jewish Literature* 34, no. 2 (2015): 231–56.

Goren, Arthur A. *The Politics and Public Culture of American Jews: The Modern Jewish Experience* (Bloomington: Indiana University Press, 1999).

Granick, Jaclyn. *International Jewish Humanitarianism in the Age of the Great War* (Cambridge: Cambridge University Press, 2021).

Griswold, Wesley S. *Train Wreck!* (Brattleboro, VT: Stephen Greene, 1969).

Grossman, Atina. *Jews, Germans, and Allies: Close Encounters in Occupied Germany* (Princeton, NJ: Princeton University Press, 2007).

Gruber, Ruth. *Israel Without Tears* (New York: A. A. Wyn, 1950).

———. *Witness: One of the Great Correspondents of the Twentieth Century Tells Her Story* (New York: Schocken, 2007).

Gruenberg, Sidonie Matsner. *Radio and Children* (New York: Radio Institute for the Audible Arts, 1935).

Gurock, Jeffrey S. *Jews in Gotham: New York Jews in a Changing City, 1920–2010* (New York: New York University Press, 2012).

Gurock, Jeffrey S., ed. *Conversations with Colleagues: On Becoming an American Jewish Historian* (Boston: Academic Studies, 2018).

Guttenplan, D. D. *American Radical: The Life and Times of I. F. Stone* (New York: Farrar, Straus and Giroux, 2009).

Hacohen, Dvora. *To Repair a Broken World: The Life of Henrietta Szold, Founder of Hadassah* (Cambridge, MA: Harvard University Press, 2021).

Hays, Arthur Garfield. *City Lawyer: The Autobiography of a Law Practice* (New York: Simon and Schuster, 1942).

Hecht, Ben. *A Child of the Century* (New York: Simon and Schuster, 1954).

Heinze, Andrew R. *Jews and the American Soul: Human Nature in the Twentieth Century* (Princeton, NJ: Princeton University Press, 2004).

Henry, Susan. "Anonymous in Her Own Name: Public Relations Pioneer Doris E. Fleischman," *Journalism History* 23, no. 2 (1997): 50–62.

Hobson, Laura Z. *Gentleman's Agreement* (New York: Simon and Schuster, 1947).

Howe, Irving. *A Margin of Hope: An Intellectual Autobiography* (San Diego: Harcourt Brace Jovanovich, 1982).

Hurst, Fannie. *Anatomy of Me: A Wonderer in Search of Herself* (Garden City, NY: Doubleday, 1958).

Jenkins, Philip. *Hoods and Shirts: The Extreme Right in Pennsylvania, 1925–1950* (Chapel Hill: University of North Carolina Press, 1997).

Joselit, Jenna Weissman. *Our Gang: Jewish Crime and the New York Jewish Community, 1900–1940* (Bloomington: Indiana University Press, 1983).

———. *The Wonders of America: Reinventing Jewish Culture, 1880–1950* (New York: Hill and Wang, 1994).

Kahn Jr., E. J. "Democracy's Friend: Bewilderment in Sedalia," *New Yorker* (26 July 1947): 28–39.

———. "Democracy's Friend: Smears, Sneers, Snarls, Snorts, and Snaps," *New Yorker* (2 August 1947): 28–35.

Katz, Emily Alice. *Bringing Zion Home: Israel in American Culture, 1948–1967* (Albany: SUNY Press, 2015).

Kazin, Alfred. *A Walker in the City* (New York: Harcourt Brace, 1951).

———. *Starting Out in the Thirties* (Boston: Little, Brown, 1965).

Kessner, Carole S. *Marie Syrkin: Values Beyond the Self* (Hanover, NH: Brandeis University Press, 2008).

Klapper, Melissa R. *Jewish Girls Coming of Age in America, 1860–1920* (New York: New York University Press, 2005).

———. *Ballots, Babies, and Banners of Peace: American Jewish Women's Activism, 1890–1940* (New York: New York University Press, 2013).

Klein, Kathleen Gregory. *The Woman Detective: Gender and Genre* (Urbana: University of Illinois Press, 1988).

Kranson, Rachel. *Ambivalent Embrace: Jewish Upward Mobility in Postwar America* (Chapel Hill: University of North Carolina Press, 2017).

Kroeger, Brooke. *Fannie: The Talent for Success of Writer Fannie Hurst* (New York: Random House, 1999).

Lazin, Frederick A. "The Response of the American Jewish Committee to the Crisis of German Jewry, 1933–1939," *American Jewish History* 68, no. 3 (1979): 283–304.

Lee, Albert. *Henry Ford and the Jews* (New York: Stein and Day, 1980).

Levin, Harry. *I Saw the Battle of Jerusalem* (New York: Schocken, 1950).

Levine, Peter. "The *American Hebrew* Looks at 'Our Crowd': The Jewish Country Club in the 1920s," *American Jewish History* 83, no. 1 (1995), 27–49.

MacKay, Kenneth Campbell. *The Progressive Movement of 1924* (New York: Columbia University Press, 1947).

Mazower, Mark. *What You Did Not Tell: A Father's Past and a Journey Home* (New York: Other, 2018).

McEuen, Melissa A., *Making War, Making Women: Femininity and Duty on the American Home Front, 1941–1945* (Athens: University of Georgia Press, 2011).

Mendelsohn, Daniel. *The Lost: A Search for Six of Six Million* (New York: Harper, 2006).

Meyerowitz, Joanne. "Beyond the Feminine Mystique: A Reassessment of Postwar Mass Culture, 1946–1958," in Joanne Meyerowitz, ed., *Not June Cleaver: Women and Gender in Postwar America, 1945–1960* (Philadelphia: Temple University Press,1994), 232–37.

Moore, Deborah Dash. *At Home in America: Second Generation New York Jews* (New York: Columbia University Press, 1981).

Morse, Arthur D. *While Six Million Died: A Chronicle of American Apathy* (New York: Random House, 1968).

Morton, Leah [E. G. Stern]. *I Am a Woman—and a Jew* (New York: Markus Wiener, 1986 [1926]).

Nadel, Ira B. *Leon Uris: Life of a Best Seller* (Austin: University of Texas Press, 2010).

Nadell, Pamela S. *America's Jewish Women: A History from Colonial Times to Today* (New York: W. W. Norton, 2019).

Nasaw, David. *The Last Million: Europe's Displaced Persons from World War to Cold War* (New York: Penguin, 2020).

Nora, Pierre. "Entre mémoire et histoire," in Pierre Nora, *Les Lieux de mémoire*, t. 1 (Paris: Seuil, 1984), xvii–xlii.

Novick, Peter. *The Holocaust in American Life* (Boston: Houghton Mifflin, 1999).

Perry, Elisabeth Israels. *Belle Moskowitz: Feminine Politics and the Exercise of Power in the Age of Alfred E. Smith* (New York: Oxford University Press, 1987).

———. *After the Vote: Feminist Politics in La Guardia's New York* (New York: Oxford University Press, 2019).

Pizer, Donald. *American Naturalism and the Jews* (Pittsburgh: University of Pittsburgh Press, 2008).

Popkin, Henry. "The Vanishing Jew of Our Popular Culture: The Little Man Who Is No Longer There," *Commentary* (July 1952).

Popkin, Jeremy D. "A Forgotten Forerunner: Zelda Popkin's Novels of the Holocaust and the 1948 War," *Shofar* 20 (2001): 36–60.

———. *History, Historians and Autobiography* (Chicago: University of Chicago Press, 2005).

———. "History, a Historian, and an Autobiography," *Rethinking History* 14 (2010): 387–300, reprinted in Alun Munslow, ed., *Authoring the Past: Writing and Rethinking History* (London: Routledge, 2013), 183–95.

———. "Family Memoir and Self-Discovery," *Life Writing* 12, no. 2 (2015): 127–38, reprinted in Paul Arthur and Leena Kurvet-Käosaar, eds., *Border Crossings: Essays in Identity and Belonging* (New York: Routledge, 2018).

———. "From Displaced Persons to Secular Saints: Holocaust Survivors, Jewish Identity, and Gender in the Writings of Zelda Popkin," *Studies in American Jewish Literature* 37, no. 1 (2018): 1–20.

Popkin, Juliet. "Another Era, Another Train Wreck," *Los Angeles Times*, 16 January 1987.

Popkin, Louis. "Who's Who in Philanthropy—1920," *American Hebrew* 108 (3 December 1920): 65.

———. "The Problem of the Jewish Youth in America. An Interview with Justice Irving Lehman," *American Hebrew* 109 (8 July 1921): 196.

———. "Shifters," *New York Times*, 25 March 1922.

———. "Shifters No Longer Appeal to Flapper," *New York Times*, 26 March 1922.

———. "The Future of the Jew in America, interview with Nathan J. Miller," *American Hebrew* 115 (31 October 1924): 779.

———. "Interesting People: Henry J. Gaisman, the Edison of the Safety Razor Field," *Jewish Tribune* 97 (29 August 1930): 4–5, 16.

Popkin, Richard H. *The Second Oswald* (New York: Avon, 1966).

———. "Intellectual Autobiography: Warts and All," in Richard A. Watson and James E. Force, eds., *The Sceptical Mode in Modern Philosophy: Essays in Honor of Richard H. Popkin* (Dordrecht: Nijhoff, 1988), 103–49.

———. *The History of Scepticism: From Savonarola to Bayle* (New York: Oxford University Press, 2003).

Prell, Riv-Ellen. *Fighting to Become Americans: Assimilation and the Trouble between Jewish Women and Jewish Men* (Boston: Beacon, 1999).

Radway, Janice A. *A Feeling for Books: The Book-of-the-Month Club, Literary Taste, and Middle-Class Desire* (Chapel Hill: University of North Carolina Press, 1997).

Reznikoff, Charles. *Louis Marshall: Champion of Liberty*, 2 vols. (Philadelphia: Jewish Publication Society of America, 1957), 1:374–81.

Ribalow, Harold U., ed. *Mid-Century: An Anthology of Jewish Life and Culture in Our Times* (New York: Beechhurst, 1955).

Rossi, Helen. "Army Goes in for Art: Posters for Psychological Warfare," *Palestine Post*, 27 August 1948.

Schott, Ben. "A Ponzi Scheme for Flappers," *New York Times*, 30 November 2012.

Selengut, Suzanne. "Quietly Ahead of Her Time," *Jerusalem Post*, 3 February 2006.

Seliger, Yael. "After 'Postmemory': Coping with Holocaust Remembrance in Postmodern Hebrew Literature," PhD dissertation, York University, 2015.

Seltzer, Robert M., and Norman J. Cohen, eds. *The Americanization of the Jews* (New York: New York University Press, 1995).

Shandler, Jeffrey. "Religion, Democracy, and Radio Waves: *The Eternal Light*," in J. Hoberman and Jeffrey Shandler, eds., *Entertaining America: Jews, Movies, and Broadcasting* (Princeton, NJ: Princeton University Press, 2003), 130–32.

Shapiro, Edward S. "World War II and American Jewish Identity," *Modern Judaism* 10, no. 1 (1990): 65–84.

Sicherman, Barbara. "Reading *Marjorie Morningstar* in the Age of the Feminine Mystique and After," in Diner, Kohn and Kranson, eds., *A Jewish Feminine Mystique? Jewish Women in Postwar America* (New Brunswick, NJ: Rutgers University Press, 2010), 194–204.

Silver, M. M. *Our Exodus: Leon Uris and the Americanization of Israel's Founding Story* (Detroit: Wayne State University Press, 2010).

———. *Louis Marshall and the Rise of Jewish Ethnicity in America: A Biography* (Syracuse, NY: Syracuse University Press, 2013).

Simon, Kate. *Bronx Primitive: Portraits in a Childhood* (New York: Penguin, 1997 [1982]).

———. *A Wider World: Portraits in an Adolescence* (New York: Harper and Row, 1986).

Smith, Eric R. *American Relief Aid and the Spanish Civil War* (Columbia: University of Missouri Press, 2013).

Sochen, June. *The New Woman: Feminism in Greenwich Village, 1910–1920* (New York: Quadrangle, 1972).

Sollors, Werner. *The Temptation of Despair* (Cambridge, MA: Harvard University Press, 2014).

Spacks, Patricia Meyer. *Imagining a Self: Autobiography and Novel in Eighteenth-Century England* (Cambridge, MA: Harvard University Press, 1976).

Stansell, Christine. *American Moderns: Bohemian New York and the Creation of a New Century*, new ed. (Princeton, NJ: Princeton University Press, 2000).

Stone, I. F. "Born Under Fire," *New Republic* (31 May 1948): 12–14.

———. "Against All Rules," *New Republic* (14 June 1948): 14–17.

Szajkowski, Zosa. "The Jews and New York City's Mayoralty Election of 1917," *Jewish Social Studies* 32, no. 4 (1970): 286–306.

Terkel, Studs. *"The Good War": An Oral History of World War Two* (New York: Ballantine, 1984), 114–16.

Teveth, Shabtai. *Ben-Gurion's Spy: The Story of the Political Scandal that Shaped Modern Israel* (New York: Columbia University Press, 1996).

Tye, Larry. *The Father of Spin: Edward L. Bernays and the Birth of Public Relations* (New York: Crown, 1998).

Uffen, Ellen Serlen. *Strands in the Cable: The Place of the Past in Jewish American Women's Writing* (New York: Peter Lang, 1993).

Umansky, Ellen M. "Representations of Jewish Women in the Works and Life of Elizabeth Stern," *Modern Judaism* 13, no. 2 (1993): 165–76.

Urofsky, Melvin I. *A Voice That Spoke for Justice: The Life and Times of Stephen S. Wise* (Albany: SUNY Press, 1982).

Waite, Robert G., "'Raise My Voice Against Intolerance': The Anti-Nazi Rally in Madison Square Garden, March 27, 1933, and the American Public's Outrage over the Nazi Persecution of the Jews," *New York History Review* (online), 20 October 2013.

Weiss, Amy, "1948's Forgotten Soldiers? The Shifting Reception of American Volunteers in Israel's War of Independence," *Israel Studies* 25, no. 1 (2020): 149–73.

Weissbach, Lee Shai. *Jewish Life in Small-Town America: A History* (New Haven, CT: Yale University Press, 2005).

Wenger, Beth S. *New York Jews and the Great Depression: Uncertain Promise* (New York: Syracuse University Press, 1999).

———. "Federation Men: The Masculine World of New York Jewish Philanthropy, 1880–1945," *American Jewish History* 101, no. 3 (2 August 2017): 377–99.

Whitfield, Stephen J. *In Search of American Jewish Culture* (Hanover, NH: Brandeis University Press, 1999).

Wilkman, Jon. *Screening Reality: How Documentary Filmmakers Reimagined America* (New York: Bloomsbury, 2020).

Wilson, Ross J. *New York and the First World War: Shaping an American City* (Farnham: Ashgate, 2014).

Wyszkowski, Yehezkel. "'The American Hebrew': An Exercise in Ambivalence," *American Jewish History* 76, no. 3 (1987): 340–53.

Yagoda, Ben. *About Town: The New Yorker and the World It Made* (New York: Scribner, 2000).

Yellin, Emily. *Our Mothers' War: American Women at Home and at the Front During World War II* (New York: Free Press, 2004).

Zerwick, Phoebe. "Memory: Father's War Tales Masked a Dark Truth," *Winston-Salem Journal*, 27 May 2001.

INDEX